BANNING DDT July 2014

To Johnny,

Do Good Work!

Bill Berry

BANNING
DDT

HOW CITIZEN ACTIVISTS
IN WISCONSIN
LED THE WAY

Bill Berry

WISCONSIN HISTORICAL SOCIETY PRESS

Published by the Wisconsin Historical Society Press
Publishers since 1855

© 2014 by the State Historical Society of Wisconsin

Publication of this book was made possible in part by a grant from the Alice E. Smith fellowship fund.

wisconsinhistory.org

Photographs identified with WHi or WHS are from the Society's collections; address requests to reproduce these photos to the Visual Materials Archivist at the Wisconsin Historical Society, 816 State Street, Madison, WI 53706.

Printed in Canada
Design and production by Mighty Media, Inc.
Interior and text design by Chris Long
Cover design by Anders Hanson

18 17 16 15 14   1 2 3 4 5

Library of Congress Cataloging-in-Publication Data
Berry, Bill, 1951–
  Banning DDT : how citizen activists in Wisconsin led the way / Bill Berry.
      pages   cm
  Includes bibliographical references and index.
  ISBN 978-0-87020-644-3 (pbk. : alk. paper)—ISBN 978-0-87020-645-0 (ebook)
  1. DDT (Insecticide)—Environmental aspects—History—20th century. 2. Environmental protection—Wisconsin—Citizen participation—History—20th century. 3. Environmentalism—United States—History—20th century. I. Title.
  TD196.P38B47 2014
  363.738'498—dc23

                                                                    2013036819

∞ The paper used in this publication meets the minimum requirements of the American National Standard for Information Sciences—Permanence of Paper for Printed Library Materials, ANSI Z39.48–1992.

To members of my family, who offered encouragement and support

Soldiers in World War II carried DDT dust cans with them to fend off a variety of insect pests. After the war, DDT was a popular household and garden product. *WHS Museum 1999.143.20; photo by Joel Heiman*

CONTENTS

FOREWORD

THIS ACCOUNT OF CITIZEN ACTIVISM IN WISCONSIN IN THE 1960s is a powerful testament to the effectiveness of grassroots advocacy in creating substantive social change. The players in this drama are not corporate titans or conservation NGO leaders, but concerned citizens and dedicated scientists whose passion and determination helped pave the way to banning DDT.

It's an important story because DDT would not have been banned quickly—or maybe at all—without citizens and scientists committed to participatory democracy. Author Bill Berry's focus on ordinary citizens rather than policy makers is something you seldom see in history books. Here Senator Gaylord Nelson is a bit player while Lorrie Otto, a Milwaukee-area housewife, is a star.

As has been clear since the National Audubon Society launched more than a hundred years ago, a handful of dedicated citizens can and do make a difference. Audubon's roots are in a small group of men and primarily women who came together to protect birds from slaughter at the hands of plume hunters. This happened at a time when hats sporting feathers—sometimes even entire birds—were the height of fashion. It was these early conservationists who founded the National Audubon Society.

Today, Audubon continues its legacy of protecting birds and other wildlife through a combination of science, advocacy, and grassroots activism. Organizations like Audubon depend on people like Lorrie Otto to make collective action possible. If we are going to accomplish any of our conservation goals, people must remember the successes of committed Americans like Otto—and the others whose stories are told in these pages, including scientist Joseph Hickey, her fellow Audubon Medal recipient—in driving policy change.

This account also shines a light on the role birds can play in signaling when something is wrong in our environment. Among the earliest to see that something was wrong after neighborhood trees were sprayed with DDT were bird-watchers and gardeners in cities and suburbs who noticed the death and disappearance of songbirds. In fact, as Mr. Berry points out in this account, bird-watchers had issued warnings about the environmental impacts of DDT as early as 1945, when Richard Pough, then with the National Audubon Society, raised the alarm in the *New Yorker*. But it was the publication of Rachel Carson's world-changing *Silent Spring* in 1962 that galvanized a nation of grassroots activists and launched the modern environmental movement.

Scientists tell us that, increasingly, nature is out of sync. Birds are arriving too early at their summering grounds to find adequate food and many species are running out of habitat. We are seeing many of the effects of climate change sooner than we expected. The challenges we face now are bigger than ever before. Whether you're concerned about birds, biodiversity, or people, every single thing you do can make a difference.

So, raise your voice for birds, for people, and for the future of our planet. Inspired examples of making a difference can be found in this story of engaged citizen activists who, through a combination of passion and grassroots activism, sought and achieved change in Wisconsin and beyond.

—DAVID YARNOLD,
PRESIDENT & CEO, NATIONAL AUDUBON SOCIETY

PREFACE

ONE DAY IN 2008, WHILE WALKING THROUGH CHERRY CREEK Canyon in New Mexico with a lifelong friend who made his living as a wildlife biologist, we heard the fierce screams of a couple of peregrine falcons echo off ancient rock formations.

We strained to see the birds, but to no avail. The screams and streaks of "whitewash" below falcon perches would have to do that day. That didn't diminish the thrill. It seemed almost fitting that the birds should take on this ghostly presence.

That day we were on a bird-watching tour led by a National Audubon Society guide. He confirmed what we already knew: the peregrines were making a comeback decades after the use of the pesticide DDT—dichlorodiphenyltrichloroethane—had been banned in the United States.[1]

Cherry Creek Canyon is near the Gila Wilderness, the nation's first wilderness area, for which Aldo Leopold had lobbied in the days he worked for the US Forest Service. It was designated so in 1924, the same year Leopold left the Southwest for a position at the US Forest Products Laboratory in Madison, Wisconsin. In 1933, he was named professor of game management in the Department of Agricultural Economics of the College of Agriculture at the University of Wisconsin in Madison.

The story of Leopold and his classic book, *A Sand County Almanac*, is oft told. The power of the collection of essays, penned mostly on family outings to the "shack" and its surrounding worn-out farmland where Leopold set out to undertake an exercise in ecological restoration, still resonates across the world. Leopold died in 1948, and the book was published a year later, but his concept of a "land ethic," or a responsible relationship between people and the land they inhabit, guides the work of natural resources professionals and conservation-minded citizens to this day. Leopold's impact is felt in the pages of this book. Although he was dead nearly two decades before the use of DDT was challenged in Wisconsin, his name and lessons were often cited by a gutsy band of early citizen environmental activists. Among them were scientists who had worked with or known Leopold. His lessons may have helped them step out of the comfort zone that academia can provide and into the public fray, sometimes with painful consequences.

It was Leopold who, in 1947, convinced a lanky easterner he had advised as a graduate student to join him as a professor in Madison. The man was Joseph Hickey, and his name is now forever tied to the Wisconsin DDT battles of the late 1960s. Hickey was a lifelong bird-watcher whose childhood companions in the endeavor included Roger Tory Peterson, who would become one of America's best-known naturalists and artists, and Allan Cruickshank, who would establish himself as a pioneering wildlife photographer. Hickey also had a special affection for the peregrine falcon. This affinity would prove a crucial link in the effort to understand the impacts DDT was having on the web of life.

Hickey was a scientist. He would be joined by other scientists in challenging the use of DDT. By stepping into the public fray, they were breaking the mold for scientists of the day. Few were comfortable entering the public arena, believing their place was the laboratory and, for those in universities, the classroom. Those who did were sometimes considered grandstanders out to make names for themselves. But these were the 1960s, and citizens of all ages and backgrounds were impacted by the dramatic social changes occurring around them. The story of the rise and fall of DDT is inextricably linked to this moment in time.

Wisconsin's DDT battles were one of the first chapters of citizen activism in the modern environmental era. Leopold's *A Sand County Almanac* was a prescription for a healthy land community. The citizens who engaged in the DDT battles went a step further. When they saw something out of place in the land community and its web of life, they challenged the status quo.

Banning DDT tells the story of these citizens—garden club ladies, hunters and fishers, bird-watchers, university professors and scientists, newspaper reporters and columnists, traditional conservationists— who drew attention to the harm DDT was causing.

⊠   ⊠   ⊠

I think it fair to say most authors undertake projects like this because of personal connections.

Mine are many. I came of age in the tumultuous 1960s and '70s. My growing interest in the environment was fed by Leopold's essays and countless forays along the Kinnickinnic River with college buddies at the University of Wisconsin–River Falls. The seeds planted then grew as I undertook work as a journalist. The environment became my specialty. Later in life, as I transitioned to self-employment in the fields of conservation and agriculture, I began to help compile biographies of candidates for the Wisconsin Conservation Hall of Fame in Stevens Point. I got to know many of the citizen activists in this book through that work, though several of them, including Hickey, were dead.

The connections to this book's content for me are many, but one stands out among all the others. My earliest encounter with DDT came as a teenager in a working class neighborhood of Green Bay. Tall elm trees graced the busy street out front of my home. The city was waging a fight with Dutch elm disease by following the prescribed course of action of the day, which included dousing the trees with DDT in an attempt to kill the tiny beetles that spread the disease.

It was quite the show when the DDT boys came rumbling down the street on a spring night, swirling yellow lights signaling their arrival. I recall that a pickup truck with a mounted speaker led the way. A stern voice warned us to go indoors. Spraying was about to begin. A flatbed truck followed, with a misting machine on its bed. We watched from the front windows of our home as the mister sprayed an emulsion containing DDT up to one hundred feet into the treetops.

When the trucks had passed, I was allowed to go out back to resume practicing my basketball jump shot on the hoop that hung from the garage, about fifty feet behind our home. Two scraggly elm trees leaned over a side of the garage. A chilling clamor like none I had ever heard arose from those trees. Hundreds of songbirds had congregated there, as though to escape the trees out front. They squawked and chattered and fluttered about the tree in what seemed like a panic. I was dumbfounded. What had caused the birds to gather in this way? That question would stalk me as the years went on. Obviously, the birds were seeking some sort of refuge. I was the witness at that place. It is no stretch to say that I might not have undertaken this project had it not been for that eerie night long ago.

PROLOGUE

O N A DECEMBER DAY IN 1968, DDT WENT ON TRIAL IN MAD-
ison, Wisconsin.

US senator Gaylord Nelson, who had emerged as an environmental leader in Congress, was the first witness at an administrative hearing brought by a group of citizens who challenged the use of what
had once been considered a miracle chemical. The initial phases of the
hearing were held in the ornate Assembly Chamber of the Wisconsin
State Capitol building. Later, as legislators reclaimed their chambers
for work in a new session, the hearing moved to the Hill Farms State
Office Building. The citizens used a provision in Wisconsin's administrative rules that allowed them to challenge the use of DDT on the
grounds that it was a water pollutant.

DDT was a persistent organochlorine chemical known to scientists
as dichlorodiphenyltrichloroethane. Almost everyone else just used
the handy abbreviation DDT, which, as it turned out, fit well in headlines—and of those there were plenty during the height of controversy
over the chemical. One writer speculated that other than "S-E-X" few
letters of the alphabet were drawing as much attention as DDT.

The Madison hearing served as a beginning and an end. Environmental historians frequently cite it as the first big skirmish of the
modern environmental era. Closer to home, the hearing was the cul-
mination of years of agitating by a small but determined group of citizens called the Citizens Natural Resources Association of Wisconsin.

The CNRA had been focused on drawing attention to the increasing use of chemicals to deal with everything from roadside weeds to the insect pests that were ravaging city elm populations across the state.

The hearing would drag on into 1969. On May 21, 1970, Hearing Examiner Maurice Van Susteren—who possessed a strong legal mind and a penchant for challenging convention—ruled that DDT was, indeed, polluting state waters. By then, Michigan had become the first state to ban DDT, and Wisconsin's legislature already had followed suit.

The Wisconsin DDT hearing may have seemed tame compared to other conflicts raging across the country in the 1960s. There had been no massive demonstrations calling for an end to the use of DDT. While the CNRA was formed with the intent of being a "militant" defender of the environment, there was no violence. The hearing produced more than its share of dry, highly technical testimony.

But this Wisconsin administrative hearing had been pivotal. It gave the citizen activists a national stage. Media coverage was heavy, thanks in no small part to the fact that an editor at the *Capital Times* in Madison—convinced that the hearing was of immense importance—put aggressive young reporter Whitney Gould on the story from start to finish.

America bristled with citizen activism and cultural conflict in the 1960s: Students and others took to the streets to protest an unpopular war in Vietnam; blacks demanded civil rights in the face of fierce opposition and at risk of life; the women's liberation movement demanded that society practice equality on collective and individual levels. The environmental movement was gaining its legs, thanks to voices like those of Gaylord Nelson, who was elected to the US Senate in 1962. Nelson had established a strong conservation record while serving as governor of Wisconsin. He continued to agitate on behalf of the environment upon arriving in Washington. By 1965, he was proposing a federal ban on DDT. But despite the growing stack of research indicting DDT for its impact on ecosystems, a federal ban was still years away.

In a tumultuous decade, 1968 was as white-hot as any year. For Wisconsin residents, it started out happily enough. The Green Bay Packers won their second Super Bowl in January, dispatching the Oakland Raiders in what would be Vince Lombardi's last game as coach of the Packers.

That same month, the war in Vietnam was raging. The bloody battle of Khe Sanh and North Vietnam's Tet Offensive served to galvanize an already burgeoning antiwar movement, and the University of Wisconsin in Madison was a hotbed of antiwar activity. Vietnam had become the first TV war, with nightly news reports served up along with dinner for people across the country.

On June 6, Americans awakened to news that Senator Robert F. Kennedy had been fatally wounded by assassin Sirhan Sirhan in Los Angeles, during a celebration marking his victories in Democratic primaries in California and South Dakota. As the Democratic Party convened in Chicago that summer, the nation would watch live as antiwar protesters were battered by Chicago police outside the convention. Vietnam would lead to the demise of Lyndon Johnson's presidency and the birth of Richard Nixon's in 1968.

Meanwhile, the civil rights movement that had begun earlier in the decade continued to be propelled by demonstrations and strikes across the country, and frequent violence associated with this citizen uprising was also a staple on the nightly news. Three college students died in February when highway patrolmen were called in to quell a demonstration in Orangeburg, South Carolina. In that same month, black sanitation workers in Memphis, Tennessee, went on strike, bringing Reverend Martin Luther King Jr. to the city several times. On April 4, King was assassinated as he stood on the balcony outside his room at the Lorraine Motel in Memphis, Tennessee. Across the country, blacks took to the streets to protest in a massive wave of riots.

In Milwaukee, Father James Groppi was calling attention to housing segregation and other inequalities. He led marches and other activities to draw attention to the cause.

President Johnson would sign the Civil Rights Act in 1968.

Women's rights had emerged as another social uprising, and when
the Miss America Pageant got underway that September in Atlantic
City, New Jersey, hundreds of women were on hand to protest what
they saw as the pageant's exploitation of women. Later that year, Yale
University announced it would admit women students.

It was clear in the early 1960s that something was afoot in America. While Earth Day was still a decade off, everyday citizens were
awakening to a new understanding about human impacts on the environment. Prior to Rachel Carson's world-changing *Silent Spring*, published in 1962, the impact of pesticides on the environment was being
documented by some scientists, but the information was scattered
and not well understood by the general public. *Silent Spring* shook
a nation from its unflagging reliance on the perceived magic of pesticides by drawing attention to the dangers of their indiscriminate use.
Renowned Harvard biologist Edward O. Wilson would later describe
the book's impact this way: "*Silent Spring* delivered a galvanic jolt to
public consciousness and, as a result, infused the environmental movement with new substance and meaning."[1] Others were less impressed.
Carson was excoriated in many quarters, especially the agricultural
sector, for her book. It remains a target of criticism to this day, with
some charging that her science was flawed.

In Wisconsin, the CNRA and other groups had been pointing out
the danger of pesticides for several years prior to Carson's book. Some
of the earliest to raise concerns were both the least and most likely.
They were garden club enthusiasts from upscale suburbs and well-kept
cities—most of whom were housewives unaccustomed to "stepping
out" into the public fray—who began to notice that DDT spraying to
control Dutch elm disease was decimating songbird populations. The

Wisconsin activists weren't the first to draw attention to the impacts of DDT on a variety of species. Bird-watchers had issued warnings as early as 1945, when Richard Pough, then with the National Audubon Society, related his concerns to the *New Yorker*.

Acute toxicity caused by DDT and leading to songbird deaths was a concern, but so was the loss of beloved elm trees that lined the streets of cities across the eastern United States. At first, concerns about DDT use in Wisconsin were directed at the local governments that authorized spraying. Those local elected officials found themselves in a quandary: many citizens demanded action to save their elm trees, but when DDT was employed, there was a strong backlash.

Eventually, these citizen activists realized that the matter went beyond confrontations with city, village, and town boards. University agriculture departments, state agricultural agencies, the US Department of Agriculture, and multinational corporations that made millions from pesticide sales were all in agreement: pesticide regulation was sufficient, economic entomologists were the experts, and the control of disease and elimination of agricultural and forest pests depended on chemicals like DDT.

Meanwhile, the little cadre of Wisconsin activists forged ahead, seeking a ban on DDT use. In 1968, after a series of setbacks, the door opened.

Research by ecological scientists slowly uncovered an even more dramatic discovery: DDT concentrations built up as they moved up the food chain, and they were decimating populations of raptors and other species by disrupting their reproductive cycles. By the time of the Wisconsin hearing, it had also become clear that DDT was accumulating in lakes and rivers and threatening the state's billion-dollar sportfishing industry.

In Wisconsin, the CNRA had found a cause worth fighting for, and at the same time, a group of eastern environmental activists was fishing around for a DDT test case. The upstart Environmental Defense

Fund, incorporated in New York State in 1967, had a simple motto in those days: "Sue the bastards." True to its word, the EDF sought to advance its arguments in courts of law and hearing rooms.

The two groups found one another in 1968. In August of that year, Lorrie Otto, a suburban Milwaukee housewife later derisively referred to by one local politician as "the little lady in tennis shoes,"[2] spied a notice in a local paper: the Wisconsin Department of Agriculture had again recommended DDT for Dutch elm disease control in Milwaukee and some of its suburbs. Otto called Joseph Hickey, a professor in the Department of Wildlife Management in the College of Agriculture at the University of Wisconsin in Madison, who was coming around to the belief that it was time for scientists to act. Otto and Hickey were by then members of the CNRA, and Hickey agreed that a suit was the group's only recourse.[3]

Soon the CNRA was raising money to bring the EDF to Wisconsin. The CNRA filed a complaint with the Wisconsin Department of Natural Resources over the city of Milwaukee's plan to spray DDT for Dutch elm disease control. The two groups planned to sue the city and Buckley Tree Service of Waukesha. Maurice Van Susteren, chief hearing examiner for the DNR, presided. The hearing in Milwaukee quickly fizzled: the city and the tree service agreed not to use DDT, and thus argued that no contract for spraying existed between them. Van Susteren told the litigants the case was moot: without a contract for spraying there was no basis for a suit.

In effect, the citizen activists had won. The city would not spray DDT. But the citizens were not pleased. Picking up on this, Van Susteren asked the "winners" why they were disheartened. EDF attorney Victor Yannacone explained that his organization wanted a forum to present scientific evidence against DDT and to get a judgment on its use.

Van Susteren told the citizens' group that if they really wanted to press forward with their concerns about DDT spraying, Wisconsin law provided for a declaratory hearing procedure in which Wisconsin citizens could ask a government department for a ruling on the applicability of a particular set of facts on any rule enforced by that agency.[4] Essentially, CNRA members could simply ask the DNR if DDT was a water pollutant under the state's water-quality standards and thereby set in motion a hearing, complete with testimony, which would ultimately result in a ruling by that department's hearing examiner.

On October 28, 1968, Frederick L. Ott, a Milwaukee businessman and an early member of the CNRA who also would serve as its chief fund-raiser for the DDT hearing, asked the DNR for a ruling on whether DDT was a water pollutant. Van Susteren assigned himself to the action and set a hearing for December.

Van Susteren's own interest in the topic and for the environmentalists' cause was but one example of Wisconsin DNR employees advocating on behalf of the citizen activists and for the environment. It also underscored a split between state agencies. The Department of Agriculture continued to promote the use of DDT even as the DNR had suspended its use on state lands and recommended against its use in other settings.

The hearing also highlighted differences within the scientific community, with most of the University of Wisconsin College of Agriculture faculty proclaiming the need for DDT even as other colleagues, such as Hickey, saw the pesticide as a major threat to the environment.

The CNRA engaged the EDF and Yannacone, a brilliant and flamboyant Long Islander, for the hearing. He and his wife, Carol, had already undertaken localized legal actions in their own state to halt the use of DDT. CNRA members dug into their own pockets and pried funds from friends and neighbors to cover air travel and other expenses. Group members also hosted EDF staff in their homes during the hearings.

The chemical industry and its supporters initially underestimated the potential impact of the hearing. But the EDF had crafted a careful strategy supported by testimony from experts around the country and beyond. By the time the industry realized the score, the game was over. The hearing would last for six months and produce 4,499 pages of testimony weighing forty pounds.

The *Capital Times*'s Gould was far from the only reporter on hand. The *New York Times* and other major newspapers, news services, and other media outlets covered the hearing. The coverage focused national and international attention on DDT and the unfolding story of its impact on a variety of species. The hearing and resulting ruling were considered a major victory for modern-day environmentalists. And the environment was emerging as a beat worthy of attention, be it from the local newspaper or the most powerful media outlets on Earth.

The actions of the activists whose deeds fill the following pages were—and continue to be—questioned by many. Today, foes of the DDT bans claim that uninformed people guided by pseudoscience removed one of the world's most important pesticides from the public health and agriculture and forestry toolboxes. They say millions died from malaria in developing countries once DDT use was scaled back. They decried the marriage of science and citizen activism, often characterizing the activists as food faddists (a then popular term for organic food advocates opposed to pesticide use), nature lovers, and Marxists.

Many of those who sought to ban DDT maintain that they recognized the need for the compound in certain situations, especially where human health was at stake. Most of those who supported a DDT ban also said that other chemicals and pest management strategies were as effective or more so in addition to being safer. They pointed out that numerous insect species had developed resistance to the chemical. And they maintained that DDT's persistence and impact on whole ecosystems made its use too dangerous. Supporters of the ban also said that lessons learned from the DDT battle underscore the importance of interdisciplinary scientific review of pesticides. More important, they said citizens deserve a voice on the health of the land and water that sustain us. They were adhering to a simple idea that, in a democracy, citizens have not only the right but the responsibility to be informed and involved.

What is clear about Wisconsin's DDT battles is that a handful of citizens did make a difference. That is a lesson worth revisiting.

CHAPTER ONE

"MIRACULOUS PESTICIDE" COMES TO TOWN

THE INSECTICIDE DDT WAS CONSIDERED A WONDER CHEMical when first introduced to the world, and as well it should have been, given the early successes associated with its use.

It was effective, inexpensive, and had many applications.

These very properties led to its widespread use, and, it could be argued, its demise. When it was employed in the effort to save America's elm trees, it came face-to-face with a public that might not have otherwise given it much thought. A generation of city dwellers got to see some of DDT's darker sides.

A member of the chlorinated hydrocarbon family, DDT was first synthesized in 1874. It wasn't until 1939, though, that a team of investigators working for Geigy Chemical Company of Switzerland would identify its powerful pesticide punch. The team's leader, Paul Muller, won the 1948 Nobel Prize in Physiology or Medicine for the discovery.

Little wonder. DDT was credited with saving tens of thousands of human lives. It was first put to use in World War II and helped protect thousands of US military personnel who would otherwise have been exposed to malaria, typhus, and other insect-borne diseases. Dichlorodiphenyltrichloroethane, wisely shortened to DDT, quickly earned its stripes.

Muller was saluted in the Nobel presentation speech by Professor G. Fischer, member of the Staff of Professors of the Royal Caroline Institute:

"The story of DDT illustrates the often wondrous ways of science when a major discovery has been made. A scientist, working with flies and Colorado beetles discovers a substance that proves itself effective in the battle against the most serious diseases in the world. Many there are who will say he was lucky, and so he was. Without a reasonable slice of luck hardly any discoveries whatever would be made. But the results are not simply based on luck. The discovery of DDT was made in the course of industrious and certainly sometimes monotonous labour; the real scientist is he who possesses the capacity to

Communities seeking to control Dutch elm disease sometimes resorted to spraying DDT by helicopter. Citizens in many communities were alarmed when the insecticide led to songbird deaths due to acute exposure. *WHi Image ID 72978*

A familiar sight on many American streets in the 1960s: the spraying of elm trees with DDT in an effort to halt the spread of Dutch elm disease. Spraying often took place at night, and citizens were warned to go inside as trucks pulled misting machines that launched an emulsion containing DDT to the tops of trees. *WHi Image ID 73014*

understand, interpret and evaluate the meaning of what at first sight may seem to be an unimportant discovery."[1]

The same might be said of the ecological scientists who years later uncovered the mystery of how DDT was seriously impacting wildlife.

Fischer's reference to the flies failed to mention another fact that would ultimately affect DDT's future: at least one species of house fly had already become resistant to the compound. Other insect species would develop similar resistance, including, DDT foes later argued, the mosquitoes that spread malaria.

But any negatives were far outweighed by positives as humans rushed into the second half of the twentieth century. DDT and other related compounds—chlorodane, toxaphene, aldrin, and dieldrin—were the dominant family of insecticides used after World War II.[2]

To combat mosquitoes, DDT was often sprayed in places where water gathered. The persistent pesticide is toxic to a wide range of living organisms, including many species of fish. DDT, through its metabolite, DDE, causes eggshell thinning in a number of birds of prey and certain other bird species. Some species, such as the bald eagle and peregrine falcon, experienced drastic population declines during years of heavy DDT use. *WHi Image ID 60301*

DDT quickly earned favor as a preferred and effective agent for chemical control of pests on agricultural, forest, and city landscapes in the United States, Europe, and other developed regions.

Children of the 1960s in eastern US cities—where DDT was aimed at the Dutch elm beetle—recall riding their bikes through the mist behind DDT foggers. They did not die, although countless songbirds around them did. The apparently negligible impact on humans served as one of the major arguments for widespread use of the pesticide: direct human exposure at high levels did not seem to produce serious symptoms. Even Rachel Carson's *Silent Spring* failed to make a strong case that DDT and other chemicals were harmful to humans.

Thomas Dunlap, author of *DDT, Scientists, Citizens and Public Policy*, captured the cultural and scientific realities that helped usher in the era of DDT and other chemicals when he wrote, "The failure of other methods to meet public demands for ways to stop insects without long, expensive research, changes in farming practice or long-term planning paved the way for chemicals. The triumph of chemical insecticides was due not just to the visible results they gave, but to their acceptance by a public and a farming community that valued, above all else, convenience, simplicity and immediate applicability."[3]

DDT was introduced in 1942, and it drew raves from those looking for better insecticides. Dunlap's book notes that one economic entomologist who tested DDT on potatoes described the results years later, saying DDT was "a miraculous pesticide."[4]

With the rise of DDT came the corresponding rise of a new breed of scientist: the economic entomologist, whose job it was to save humankind and wrestle control of the earth—including the elm-lined streets of the eastern United States—from insects. The entomology department in the College of Agriculture at the University of Wisconsin in Madison flourished in this post–World War II environment.

Public debates about the use of chemicals in food production took place not long after DDT was introduced. Some scientists had warned of DDT's chronic impacts almost immediately, but these discussions eluded average Americans.

Then came Carson's seminal book, which paralleled the growing use of DDT in populated settings. Soon, another new breed of experts, ecological scientists, were talking about widespread impacts of insecticides on the environment. They established with growing scientific certainty that, in addition to acute toxicity to many species—notably songbirds—DDT packed a heavier punch in other bird species higher on the food chain through chronic exposure. DDT was mobile and persistent, and it accumulated in nontarget species. Ecological scientists began to establish that in sufficient levels of accumulation, DDT's metabolites caused reproductive problems in a number of species. This led to a quiet but deadly decline in scores of species, a heretofore unheard of phenomenon and one that escaped the immediate attention of wildlife biologists because such species, including raptors, are long-lived, and their population declines were not initially obvious because live birds were still seen.

The chemical industry, backed by its own stable of respected and knowledgeable scientists, fought back with vigor. They had the financial resources to do so, and they used them.

But science is only part of the DDT story. Among the earliest to see that something was off-kilter were bird-watchers and gardeners in cities and genteel suburbs who took note of population declines in songbirds. If they had a hard time connecting with scientists on the issue of DDT use, they had less luck with municipal officials who were following USDA and state agricultural agency advice about how to handle insect pests and struggling to save the monoculture urban elm forests. Saving elm trees was also important to local governmental budgets: removing and properly disposing of dead trees was costly and time-consuming. Urban foresters were pressed into using DDT as a cost-effective if not entirely successful means to control the spread of Dutch elm disease.

But backyard naturalists persisted. Aldo Leopold had reminded the world that "to keep every cog and wheel is the first precaution of intelligent tinkering."[5] Bird-watchers and gardeners like Lorrie Otto were among the first to notice that we were losing some of the parts. They would lead efforts to literally put DDT on trial in the public arena. It can be said that it all started with the robin.

CHAPTER TWO

DEAD ROBINS

IT IS NOT MUCH OF AN EXAGGERATION TO ATTACH THE ADVENT of the modern environmental movement to the time when American robins started twitching and dying in citified gardens, yards, and boulevards across the eastern United States.

It is also fitting that some of the earliest modern-day environmental skirmishes should be in Wisconsin, where schoolchildren voted *Turdus migratorius*—the American robin—the state bird in 1927.[1]

Acute DDT exposure, which dropped robins and other songbirds on lawns, wasn't the ultimate reason for the pesticide's demise, but it served as the first warning of its toxicity as birds began perishing in great numbers.

It was an elderly woman who first told Charles Wurster, who was at the time a biology postgraduate fellow at Dartmouth, in Hanover, New Hampshire, that DDT was killing birds. Like so many other towns across the eastern United States, Hanover was engaged in a determined if futile effort to control Dutch elm disease with DDT.[2] "Her name was Betty Sherrard," Wurster recalled. "She was certainly interested in birds." In 1960, Sherrard invited Wurster and others to a party at her home, intending to share more than nosh. "She passed around this petition to the town fathers in Hanover, asking them not to spray because it killed birds," Wurster said. "Well, the petition went to the town managers, and they said they were real careful, and their

Charles Wurster was a scientist and cofounder of the Environmental Defense Fund. He and EDF played key roles in Wisconsin's DDT hearing. *Courtesy of Stony Brook University*

spray didn't kill birds, and it was some kind of nerve disease that killed the birds."[3]

That party would change Wurster's life. He and some colleagues undertook what he called "a little study and found out what was happening." Their work eventually led the town to halt the spraying. Betty Sherrard the citizen activist had found her man. In 1967, Wurster, who had moved on to the State University of New York at Stony Brook, helped found the Environmental Defense Fund. It was an organization that wasn't interested in pussyfooting around on matters that concerned the environment. Early in its existence, the EDF believed the best way to achieve victories for the environment was in legal settings. Similar to many early environmental organizations, the EDF moderated its positions over time.

Wurster had learned something else when he began to poke into the mystery. For years, citizens had been taking note of bird deaths in other populated areas where elm trees were sprayed with DDT, primarily in the East and Midwest. It was especially true in the Midwest, where the connection had been noted much earlier than in Hanover, he discovered.

An early Wisconsin environmental activist, Dixie Larkin of Milwaukee, told the Wisconsin Society for Ornithology at its 1957 meeting in Green Lake that "the D.D.T. used to destroy the Dutch Elm Disease is killing many birds."[4] At the meeting, Walter Scott, who served in the position of "custodian" for the group, said he felt the right way to treat the disease without killing birds would be found. Scott would go on to play a major role in efforts to ban DDT. A long-time staff member of the Wisconsin Conservation Department, which evolved into the Wisconsin Department of Natural Resources in 1968, Scott flooded people like Lorrie Otto with new research, insider tips that helped the citizens' cause, and leads on where to look for more information, all while serving as assistant to the director of the department and in other positions. He was also one of the founders of the Citizens Natural Resources Association.

Indeed, the first alarms were being sounded across the eastern United States and in midwestern cities like Milwaukee and its suburbs, prompting letters to newspaper editors and this 1957 communication from Marie Thompson of Milwaukee, president of the Animal Protective League, to John Beale, chief forester of the Wisconsin Conservation Department: "Dear Mr. Beale: We implore you to stop the use of all DDT spraying—which is a complete violation of all of our laws and treaties re: migratory birds, game birds and wild animals taken out of season. The death toll is shocking & we all have the right to protect our birds and wildlife."[5]

Complaint upon complaint piled up in urban areas where DDT was used. The complaints, though, were mostly anecdotal, and some were easily dismissed. But local officials were under pressure: other citizens were imploring them to save the beloved cathedral elms that arched over their streets, cooling summer days and cutting winter winds. In the face of protests about bird deaths, many city dwellers agreed with the village of Bayside official who asked the now infamous question of Lorrie Otto, "What do you want, Mrs. Otto, birds or trees?"[6]

The question itself was not completely out of line. Even though wildlife researchers including Clarence Cottam and Elmer Higgins with the US Department of the Interior had warned as early as 1946—

Dutch elm disease struck hard and fast once it arrived. In this photo, trees on one side of a street in Shorewood Hills, Wisconsin, are dead. Those on the other side of the street would suffer a similar fate despite efforts to control the disease with DDT and other compounds. *US Forest Service*

the year widespread use of DDT began in the country—of the effects DDT had on fish and other wildlife,[7] other respected scientists argued that the benefits of DDT outweighed any potential risks. Some predicted dire consequences for US agricultural crops and forests if DDT was banned. The work of Cottam and Higgins anticipated the coming push and pull among agencies such as the Department of the Interior, which had managing wildlife populations as part of its mission, and the Department of Agriculture, which was focused on agricultural production and feeding the public. With such divergent missions, it should be of little wonder the two departments did not see eye to eye. The same tension was obvious in the states—Wisconsin not the least of them—where conservation and agriculture departments often held conflicting views and offered contradictory advice to their stakeholders.

For his part, Cottam, a long-serving government biologist unafraid of a tussle,[8] had warned of looming danger in 1945. Excessive use of DDT, he said, could kill an array of species, from birds and fish to turtles and frogs. DDT "will kill a lot of things we don't want killed," Cottam warned. "It kills beneficial insects as well as obnoxious insects. Therefore, it should be used with understanding, intelligence and caution. If used in excess, it will be like scalping to cure dandruff."[9]

Cottam's choice of colorful language underscored the fact that scientists were split on the topic, often by discipline. Even as Joseph Hickey's work at the University of Wisconsin in Madison became a crucial link to understanding the full impacts of DDT, a prominent scientist and administrator at the school took a different position. Dr. Ira Baldwin, a plant bacteriologist who spearheaded US chemical warfare research in World War II, would write a critical review of *Silent Spring* in *Science* magazine in 1962. Faculty at the university would continue to be divided—sometimes angrily so—as the DDT story unfolded. At times, it seemed as though the message on a plaque at the entrance of Bascom Hall, the main administrative building at the university, might be compromised: "Whatever may be the limitations which inhibit inquiry elsewhere, we believe that the great state university of Wisconsin should forever encourage that continual and fearless sifting and winnowing by which alone the truth can be found."

Meanwhile, citizen complaints continued. The early tales of bird deaths and citizen concerns are eerily similar. They often involve a disgruntled citizen dropping off a batch of dead birds at a local governmental office. Wisconsin author Jerry Apps was a county extension agent in Green Bay in the early 1960s and a member of the local National Audubon Society chapter (Northeastern Wisconsin Audubon Society). A fellow club member approached him in his office one day with a basket of dead birds.[10] She asked why the Extension Service offered instructions on the use of DDT to control lawn and garden pests when it killed birds so readily. Apps recalled not having a ready answer.

In the upscale Milwaukee suburb of Bayside, Lorrie Otto was springing into action. She had been pestering people with her environmental activism for years by the time she dropped off a load of twenty-eight dead robins at the Bayside village offices. A housewife with a penchant for gardening and native plants, Otto became dogged in her efforts to put an end to DDT spraying. She was frequently frustrated with the response her work received and often ran out of patience with or didn't trust bureaucrats going by the books, but she continued undeterred.

She was not, as it turns out, one to trifle with. She had already tangled with officials over efforts to save a twenty-acre wooded area along the Lake Michigan shore that was being eyed for a subdivision. As she edged toward action on DDT, she was encouraged by the likes of George Wallace, a Michigan State University zoologist who had conducted pioneering studies on DDT bird mortality in Michigan in the mid-1950s. In 1966, responding to a letter and other materials from Otto, Wallace wrote her: "I think you 'gals' have more influence on

public opinion than you realize. Many a battle has been lost or won
by pressure from the local citizens, especially women. People like me
dig up the facts, by research, then publish the results in some obscure
journal which nobody reads, except a few people who already know
the story."[11]

So the citizens' uprising went from community to community, with
people complaining about dying birds and municipal officials desper-
ately trying to save the cathedral elms.

The uprising came in fits and spurts at first, mostly reported by
"Audubon ladies"—Hickey's reference to Illinois women who reported
robin deaths in the journal of the Illinois Audubon Society[12]—who
noticed the decline in bird numbers; by gardeners, who witnessed robins flopping about in fits and dying in their yards; and by children,
who picked up dead birds on the tree-lined boulevards of their eastern and midwestern neighborhoods.

Hickey would later recount his own early introduction to the
matter of DDT and birds. "It started when I went to a funeral in
Kenilworth, Illinois, in June 1958," he told author Thomas Dunlap.
"There was a mulberry tree in front of the house. It was loaded with
berries and there were no birds. I realized something was extraordi-
narily wrong, so I asked the local people 'Where are the birds? Where
are the robins?' They said there were robins earlier in the spring but
they all went north. When we got out of town and to a golf course in
the next town, I saw robins."[13]

Kenilworth, an affluent suburb, had a problem. Hickey knew something was wrong, but at that time he could not envision what the next
decade-plus would produce. A careful scientist, he was loath to go too
far in his assessment of the bird deaths until he had all his facts. And
he had little or no idea about DDT's other face: the chronic, sublethal
dosage that would wreak havoc on birds of prey and other species. He
returned to his work back in Madison, where the university was spraying DDT in an effort to save its iconic elms. The next decade would

produce a remarkable unraveling of a scientific mystery, and he would
be in the center of it.

As Hickey carefully edged closer to action in the 1960s, Otto was
carrying on a sort of one-woman campaign in her suburb and throughout the Milwaukee area. The record indicates that she didn't hook up
with the CNRA in these early efforts. The trail of correspondence
from her files shows she reached out first to Wallace and Wurster, who
in turn linked her back to Hickey and the CNRA folks—some of
them her neighbors.

Wurster, already convinced of DDT's danger and less cautious than
Hickey, was ready for action. In response to a letter and other materials
from Otto in 1965, he replied: "This whole pesticide business is a real
problem, and the forces at work are hard to beat. If the city sprays your
trees without your permission, can't you sue them? Gather the garden
clubs and bird clubs together and hit the city with 100 lawsuits. You
can produce buckets of evidence to prove that DDT is killing desirable wildlife. The biggest problem is to inform people of the facts."[14]

In the same letter, Wurster steers Otto to Wallace and Hickey.

So it appears that the 1965 exchange between two activists—one
a scientist, the other a housewife—played a crucial role in the coming
together of a group of Wisconsin and New York environmental activists. The story unfolded rapidly in the next few years, though time
seemed to be moving slowly for those, like Otto, who wanted immediate action. Joseph Hickey was not among them. He had more work
to do.

CHAPTER THREE

JOSEPH HICKEY WEPT

O N A RAINY SPRING DAY LONG AFTER JOSEPH HICKEY HAD died, an associate recalled how the wildlife professor had wept about the suppression of some of his early research on DDT. Sitting in a café not far from the UW–Madison campus, Gene Roark sipped coffee and tugged on his gray goatee as he revisited events that took place when he was a young man.

Roark, who later went on to work as a communications specialist with the Wisconsin Department of Natural Resources and become a longtime Wisconsin conservation leader,[1] was harking back to what happened one day in 1959 in Hickey's office. Roark was a journalism graduate student and graduate assistant in the university's news service office, where his duties included covering natural resources issues. "Hickey wept that day as we talked," recalled Roark. "He had all this research about the impact of DDT on birds. But his work was being suppressed. The Agriculture College was in complete denial. Of course, the university was spraying DDT to protect its historic elms from the beetle, and there were dead robins everywhere."[2]

Hickey was a frustrated professor and researcher in the Department of Wildlife Management in the College of Agriculture at the University of Wisconsin in Madison. "He literally said, 'I can't let you publicize this, under orders of the dean,'" Roark recalled.

The research Roark was referring to had been done by Hickey and a graduate student, Barry Hunt, and focused on the effects of DDT

Joseph Hickey's interest in birds began when he was a boy growing up in the Bronx and continued throughout his life. A professor of wildlife management at the University of Wisconsin in Madison during the Wisconsin DDT hearing, Hickey's research on eggshell thinning caused by DDT in certain bird species was pivotal in efforts to ban the pesticide. *Courtesy of Susan Nehls*

spraying on songbird populations. One of their research sites was the University of Wisconsin. Years later, Hickey recalled the events: "They used tons of DDT. There were robins dying all over the place. Even our screech owls died. The screech owls died only after rainstorms, when the rains force the earthworms up. We found the cuticles of the worms in the screech owls' stomachs."[3] It was an important link. Earthworms accumulated DDT from the soil around trees that had been sprayed. Screech owls, well named for their tremulous wails, are among the smallest in the owl family, and their cosmopolitan diets include invertebrates like worms. The cuticles—the tough, protective outer layer of worms—would have taken longer to digest.

Hickey and Hunt found that robin mortality on the Madison campus was about 90 percent. Hunt had also been conducting bird censuses in other Wisconsin communities—some that had sprayed DDT, some that had not. The research showed that the density of songbirds in these communities was inversely proportional to the number of trees per acre sprayed with DDT. "In other words, if they had only one tree the density was only lightly reduced, but if it had 10 trees, it was essentially a silent spring. So we saw a silent spring in the spring of 1959," Hickey would recall years later.

Hickey's comments show how the drama surrounding DDT played out step by step, like the pages of a mystery novel. In 1959, Hickey and other scientists had yet to make the full leap from the acute toxicity that killed songbirds to recognizing its buildup in the food chain, which was already decimating raptors and other species.

But even in 1959, the academic differences at the University of Wisconsin were distinctly marked. Indeed, the voices of some of Hickey's College of Agriculture colleagues were being heard on the use of DDT and had been heard for years. Most who spoke felt DDT was necessary and valuable. It is not surprising that much of the college's faculty leaned in this direction. The College of Agriculture, like none other on campus, worked closely with the agricultural sector to support the state's bedrock industry. The school's researchers were focused on feeding a growing population and relying on an array of modern tools, many only introduced after World War II. From their perspective, DDT was essential for use on crops. It was a broad-spectrum pesticide that could be used to fight a number of insect pests, and it was less expensive than alternatives. The college was also on the receiving end of money from chemical companies and agricultural interests for research.

The college's entomology department held more than its share of DDT proponents. One was Ellsworth Fisher, who was steadfast in his belief that DDT was an important weapon in the pest-control arsenal. Fisher and C. L. Fluke, another economic entomologist in the college, were authors of a special circular, "DDT: Its Present Uses and Limitations," published by the College of Agriculture's Extension Service in 1945.

The publication alternated between advising caution and encouraging use of the newly introduced chemical. On some matters, it was quite clear: "It is safe to recommend the use of DDT in specific preparations for the control of most flies that frequent the house and barn, mosquitoes, most cockroaches, some ants, fleas, sand flies, bedbugs, lice, and brown dog ticks."[4] Given the Extension Service's mission of extending the university's resources to all citizens, the circular most certainly found its way into extension offices across the state, including in Brown County, where Jerry Apps was presented with a basket of dead robins and a question about why DDT was being recommended.

While citing the reason DDT was valuable, the entomologists unwittingly indicted it in the same circular: "The chief advantage of DDT is in its ability to remain toxic on a sprayed or dusted surface for days and even months, depending upon conditions." Still, they advised caution, since "there are yet numerous problems to be solved especially as to its effects upon man, livestock, pets, food plants, beneficial insects, wildlife, and soil organisms which are beneficial to man in aiding better crop production."

Fisher continued advocating for DDT use even as new information on its impacts became available. He would testify in support of it at the DNR hearing, almost a quarter century after the extension circular made its rounds, and he also sat through the hearing with the Task Force for DDT, the advisory group of the National Agricultural Chemicals Association that intervened in the Madison case.[5]

Fisher was by no means alone, but many others in the college declined to get into the public fray—or at least declined to be named. Attributed or not, sentiments within the entomology department erupted in 1962, when WHA Radio, the flagship of the state public radio network, brought Rachel Carlson's *Silent Spring* to its listening audience.

Karl Schmidt, host of "Chapter A Day," read the book over the air. Schmidt was no stranger to DDT. He and others in his Madison neighborhood had already protested the city's spraying of DDT by helicopter.[6]

The reaction to "Chapter A Day" was anything but silent. Schmidt and his bosses at WHA fielded a slew of complaints.

Schmidt responded to the controversy by hosting a panel discussion, "Insecticides and People," in Madison in November 1962. Professors on the panel included botanists Hugh Iltis and Grant Cottam,[7] limnologist Arthur Hasler, chemist Aaron Ihde, medical geneticist James F. Crow, and biochemist Van R. Potter.[8]

None of the panelists came from the College of Agriculture. The discussion clearly leaned in the direction of defending *Silent Spring* and warning about overuse of broad-spectrum and persistent pesticides such as DDT.

The College of Agriculture Department of Entomology complained, leading to a subsequent forum, "The Use of Pesticides," moderated by Ira Baldwin. Baldwin is a captivating figure in his own right, having served as scientific director of the US biological weapons program during World War II, where the focus was on how to turn anthrax and botulinum toxin into weapons of mass destruction. In

1960, he had chaired a committee of the National Academy of Sciences' National Research Council that studied the use of pesticides and concluded that the benefits of DDT outweighed its risks. In the midst of that study, he was asked by *Science* magazine to review *Silent Spring*. He did so in the September 1962 issue, claiming that Carson chose to be the "prosecuting attorney" and thus failed to present both sides to the issue.[9]

Baldwin's panel of entomology, oncology, wildlife management, and zoology faculty wasn't enough to settle the score in the eyes of the entomology department. The department issued a cover letter written by Chairman Robert Dicke and a blistering eighteen-page critique charging that Schmidt and WHA had violated station policies under which it operated by the authority of the UW Board of Regents, "ignoring their responsibility toward programming in areas of 'special interest.'" As for the "Insecticides and People" panelists, the critique named the men, noting "none of whom is competent in the field of pesticides." The letter went on to say, "We are disturbed by the continuing spread, from this campus, of false and misleading information in our field. We, who have collectively over 200 years of experience in the study of insecticides, regret that it has become necessary to correct some of the more glaring, misleading and erroneous statements broadcast over the state network." It was the entomology department's belief that WHA staff had "directed its efforts entirely to present the Carson story of pesticide dangers as an authentic, scientific document without notifying or consulting with the appropriate departments." As a result, they added, "Our considered opinion to ignore *Silent Spring*, as it deserves, has been thwarted by the actions of the University of Wisconsin personnel who are neither trained nor skilled in the field of pesticides, primarily by the staff of WHA and especially Karl Schmidt."[10]

Members of the "Insecticides and People" panel fired back, writing letters to Dicke and H. B. McCarthy, director of the Division of Radio-Television Education at the university. In his letter, Iltis accused the Department of Entomology of "an attempt at censorship by one department of the opinions and concerns of scientists in other departments with which they do not agree."[11]

The battle was on, and it would continue for the next several years as Wisconsin's DDT story unfolded. An exchange between College of Agriculture dean Glenn Pound and Wisconsin Conservation Department director Lester Voigt shows how the battle lines had formed. Pound, dean during much of the DDT debate, steadfastly maintained that the college took no official position on the chemical. But his back-and-forth correspondence with Voigt shows he wasn't about to back down on the topic, either.[12]

In a December 14, 1966, letter, Voigt politely but firmly criticized the College of Agriculture for its sponsorship of the Wisconsin Shade Tree Conference and the annual Pesticide Conference with Industry, which presented what he deemed "a one-sided approach to the total problems as related to environmental pollution and especially side effects on fish and wildlife."

Pointing to his department's concerns about DDT concentrations in Wisconsin waterways and other warnings about pesticide residues, Voigt added, "It is inconceivable that this mass of evidence and obvious reasons for concern by all conscientious citizens can be ignored—or should be hidden—from individuals attending conferences sponsored by the College of Agriculture."

Voigt believed that the conference bias had wide-ranging effects. "Because of this incomplete and one-sided approach to a problem with serious ecological implications to our entire environment, we now have a movement toward increased use of DDT by many communities."

Pound responded on February 2, 1967, relating that faculty and staff had met to discuss Voigt's concerns, which he termed "rather strong indictments of our public programs." He noted: "Our scientists made it very clear to me that their concept of a program for Dutch Elm disease control is not totally a DDT program" and that "it is only under certain conditions involving the time of the year and the number of trees to be protected that DDT spraying is recommended as the

only feasible method to secure satisfactory control." He added that
Wisconsin Conservation Department engineer Laurence Motl was in
fact given an opportunity to present his views at the Wisconsin Shade
Tree Conference.

That elicited a three-page letter from Voigt. In his February 16
response, he pointed out that his criticism of information provided at
the conference came "because the Conservation Department has made
great effort to minimize the use of DDT, particularly in connection
with its spring usage for Dutch elm disease control" and acknowledged
that the department had made "considerable progress in this direction last year." He noted that after the conference "a number of large
municipalities have informed us that they have gone back to the use of
DDT for spring spraying and that they intend to continue its usage."

As for Motl, Voigt wrote that Motl's sense was that his participation in the conference would have been extremely limited, noting,
"Mr. Motl assures me that there was no provision for such presentation except that he would have stood up from the floor and forcibly
announced Conservation Department policies contrary to the tone
of the conference."

Voigt noted in his communications that the official position of the
Conservation Department concerning the use of DDT was of great
interest to the general public because the department had the responsibility of issuing permits for pesticide use by municipalities. Voigt went
on to say: "It has been a recognized tradition of the university for a
great many years to encourage the 'winnowing and sifting' of factual
information in an effort to discover the truth, whatever that may be. I
believe the impression given to most all who attended the conference
was that the information was all in favor of DDT usage and no information was presented representative of objections to its use."

Pound's April 25 reply was: "I should like to make it very clear that
the College of Agriculture has no 'official position' on Dutch Elm
disease control. Our scientists assure me that we have given adequate
recognition of the hazards in usage of DDT for Dutch Elm disease

control and their public service programs have presented a comprehensive view of Dutch Elm disease control. I must, therefore, reject your inference that we have failed to encourage the 'winnowing and sifting' process by which the truth is found."

But Pound was juggling a hot potato. In a November 11, 1966, speech in Washington, DC, he had said, "We have too much indiscriminate and unilateral use of agricultural pesticides. We in agriculture can no longer let commodity production be our only relationship to pesticides. We must become deeply involved in ecological and sociological relationships."[13]

⊠   ⊠   ⊠

Joseph Hickey was doing his own sifting and winnowing as he learned more about DDT. He had remained relatively quiet during the early 1960s. But by 1964, as research began to show the connection between chronic exposure to DDT and the population declines of peregrine falcons and a number of other bird species, he saw the need for a conference to pull the disparate research together. The international conference on peregrine falcon populations would be held in Madison in 1965, and Hickey recounted later how he had trouble finding funding to bring together scientists from two continents to share their information. A donation of more than eight thousand dollars from the National Audubon Society made it possible, and he speculated that his longtime friend Roger Tory Peterson—an Audubon board member—probably engineered the donation.

That Hickey endured difficulties in the College of Agriculture is clear. That he chose to remain relatively quiet until he had his research in order, to the chagrin of friends and colleagues like Peterson, is also clear. Two things are obvious: He gained confidence as his own research coalesced with that of respected colleagues. And once there was the data behind him, Hickey would become a fearless if reluctant warrior. Dan Anderson, a Hickey graduate student who played a key role in locking down the crucial data on eggshell thinning as the cause of steep population declines in raptors and other bird species, was surprised years after the fact to hear of Roark's story of Hickey weeping. "Joe probably got over that pretty fast," Anderson recalled. "The Joe I knew wouldn't back down."[14]

But there was no doubt that scientists who pushed the envelope on DDT encountered academic isolation.

Anderson, who would land a job at University of California, Davis, as a professor of wildlife biology—despite being referred to as "that egg shell son of a bitch" by one of the faculty members—recounted the experience of his colleague, University of California, Davis, zoologist Robert Rudd. Work by Rudd at Clear Lake, California, in the 1960s showed the impact of DDT on fish-eating western grebes. "He was persecuted and shunned so bad," Anderson said. Undeterred, Rudd ended up being a key witness at the Wisconsin DNR hearing and wrote *Pesticides and the Living Landscape*, an important work published in 1964 by the University of Wisconsin Press.

Charles Wurster, Environmental Defense Fund cofounder and biologist/biochemist at the State University of New York at Stony Brook, recalled a similar fate for combining his academic duties and civic activism. "I wasn't promoted to full professor. I was an associate professor, and my salary was kept low." He retired in 1996. Chuckling, he later noted the irony, "In 2009, the State University of New York, of all things, awarded me an honorary doctor of science degree."[15]

Joseph Hickey never said much about his own struggles. His papers include no direct references to any personal difficulties.

But as tributes rolled out after Hickey's death in 1993, so did long-held secrets. Bill Foster, a friend and professor in the UW–Madison School of Law who chased bird-watching lists with Hickey, was most direct. In remarks at Hickey's memorial service, Foster recalled the days after *Silent Spring* was published. He noted, "From the College of Agriculture at Wisconsin, criticism of Miss Carson was quick to come and harsh: She was an irresponsible fear-monger, utterly with-

out proof that these chemicals caused the harms she suspected. . . .
WHA, the university's public radio station, soon discovered that Joe
Hickey was, quite literally, the only member of the Ag School faculty
who would appear on the air in defense of Miss Carson. Her critics
landed on him: Where are your proofs that Miss Carson is right? You
have none and you are as irresponsible as she."[16]

Recalling his friend's fielding of such criticism, Foster said, "Joe's
response was that the critics couldn't prove their case, either—and evidence suggesting links between these chemicals and harm was mounting. On our list-chasing trips these days, Joe spoke of his loneliness in
the Ag School."

In many ways, Joseph Hickey was misplaced in the College of Agri-
culture. Wildlife management had little directly to do with agricul-
ture, but natural resources programs sometimes found themselves in
those settings in the mid-twentieth century. As the story played out,
Hickey found collaborators elsewhere at the university: Hugh Iltis and
Orie Loucks, another botanist, would join Hickey as members of the
Citizens Natural Resources Association. Both were members of the
College of Letters and Science.

The differences between the two colleges—Agriculture and Letters and Science—would be a subplot throughout the DDT battles. It shouldn't have been a surprise. Many of those in the College
of Agriculture were charged with improving efficiency and crop production, which was assisted by chemicals. Those in Letters and Science were intensely interested in ecological science: the relationships
living organisms have with the environment. Other influences were
noted, too. "What was different at the College of Letters and Science
was there was a fair sprinkling of people who admired Aldo Leopold,"
Loucks recalled. "He had been dead twenty years, and, although his
book was not national then, he was very respected."[17]

In the mid- to late 1960s, the tension over the activities of scientists
such as Hickey, Iltis, and Loucks was palpable at the university. But
years later, when looking back on that time, Loucks said he believed

that the University of Wisconsin was one of the few schools in the nation where citizen scientists could work with any measure of security. He recalled colleagues at other universities losing their jobs over involvement in contentious issues.

Victor Yannacone, the fiery EDF attorney who would come to Wisconsin for the DDT hearing, agreed. "Wisconsin was one of the few places that hearing could have taken place," he recalled. "The political climate there was right for it."[18]

CHAPTER FOUR

"MILITANT" ACTIVISTS

I T MIGHT BE EXPECTED THAT A GROUP OF CITIZENS WHO
boldly proclaimed a need for "a militant and democratic citizen-
based state resource-use organization"[1] at the midpoint of the twentieth century would encounter opposition at its very founding. Such
was the case for the upstart Citizens Natural Resources Association
of Wisconsin.

The CNRA was established in 1950 by a small group of citizens
concerned about plans to cut down an alley of large hackberry trees
during construction of Highway 30 near Oconomowoc.[2]

Among the founding members was Frederick L. Ott, a paper salesman of old Milwaukee wealth. "We were mad. Some letter writing,
then get-togethers—all-day sessions—then [we] decided to become
citizen watchdogs," he said, recalling the tree controversy. "We wanted
something different from other conservation organizations. More militant. Ready to mobilize."[3]

The hackberry battle was the opening salvo for these citizens, who
believed "there are forces at work in Wisconsin which tend to emphasize only the economic values of natural resources under a philosophy
of resource-use which evidently is based upon a short-sighted immediate policy at the expense of sound long-term use."[4] But even before
that, the CNRA found controversy.

The invitation to the group's organizational meeting, scheduled
to be held December 16, 1950, at the Milwaukee Public Museum,

is telling in itself. It came on paper with the letterhead of the Wisconsin Conservation Commission, the citizens' board that oversaw operations of the Wisconsin Conservation Department, and was most likely penned by Walter Scott, who served as an administrative assistant with the commission.

Scott had compiled a list of state residents who were to be invited to the organizational meeting.[5] In addition to the 350 names he submitted to fellow CNRA organizers, letters informing recipients of the meeting were sent to another 350 addresses, according to a letter to Scott from the museum staff who handled the mailings. Citizens invited to the meeting came from all walks of life and all corners of the state. Many had deep roots in Wisconsin's conservation community. Some were academics, while others were influential politicians, including governor-elect Walter J. Kohler, and iconic newspaper figures, such as William T. Evjue, publisher of the *Capital Times* in Madison.

Scott's involvement is telling. Even though he was an employee of the Wisconsin Conservation Department (later the Wisconsin Department of Natural Resources), Scott would play an influential role throughout the DDT battles. He seemed to make no effort to hide his activities: numerous documents from the period show Scott wasn't much inhibited by his state job when it came to being active on natural resources issues. Still, while Scott was dedicated to the establishment of the CNRA and its campaigns, some of the environmentalists who fought DDT distrusted the state agency that employed him or criticized it in the belief it moved too slowly on the pesticide. Not unlike Dean Glenn Pound of the College of Agriculture, Scott had a daily balancing act.

The CNRA's pre-organizational committee included Scott and a handful of other activists. Among them were Charles "Chappie" Fox of Oconomowoc, an ardent conservationist better known for his connections to the Circus World Museum in Baraboo; well-known conservation activists Wallace Grange of the Sandhill Game Farm in central Wisconsin and Aroline Schmitt of Milwaukee; along with Milwaukee Public Museum leaders such as Albert Fuller, its curator of biology, and Owen Gromme, an artist and a curator of mammals and birds. Alvin L. Throne, then a professor of botany at Milwaukee State Teachers College, was the only academic on the committee.

The committee anticipated pushback from other conservation groups, and the invitation to the December 1950 organizational meeting made this clear. "No doubt your immediate reaction to this proposal will be 'we don't need any more conservation organizations in Wisconsin, especially if the present groups function as intended.'"[6] The invitation noted that members of the pre-organizational committee were themselves affiliated with other groups and sought to define the differences, noting that "this new group will work with (and not against) all other conservation organizations in the state having similar plans and purposes."

That wasn't enough to appease leaders of the Izaak Walton League of America, who strongly objected to the new group. The IWLA and its local divisions had long been a major force on behalf of conservation in Wisconsin and across the country. One of the first national conservation organizations with individual membership, the IWLA was formed in Chicago in 1922 by anglers who wanted to protect fishing waters. The IWLA, whose members were referred to as "Ikes," had one hundred thousand supporters in the 1920s, but its membership was declining by 1950. In Wisconsin, the Ikes had fought early conservation battles, including efforts to protect Horicon Marsh and Wisconsin's scenic rivers. Ikes who attended the CNRA's December organizational meeting to voice opposition included William Voight Jr., national executive director of the IWLA; A. D. Sutherland and Virgil Muench, past presidents of the Wisconsin Division of the IWLA; and A. M. Buechel, then president of the Wisconsin Division of the IWLA. All the Wisconsin leaders had solid reputations in the Wisconsin conservation community. Indeed, Muench and Sutherland would later be inducted into the Wisconsin Conservation Hall of Fame for their conservation work in the state and beyond.

Perhaps it was the decline in membership and influence that led IWLA officials to challenge the formation of a new organization. They pointed out at the CNRA's organizational meeting that membership in the Milwaukee IWLA division had declined from about a peak of 3,600 to about 400 by 1950.

The Ike leaders clearly ruffled feathers of members of the new organization that day. On December 17, Throne sat down to pen a sizzling letter to the four Ikes regarding their "regrettable action" at the meeting the previous day. "Had you gentlemen appeared at that meeting as individual citizens, your actions might be understandable and perhaps excusable," he wrote. "But appearing in your several official capacities, as you gentlemen did, it is my opinion that your actions are indefencible [*sic*], highly unethical, and gave to the Izaak Walton League of America the greatest black eye the League has ever received." He continued, "You gentlemen exhibited before the people assembled so extreme a case of jitters and bitter jealousy as to raise in their minds the reason for those jitters and jealousy."[7]

Throne questioned whether the IWLA was "skating on so thin ice that it cannot stand the competition that you gentlemen imagine the new organization will give you? Is it that the principles of the new organization are so sound and your own so weak that you fear it? Is it that the plan to put a full-time executive secretary in Madison [something that did not materialize] is so good an idea that petty jealousy prompts you to desire that the League should be the one to do so? Or is it that the conservation of you gentlemen and the League is so narrow as to hold that any ideas not fostered by your brains are worthless?"

He went on to paint the CNRA as a potential partner for the IWLA, writing, "In my opinion, if the League is truly concerned about conservation, it should embrace the new Association as a brother ally, both fighting for the same cause, hand in hand."

A few days later, Sutherland answered Throne by letter. He noted that he had to leave the meeting early and didn't speak, for he was there to listen. The letter outlined the Ikes's ongoing efforts in Wisconsin, noting, "Apparently you have not heard of the enactment of the Pollution law which was opposed by the most powerful influential combinations that the Izaak Walton League ever combated. Our bill passed unanimously in both Houses."[8]

Sutherland appealed for support for the IWLA's own efforts to hire "a full-time man to co-ordinate the many Chapters' activities and I trust you will help us in trying to get such a man."

In the last paragraph, Sutherland raised the issue of Walter Scott's involvement. "I am wondering if the meeting I attended which was presided over by a full time employee of the Conservation Department in the presence of the Chairman of the Conservation Commission didn't suggest that the Conservation Commission intended to control the proposed new Conservation organization."[9]

For his part, Scott was criticized by some for letting the Ikes have their say during the organizational meeting. Responding to Roy Swenson, a CNRA supporter and conservation coordinator for Milwaukee Public Schools, Scott defended his approach. "It was more or less unexpected to see so many of the top flight IWLA members come into the meeting, obviously determined to present a negative approach. It seemed that there was no other way to handle the situation than to let them speak their piece, unfortunate as it was, I believe, for their organization."[10]

The Ikes weren't the only opponents of the new organization. William J. Knoll, editor of the *Badger Sportsman* in Wausau, said so in the January 1951 issue of his publication. Lauding Muench's comments at the meeting, Knoll wrote: "Mr. Muench has taken a similar view to that of *The Badger Sportsman*, which has contended for years that we need less such organizations and more support given to those that have been doing a good job for the past many years. The aim of the new Organization is to sponsor an educational program of conservation. This paper has been carrying on this program for years and has over 32,000 readers to whom such a message is being reached. . . . What we need are fewer organizations but more effective ones, rather than one organization working opposite the other." Knoll went on to invite the CNRA to back his publication, writing, "If only the recently organized Citizens Natural Resources Association would put their effort in backing our program, they would have a means of reaching the sportsmen, and help to get many more to support their program. The columns of this newspaper are open to any organization new or old who are fighting for better conservation."[11]

Scott conveyed his reaction to other CNRA founders in a note: "We have now made the 'social column.' We have had a backhanded invitation to use this yellow sheet to gain new members and fight our battles. I, for one, am very pleased to see that Knoll has chosen to be on the other side—it would be impossible for me to be on the same side with him even if he were right—which he is very seldom."[12]

The early squabbling was a hint of a deeper split to come in future decades, one that divided traditional conservation organizations—especially those of the hook-and-bullet crowd—and modern-day environmental organizations. The camps shared many of the same concerns, such as habitat loss, pollution, and exploitation of natural resources. But some basic differences split them, including hunter and nonhunter friction, variances in rural and urban mindsets, and, surely, determining which natural resources issues were most pressing and then deciding how to address them. Another split would rear its head as the environmental movement grew: women were drawn more to environmental groups than those of the sportsmen. This led to the CNRA becoming an organization in which women played major roles, both as leaders and members.

Protests aside, the CNRA was indeed organized that December day in Milwaukee: "The new organization was to be militant in nature, follow the principles of Aldo Leopold, and remain a group of committed conservationists."[13]

Dues were five dollars and trial memberships one dollar. Wallace Grange would become its first president. Aroline Schmitt became president a decade later as the CNRA began to focus on pesticides. In addition to those who formed the pre-organizational committee, other founding members were W. C. McKern, Emil Kruschke, and Trudi Scott, Walter's wife.

Joseph Hickey was on the group's first advisory committee, but after a short time he had second thoughts. His actions would hint of pressure from other quarters.

Hickey had informed Walter Scott that he needed to resign from the committee and possibly from the CNRA altogether. A February 20, 1951, letter from Scott to CNRA president Grange provides insight. "When he could not give me any good reason for wishing to retire from our advisory committee (and he even seemed to want to divorce himself from membership) I kept after him until he indicated that he had been told by his superiors [at the University of Wisconsin] that continued relationship with the CNRA constituted a form of lobbying and that he would have to sever such relationships," he wrote. "He indicated that [R. J.] Muckenhirn [a University of Wisconsin soil scientist and early CNRA member] was out of town and he was anxious to secure his reaction because he no doubt would be in the same position, as he also is in the College of Agriculture."[14]

Scott went on to speculate about the status of another early CNRA member, University of Wisconsin botanist John Curtis, whose book *Vegetation of Wisconsin* would become recognized as a major contribution to the development of plant ecology. "As Curtis is in the liberal arts school [College of Letters and Science], he may not be affected as directly but that is hard to say."

The upstart organization was clearly making waves in the halls of academia.

■   ■   ■

In its first decade, with the DDT battle a few years off, the CNRA focused its attention on advocating for the designation of the state's first wilderness area, located in the Flambeau State Forest along the Flambeau River. Throughout the 1950s, its natural roadside vegetation policy guidelines served as a reference for highway crews and utilities in their removal of roadside vegetation. It protested pollution of state rivers and worked to create better state pollution-control laws.

The great cranberry scare of 1959 hinted at the rough-and-tumble decade on the horizon for the organization. It also produced some of the earliest hints that the CNRA was going to get into the row over pesticides and their impacts, real or imagined. Just days before Thanksgiving in 1959, US Secretary of Health, Education and Welfare Arthur Flemming announced that some cranberries grown in the United States had been contaminated with aminotriazole, a weed killer that was linked to cancer in laboratory animals. Acknowledging that not all berries were contaminated—those grown in Wisconsin among them—Flemming still recommended that Thanksgiving meals be served without the tart treats. It was just a recommendation, but some states went further, ordering cranberries be removed from store shelves and restaurants. Homes and restaurants across the country took the prudent path and eliminated the traditional side dish.

Critics claimed Flemming dramatically overreacted. Proponents applauded him for adhering to the "Delaney Clause," an amendment to the Food, Drug, and Cosmetic Act of 1938. The proviso said no additive could be deemed safe (or given Food and Drug Administration approval) if found to cause cancer in humans or experimental animals. The Delaney Clause was initially opposed by the FDA and by scientists, who believed an additive used at very low levels need not necessarily be banned because it may cause cancer at high levels. Proponents justified the clause on the basis that cancer experts had not been able to determine a safe level for any carcinogen. The FDA says to this day that—notwithstanding critical publicity—Flemming's action had beneficial results, particularly in convincing farmers that pesticides must be used with care. Also, to this day critics cite the cranberry scare as the first of many overreactions to chemicals in consumer products.

The CNRA jumped into the fray with a resolution calling for the agriculture committees in both houses of Congress to begin "a widespread public investigation of the present uses of chemical herbicides and insecticides."[15] It began: "Whereas—the highly poisonous effects on human life of the so-called Wonder Chemicals in cranberry and other food production have alarmed federal and other officials, and alerted our citizens of their potential danger. . . . The purpose of this investigation would be to endeavor to determine the direct and side effects of these chemicals on human and animal life with the object of enacting legislation control of the use of such chemicals."

The resolution also hinted at the coming battle over DDT. "Whereas—the entire population is literally being bombarded with poisons, in the air they breath [sic] (mosquito and tree sprays), the food they eat, and the water they drink, without their consent and in spite of their protests."

Copies of the resolution were distributed widely at the state and national level.

CNRA president Schmitt of Milwaukee went a step further, writing to Flemming on behalf of the organization: "Your action in regard to contaminated cranberries deserves the commendation and support of the people, not only of the United States, but of other countries as well."[16] In her letter, Schmitt went on to slam newspaper coverage of the matter, and shared copies of the CNRA's own pesticide materials with Flemming. (As early as 1951, the CNRA held a conference on the dangers of chemical sprays, which led to the production of a manual for roadside pesticide spraying. The organization distributed the manual to highway departments and businesses that sprayed weeds along roads, in the hope they would do so with restraint.)

An ardent conservationist, Schmitt was used to action. Though she was beset by illness and bedridden for several years, she didn't cower easily, having cruised timber for the US Forest Service during World War II. Her job was to estimate amounts of standing forestland resources available for the war effort. This job earned her some encounters with the business end of a gun, pointed by property owners who didn't want her on their land, recalled her daughter, Maxine Roberts.[17]

Perhaps this steeled Schmitt for future battles. "She wouldn't back down if she knew she was right," her daughter recalled.

Environmentalists' efforts aside, politicians were quick to show their support for cranberry growers. Vice President Richard Nixon and Senator John F. Kennedy—soon to square off in a presidential election—both publicly consumed cranberries in Thanksgiving photo ops. Nixon boldly consumed four helpings of cranberry sauce. Kennedy, from the key cranberry state of Massachusetts, drank two glasses of cranberry juice. *Life* magazine captured Kennedy taking his portion.

Back in Wisconsin, the CNRA made sure Governor Gaylord Nelson got a copy of the resolution. A few years later, in 1962, the same year *Silent Spring* was published, Nelson would win a seat in the US Senate and soon emerge as a major environmental leader. Nelson was one of the first national politicians to call for a ban on DDT.

In the end, the cranberry scare served to ignite the passions of those who saw herbicides and insecticides as potential threats to health. The CNRA was among the first groups to tap into those concerns and turn them into action. The organization would stay engaged over the decade, mostly building awareness through its newsletters and meetings. Many of its members also belonged to other conservation groups and spread the word to them. A critical mass of concerned citizens was building from the ground up.

The cranberry scare also sharpened the battle lines in the pesticide fray. Despite growing concerns among some citizens, opposing pesticides "was radical back in those days," recalled Roy Gromme, who was president of the CNRA when the group sought a hearing on DDT in 1968.[18] "People were in favor of pesticides. It was the easy way to go."

Schmitt's presidency of the CNRA ended in February 1961, not without some frustration. A few months earlier, she had written to Walter Scott, complaining that on the tenth anniversary of the organization, there was "no one willing to do the job necessary to keep it going let alone make it a strong, working body."[19] A month later, Gromme acted as secretary for a meeting at which "a discussion on the pros and cons of disbandment of the organization was held."[20] It didn't happen, and the CNRA limped along without a major cause to clamp onto.

But soon the group would find itself edging toward a bigger battle. DDT, the wonder chemical from World War II, had arrived. Dutch elm disease was marching across the eastern United States and, as cities scrambled to halt it, DDT spraying in populated areas and its visible impacts on bird life was drawing the attention of concerned citizens. It was one thing to use DDT on farm crops and forestland. Spraying it in the treetops that shaded residential homes was another matter.

Despite its earlier issues with the CNRA, the Izaak Walton League of America would later join CNRA in petitioning for the DNR hearing on DDT. Other hunting and fishing organizations across Wisconsin and the nation would also unite with the upstart CNRA environmentalists to curtail DDT use or see it banned. With garden clubs, women's organizations, civic groups, businesses and some industries also joining in, a large and influential coalition was coming together for one of the first major battles in a new environmental era.

DDT had rallied a new coalition.

CHAPTER FIVE

OFFICERS AND COUNCILORS

Lorrie Otto and Joseph Hickey will long be remembered for their roles in Wisconsin's DDT battles. But the names of other early citizen activists who worked with them aren't as well known. The Citizens Natural Resources Association officers' roster at the time of the DDT hearing reflects an interesting blend of characters from various walks of life and locations around the state.

The group's top officers hailed not from Hickey's Madison or Otto's Milwaukee suburbs, but from Stevens Point, Wausau, and Loganville, the latter lodged in Baraboo Hills country. They included President Frederick Baumgartner, a wildlife professor at what was then known as Wisconsin State University–Stevens Point (now the University of Wisconsin–Stevens Point).

The vice president, Elgis Holden "Al" Berkman, had been a soil conservationist with the Soil Conservation Service in Wausau since 1938. He also taught forestry and soils at the Wisconsin State University–Stevens Point and Northcentral Technical College and was an active member of the Wausau Kiwanis Club.

Bertha Pearson, also of Wausau, served as treasurer. She was a longtime officer at Marathon Box Company, an industrial crating manufacturer with deep roots in the Wausau area. A love of birds and other wildlife nurtured on her property along the Wisconsin River likely led her to the CNRA.

Carla Kruse of Loganville was the secretary and the crackerjack editor of the *CNRA Report*, the organization's bimonthly newsletter. She farmed with her husband, Harold, who had grown to love nature as a farm kid. He was instrumental in identifying and setting aside sensitive environmental areas in the Baraboo Hills, beginning as early as the mid-1950s, sometimes with botanist Orie Loucks from the University of Wisconsin in Madison at his side. Loucks would serve as the final witness on behalf of the petitioners at the Department of Natural Resources hearing.

A peek at the group's advisory council, or councilors, offers other insights. The group included Roy O. Gromme of River Hills, Mrs. Fred Hamerstrom of Plainfield, Mrs. Russell Rill of Clintonville, and J. J. Werner of Madison.

Gromme, son of the famed wildlife artist and curator at the Milwaukee Public Museum, Owen Gromme, headed the CNRA when it pursued its case against the city of Milwaukee and Buckley Tree Service of Waukesha. A biology teacher at Nicolet High School in Glendale, he left for an assignment in India with USAID just before the Madison hearing began.

"Mrs. Fred Hamerstrom" was Frances "Fran" Hamerstrom, who with her husband had forsaken the socialite scene in Boston to dedicate her life to saving prairie chickens on the grasslands of central Wisconsin. The Hamerstroms were colorful and eccentric Leopold disciples known internationally for their work, and Fran emerged as a nature and outdoors writer.

"Mrs. Russell Rill" was Katherine Rill, a science teacher at Clintonville High School, who would earn a master's degree in botany at the University of Wisconsin–Oshkosh in 1971. She went on to teach as a faculty assistant at the university and work for the Nature Conservancy, contacting landowners of scientifically significant property for the organization as it sought to acquire and preserve sensitive areas. She later joined the DNR, taking part in a natural areas inventory in several counties. Her husband, too, was a conservation activist.

J. J. "Doc" Werner of Madison made a living as a pharmacist, but as his son, Gary Werner, recalled, "Conservation was his life's passion."[1] Werner and his wife, Patricia, also a pharmacist, were among the associates who operated Prescription Pharmacy from the Park Hotel (now Inn on the Park) on Madison's Capitol Square.

J. J. Werner had served in the US Marines in the South Pacific during World War II. Gary, who now heads the Partnership for National Trails in Madison, recalled his dad rebuffing requests for family camping trips, saying he'd had enough of wet foxholes to last a lifetime. But in the late 1950s, J. J. Werner discovered the legacy of naturalist John Muir, whose family had homesteaded in Marquette County, Wisconsin. "It was like this sea change," his son recalled. "We were out hiking and canoeing and exploring Wisconsin."

As his interest in conservation causes grew, Werner found himself in a strategic location during work days. "The Park Hotel was the place where many of the legislators from out of town would have rooms," Gary Werner noted. "He knew many of the legislators. He also knew Gaylord Nelson when he was governor."

Soon, J. J. Werner was among those advocating for the creation of a Wisconsin chapter of the Sierra Club, to be named after Muir. The Sierra Club–John Muir Chapter celebrated its fiftieth anniversary in 2013. Werner was also among the founders of the Ice Age Trail in Wisconsin and joined a handful of other conservationists who sought to develop a state wild and scenic rivers program.

THE QUIET LEADER

Citizen movements are propelled by firebrands out front and kept on course by quiet leaders behind the scenes.

Frederick "Fred" Baumgartner of Stevens Point was in the latter category. Bespectacled and diminutive, Baumgartner's presidency of the

CNRA was marked by its brightest moment: when the DNR hearings thrust the organization into the national spotlight.

Baumgartner had risen to the presidency of the CNRA in the midst of its early legal maneuvering over DDT, as Roy Gromme left for India. Baumgartner's name seldom made its way into the thousands of news reports on the controversy. But records show he was constantly at work behind the scenes, corresponding with state and national allies, raising funds, and, occasionally, challenging opponents with letters that could draw intemperate responses. When the Wis-

Wisconsin State University–Stevens Point wildlife professor Frederick Baumgartner was president of the Citizens Natural Resources Association during the DDT hearing. *Courtesy of the University of Wisconsin–Stevens Point*

consin Legislature considered a ban on DDT in 1969, Baumgartner was among those who testified in favor.

Overall, Baumgartner comes off as a calm, confident leader who preferred personal correspondence to public pronouncements. As with several other key CNRA leaders, his spouse was also an environmental activist. Marguerite Baumgartner penned columns on ornithology and nature interpretation in the *Sunday Oklahoman* in Oklahoma City for eighteen years.[2] Her columns also ran in the *Tulsa World* and the Stillwater, Oklahoma, *Daily News Press*.

The couple arrived in Stevens Point in 1965, both holding doctoral degrees in ornithology from Cornell University. Fred took a faculty position with the rapidly growing Wisconsin State University–Stevens Point's Department of Natural Resources. He had served as an associate professor of wildlife conservation in the Department of Zoology at Oklahoma State University for twenty years before coming to Wisconsin.

Marguerite wrote columns for the *Stevens Point Journal*. The often-lengthy columns (two-thousand-plus words) focused on local, state, and national environmental issues, including the use of the popular herbicide 2,4-D. She also served as a guest lecturer at WSU–Stevens Point.

They had met at Cornell. A UW–Stevens Point news release issued upon their retirement in 1975 playfully noted: "They became engaged in a little tent under an owl's nest, which he was studying as part of his research assignment, and she was 'helping.'" Their son, Ted, put it simply: "Birds were their life. They thought the DDT situation was so bad it had to be addressed, and so they went to work."[3]

Fred Baumgartner wrote his doctoral thesis on American horned owls. His list of publications includes a paper in the 1949 *Proceedings of the Oklahoma Academy of Sciences*. DDT's post–World War II introduction was barely underway at the time, and Baumgartner found no evidence at the time that airplane spraying of a forested area near Stillwater had any impact on wildlife. "No distressed or dead individuals were observed," he wrote in "A Preliminary Study of the Effects of Certain Insecticides upon Wildlife in North-central Oklahoma." His scientific opinion would change in the coming years.

While at the helm of the CNRA, Fred Baumgartner operated much as he did in the university setting: he was low-key but professional, astute but not overly vocal, dedicated and hard working.[4] Students recall that while he wasn't flashy, he was firm in his beliefs, which he shared willingly. He was known for puffing on one pipe with another waiting in a pants pocket.

The 1975 retirement piece noted he had been heavily engaged in planning for the DDT hearing, and the trail of correspondence he left bears that out.

It was Baumgartner who penned an October 8, 1968, letter from the CNRA to "all organizations interested in conservation." It was topped with bursts of type stating "URGENT ACTION NEEDED! CONTROL PERSISTENT PESTICIDES."[5] Baumgartner sounded the alarm in his first sentence: "Wisconsin's valuable natural resources of fish, wildlife and water—as well as the potential economic benefits of both recreation and commercial fisheries on Lakes Michigan and Superior—are at stake today."

That Baumgartner chose to emphasize the economic impacts of pesticides on sport and commercial fisheries was likely no accident, and as the battle heated up, hunters and fishers and the organizations that represented them became CNRA allies. He also likely anticipated push-back from foes of a DDT ban, who would cite potential economic losses to crops and forestlands.

Baumgartner's letter recounted efforts to get a handle on the use of persistent pesticides across the Midwest and the nation. He noted that Russell Lynch,[6] the chair of the Wisconsin Natural Resources Board,[7] "even recommended that DDT should be declared a form of water pollution when sprayed in locations where it could get into public surface waters." Lynch's comments hinted at developments soon to come.

Clearly, the CNRA was spoiling for a fight. The "CNRA has decided it is time for a test case of this question of water pollution," Baumgartner wrote. The CNRA and other groups were also seeking support for legislation to create a state Pesticide Review Board. While Baumgartner's letter was primarily informational, it did include a plea for financial assistance.

And it was a fight the CNRA got, thanks to the DNR hearing in 1968–1969. An exchange between Baumgartner and Governor Warren Knowles after the hearing was underway produced the following carefully crafted message from Knowles, dated December 11, 1968: "I understand the Citizens Natural Resources Association has requested a declaratory ruling from the Department of Natural Resources as to whether the use of DDT under certain circumstances should be considered a form of water pollution. I hope these hearings . . . will bring out the facts and help us make the right decisions promptly in the forthcoming legislative session."[8]

Baumgartner replied on January 14, 1969: "We can already see some definite results from our campaign to eliminate the general use of DDT and other persistent pesticides that are polluting the waters of the world and causing alarming changes in animal life. We sincerely trust that the recent public hearings on DDT will lead to state and nationwide restrictions on the application of such chemicals for any purpose. Your continued support of such efforts is fully supported by thousands of citizens."[9]

Exchanges between the CNRA and foes of a DDT ban weren't so polite and formal. Baumgartner got under the skin of pro-DDT spokesman Ellsworth Fisher, the entomologist from the University of Wisconsin in Madison, with a letter sent March 28, 1969. Fisher was an outspoken proponent of DDT. He would testify at the DNR hearing at the behest of the environmentalists—and then only under threat of subpoena.[10]

Baumgartner challenged some of Fisher's comments and those of other DDT proponents at the Wisconsin Assembly hearing on a bill

to ban some uses of DDT. In his reply, Fisher claimed he was mis-
quoted in newspaper articles referenced by Baumgartner and denied
that his testimony had implied that another scientist—Hickey—had
falsified his data.

Fisher closed his letter with a flurry:

"Fred, I hope that there can be an orderly control of pesticides, as
further needed, based on fact. We have been operating on this basis
since the beginning of DDT. Similarly we don't want to see emotional
legislation to eliminate: robins because they eat cherries from some
people's backyard trees; some smaller songbirds because they fly into
picture windows, making a dirty blotch, sometimes breaking the win-
dow and occasionally scaring the occupants of the room; the gulls
which have caused aircraft disasters; deer which cause many automo-
bile wrecks; or many other species of living things which have a much
higher benefit than risk ratio."[11]

Hyperbole aside, Fisher's letter underscores the tension that accom-
panied disagreements among scientists who had been pulled into the
public arena, where they had to deal with politicians and journalists.

In his office in the Prairie School–design Nelson Hall at Wisconsin
State University–Stevens Point, Baumgartner was somewhat removed
from the fray in Madison. His job was to keep the ball rolling, and
that's what he did. But his work was hardly insignificant. A 1969 letter to Walter Scott, whose job title had evolved to deputy secretary, is
instructive. Baumgartner wrote:

"Fred Ott . . . strongly advises some rigid guidelines for CNRA
members on legislative matters. Apparently Fred had talked with two
more attorneys who are specialists in the field of taxes. After reviewing
our DDT hearing, both expressed real concern over the CNRA tax
status and the position of private citizens and groups who have contributed to the EDF fund. Their concern is based upon the fear that
the DDT hearing is giving CNRA a great deal of publicity. They suggest that our opponents in the use of DDT might publicly challenge
us as attempting to unduly influence legislation and thus embarrass

us. Our fund contributors might be in such a position that IRS would challenge their tax deductions. This indicates that all of us should write and speak on legislative matters as individuals rather than as official representatives of CNRA or any other organization."[12]

While Fred Ott did much of the legwork on fund-raising for the cash-short environmentalists, Baumgartner did his share, too. A February 13, 1969, letter to Dr. Elvis Stahr, president of the National Audubon Society, reveals Baumgartner's concerns about whether the CNRA and the Environmental Defense Fund would be able to raise enough funds to see the hearing and related actions through to their conclusion. The hearing was taking on a life of its own, lasting for months rather than a few weeks. Baumgartner was likely expressing the concerns of others in his camp when he noted, "We also have no assurance that the Wisconsin Department of Natural Resources will order a strict ban on the use of DDT for agricultural purposes. Court action against such a ban is a distinct possibility, perhaps a probability."[13]

That the National Audubon Society did its part becomes clear in a letter to Baumgartner later in the same year. Roland Clement, vice president of the national organization, wrote on July 7 to inform Baumgartner that the organization had allocated or raised $27,000 to be used directly in the Wisconsin action and that the Ford Foundation had also provided the national organization with $50,000 as the first half of its contribution toward the Wisconsin hearing.[14]

Much of Baumgartner's work took place in this manner: behind the scenes, in the form of quiet but essential leadership. Clearly, he worried about how to fund the DNR hearing and other activities in the state. Estimates of how much money was raised for the effort vary. Roy Gromme, president of the group until just before the hearing, reflected years later that he thought the number was as high as $257,000.[15] Other accounts are much lower.

An undated letter to the EDF's scientific advisor Charles Wurster—which notably lists Baumgartner's home address rather than that of his university office—expressed Baumgartner's feelings and those of the others who pursued a DDT ban. The letter acknowledged Wurster's personal sacrifices in the Wisconsin activities and elsewhere. Like many other scientists and academics who engaged in the DDT battles, Wurster did much of his work for little or no compensation, and often at personal cost in the academic setting. Wurster was able to chuckle later about never earning full professorship at the State University of New York at Stony Brook and being conferred emeritus status after retiring. But his correspondence with Baumgartner, Lorrie Otto, and others during the DDT battles tells the story of a man under no small amount of pressure. That Baumgartner grasped this is apparent in the letter: "The people of the world will recognize your tremendous contribution to man's health and welfare some time in the future. I can assure you that a small group of us in Wisconsin have given you a high place in the history of man's efforts to adjust and improve his environment."[16]

▨   ▨   ▨

Once DDT was banned, the Baumgartners pressed forward on new causes, as did many of the other citizen activists engaged in the DDT battles. Marguerite took her turn as president of the CNRA. She also founded Portage County Preservation Projects, an organization that called attention to concerns over the aerial spraying of potato and vegetable crops in central Wisconsin.

Upon their retirement in 1975, the Baumgartners moved to Jay, Oklahoma, where they immediately set about establishing the Little Lewis Whirlwind Nature School and Sanctuary, so named for a Cherokee boy to whom the federal government allotted the land in 1907. The boy died the following year at the age of six. "In naming our new home for its first owner, we have dedicated it to the dream of a sanctuary where all the Lewis Whirlwinds, of whatever age, ethnic background, occupation or inclination, may find inspiration and strength in the eternal values of the natural world," they said in the UW–Stevens Point news release announcing their retirement.[17]

Their work in Wisconsin had reached an end, but they left an imprint on UW–Stevens Point and the state. They continued their work in Oklahoma. In a 1982 *Oklahoma Today* article about their nature school, Fred Baumgartner said, "If people were only aware of the birds and other animals and the plants in these areas, they wouldn't need to be reminded to be more careful how they use the land."[18] A few years before Fred died in 1996, the couple collaborated on a book, *Oklahoma Bird Life.*

MISS CONSERVATION

If Lorrie Otto was the godmother of the DDT battles in Wisconsin, then Bertha Pearson was the great-aunt. She was seventy-seven and still active in conservation and numerous other causes as the DDT hearing got under way.

Bertha Ingeborg Pearson was a woman of many interests and talents who exhibited a concern for the well-being of other inhabitants of Earth, be they robins or fellow humans in need.

Her story is remarkable for many reasons. She was a longtime member of the CNRA and served as its treasurer during the DDT battles. In this role with the citizens' group, she worked with Baumgartner, Ott, and other members who worked to raise tens of thousands of dollars to bring the EDF to Wisconsin for the lengthy DDT hearing. Records show she corresponded frequently in fund-raising efforts. She was also the elder among the conservationists.

She earned the CNRA's highest honor, the Silver Acorn Award, and was named "Miss Conservation" when the Marathon County Resource Council nominated her for the Wisconsin Federation of Women's Clubs' Conservation Award in 1967. The federation was one of many examples of mainstream citizens' groups and institutions that had a commitment to conservation.

Bertha Pearson was an engaged citizen in many areas.

There was Bertha Pearson, faithful member of Wausau's Immanuel Lutheran Church, founded by Norwegian immigrants in 1883, and the home church of her parents, Jens and Greta (Olson) Pearson.

There was Bertha Pearson, a businesswoman at a time when men ruled the boardrooms. She began working at the Wausau Lumber and Box Company (later Marathon Box Company) as a teenager in 1909, and rose to become secretary-treasurer of the firm, a position she held until she was eighty-five years old, including during the years she was an officer with the CNRA.[19]

There was Bertha Pearson, who served on the state board of Lutheran Social Services in the 1930s, '40s, and '60s, and who gave time to the development of Homme Home for Boys, a Lutheran-affiliated orphanage in Wittenberg.

There was Bertha Pearson, who helped found the Visiting Nurse Association in Marathon County and served on its board for eighteen years.

Bertha Pearson of Wausau was treasurer of the Citizens Natural Resources Association during the DDT hearing. Pearson was a successful businesswoman who was active in an array of conservation and social services causes. *Courtesy of Wausau Daily Herald*

"In all of her efforts, her vision of the future was one of her greatest assets," reads her biography in the collection of the Marathon County Historical Society.

She left Wausau for a time as a young woman, first for three years of study in accounting at the University of Wisconsin in Madison and then for government service during World War I as office manager of the Illinois State Council of Defense in Chicago. This was one of the state bodies that assisted the National Council of Defense in the war effort. Why Pearson went to the Illinois council rather than Wisconsin's is left to conjecture. Perhaps adventure beckoned.

The Illinois council had many tasks related to its duty of carrying out national defense plans in the state. It engaged citizens in food, fuel, and industrial production and services, liberty loans, local Red Cross activities, and, notably for Pearson, conservation.

Appropriate citizen behavior was promoted, too. The council's final report in 1919 put it this way: "When the council came into existence, its most patent and pressing obligation seemed to be the development of a civilian morale which would insure to the nation the full and willing co-operation of Illinois in all measures required for the successful prosecution of the war."[20]

Clearly her service in Illinois and the concept of civilian morale for the greater good was something Pearson carried with her throughout her life.

After the war, the young Wausau woman moved on to New York, where she served a special assignment with the Young Women's Christian Association. Her job was to dispose of surplus properties, such as "hostess houses" for visiting guests of soldiers, which the YWCA had acquired during the war.

Following an attempted road trip to Dallas, Texas, which was foiled by winter weather, Pearson returned to Wausau and settled back into her role at Marathon Box Company, which was at the time lodged along the east bank of the Wisconsin River.

One day in the early World War II years, Pearson planted the first tree in the Wausau Senior High Forest.[21] Establishing school forests was a goal of the Wisconsin Conservation Commission. Created in 1926, this appointed commission ushered in a number of progressive reforms, going well beyond what had been called Wisconsin's "feeble pioneer efforts in conservation." The creation of school forests as educational laboratories was among the changes ushered in by the citizens' board. School forests that students visited on field trips and overnight excursions were among the earliest examples of environmental education. They were working forests that served as models of sustainable, multiple-use forestry, with regular harvests at appropriate intervals. Many school forests exist across the country today. Wisconsin was an early leader in their establishment.

Pearson's range of activities on behalf of conservation and the natural environment clearly mirror those of the conservation activists who emerged in the 1920s, '30s, and '40s. Among them was a steely-eyed professor of wildlife management at the University of Wisconsin in Madison named Aldo Leopold.

Leopold died in 1948, but Pearson lived through another evolution as environmentalists deemed that more strident measures were needed to address increasingly complex problems. She was unafraid to enter the fray, sometimes testifying at public hearings about pollution and other environmental concerns.

At a 1964 meeting of the state Water Pollution Committee in Wausau, she represented the CNRA as vice president. "Our stand is that the continued pollution of our waters is a national problem and a national disgrace, and it is up to all citizens to help solve this problem." Pearson told the committee that Wisconsin's waters "do not belong to municipalities nor to industry, but to the public as a whole."[22] The idea of federal intervention was a growing but by no means universally popular idea at the time.

Capturing the contradictions of the 1960s from the viewpoint of someone already in her seventies, she added: "Why should we, the richest country in the world, be willing to spend billions on super highways, other billions on trips to the moon, while we are complacent about the pollution of our rivers, lakes and streams? It is true today as it always has been that 'no nation can long endure whose waters are not pure.' It is time for drastic and immediate action."

Pearson's notes on the hearing clearly delineated the battle lines in the building fight over water pollution that would lead to the adoption of the federal Clean Water Act in 1972. The two-day hearing was "dignified" and "well-conducted," she reported to the CNRA, "and 95 percent of the time was given to those who were asking for leniency in any orders to be issued by the Committee on Water Pollution or State Board of Health. These were the paper mills, cheese factories, canning factories, milk processing plants, municipalities, etc."[23] Labor was well-represented, too, she noted, with "all pleading that nothing be done that would jeopardize their jobs. Chambers of Commerce and Service Clubs also raised their voices in protest against any new orders that might be contemplated on the paper mills." She observed that Clifford Krueger and Paul Alfonsi, state lawmakers from northern Wisconsin, spoke for the paper industry.

A few other voices for the environment spoke. They included William Ruth of Eagle River, president of the Federation of Wisconsin Conservation Clubs, whom Pearson quoted in her notes as saying, "Pollution is the No. 1 problem facing the nation today. Wisconsin may be doing more than other states to curb it, but it is also the No. 1 problem here." He went on to say, "If state agencies can't make reasonable orders and see that they are carried out, we will have to seek federal help."

However, the idea that the federal government should begin to play a role in water pollution cleanup was met with disdain by Pearson's hometown newspaper, the *Wausau Record-Herald*, which editorialized that federal aid was fine for research but not for loans to help river polluters build treatment facilities. Pearson made note of the editorial in her report to the CNRA board. "It would seem that pollution is much

to be preferred to federal help for its abatement!" she wrote. She concluded her report with: "I think CNRA must remain alert and militant on this subject of pollution, as halfway measures are not going to
remedy the situation."

When the CNRA honored Pearson with its top award, the Silver
Acorn, in 1967, a presenter said this of her: "Certainly this award recognizes Bertha as belonging to that very small group of people whose
whole life is one of dedication to serving the welfare of the citizenry
and the resources which support the people." The presenter also noted
she had earned the moniker "Miss Conservation."[24]

Harvey Haseltine Scholfield, a fourth-generation president at Marathon Box Company, helped paint a full picture of Pearson in an oral
history taped by his daughter, Lynne Scholfield. "Well when I came
into the business [1951] . . . I basically was responsible to my father
and his secretary, Bertha Pearson, who was a strong member of the
management team. And a strong community supporter . . . basically I
got my business education from my father and his secretary, who was
a very remarkable woman," he recalled.[25]

"[She] was very community-minded . . . and if she had been a
national figure, I am sure would have been in the forefront of wom-
en's rights. She was always advocating a greater place in business and
in the community for women. And she certainly was quite capable in
everything that she did. I think she helped my father realize that community service was as important as business service. . . . She was also
very philanthropic in her activities so she was always trying to per-
suade our corporation and other corporations to give at least 5 percent of their profits to community things. . . . She called a lot of the
shots [at work]. . . . she was a very logical, dominant woman and contributed a great deal to the survival of our business."

Bertha Pearson's frugality helped Marathon Box Company survive
the Great Depression, Scholfield claimed. She used the backs of enve-
lopes for scratch paper, saved paper clips, and avoided other expenses
by recycling and reusing office supplies.

When the work day was done—and if her many other civic en-
gagements didn't interfere—she retired to her home situated in an
eighteen-acre refuge for birds and other wildlife along the Wisconsin
River in Wausau. She named her retreat Elvestranden, an elegant Norwegian word for "river bank." Similar to other environmental activists
of her time, Pearson, a dedicated bird-watcher, likely noted the decline
of songbird populations as she wandered her wooded hideaway. She
belonged to twenty conservation organizations, but in the CNRA she
found a group willing to undertake the kind of activism she believed
necessary to address the environmental issues of the day.

MR. CONSERVATION

The CNRA awards presenter who saluted "Miss Conservation" was Al
Berkman, who also happened to be known as "Mr. Conservation"[26] in
north-central Wisconsin, where he spent much of his life.

Berkman and Pearson surely crossed paths often. Both were engaged
in a variety of civic activities in the Wausau area. Berkman got involved
in the community almost before unpacking his bags in his new north-
central Wisconsin home as World War II raged. A Marathon County
Historical Society sketch notes that the 1938 Michigan State University forestry graduate "arrived in Wausau on September 26, 1942. The
next night he joined the Wausau Symphony Orchestra with which he
played the violin and then the viola for 43 years."[27]

For Berkman, conservation was a vocation and an avocation. He
worked for forty years for the Soil Conservation Service, most of the
time as a district conservationist in Marathon County. In addition to
holding officer positions in the CNRA and other conservation organizations and teaching forestry, he served on the advisory council for
Trees for Tomorrow in Eagle River and founded the North Central
Watershed Association for protecting soil and water resources.

Berkman's arrival in Wausau came when the SCS was still a young agency, established less than a decade earlier to deal with the massive erosion problems that had led to the Dust Bowl era. Wisconsin was the birthplace of the movement, when, in 1933, the US Department of the Interior authorized the nation's first large-scale demonstration project on the Coon Creek watershed in southwestern Wisconsin. Among the scientists overseeing and implementing the project— which was based on reaching out to local farmers with technical assistance in implementing conservation measures—was Aldo Leopold. The results of the work done there reached across the country, guiding the activities of conservationists like Berkman.

Such projects relied heavily on convincing farmers to become collaborators in the adoption of soil conservation practices. By 1960, when Marathon County was honored by Goodyear Rubber and Tire Company for its conservation efforts, Berkman and his SCS coworker William Ludwig of Stratford reported that the number of farmer cooperators in Marathon County had reached almost 1,800.[28] Contour and strip cropping were established on 7,500 acres, and windbreaks on another 400. Water diversions, grass waterways to carry water from fields, and related practices to prevent erosion were established over a total of 110 miles in Marathon County.

The report on the adoption of conservation practices in Marathon County—one of Wisconsin's leading dairy farming counties—was a reminder that while the agricultural community opposed a ban on DDT, many farmers were also willing participants in land stewardship efforts, especially if government cost sharing was available.

The record doesn't address how Berkman reconciled the wants and needs of farmer cooperators with the initiatives undertaken by the CNRA. SCS employees worked closely with farmers, usually on-site, so there was plenty of interaction between him and farmer-cooperators. Perhaps he kept this work separate from his volunteer activities with the CNRA.

Clearly, Berkman was on board with other CNRA members as they decided to pursue the DDT hearing. As vice president of the organization at the time, he would have had substantial input into the organization's activities.

FREETHINKERS

Farm folks from Sauk County, the home of the Leopold family shack, Carla Kruse and her husband, Harold, embodied the enlightened stewardship of the land that Leopold envisioned.

Carla Kruse was also one to stir the pot. She sought to get the Wisconsin Farmers Union to back a DDT ban at the height of the DDT battles but was rebuffed. On November 21, 1968, just before the DDT hearing got under way, she penned a letter as secretary of the CNRA to University of Wisconsin president Fred Harrington and College of Agriculture dean Glenn Pound asking for information on the gifts, grants, and loans the university received from chemical companies that manufactured biocides. She also asked for the "limitations, if any, placed by the grantors on the use of such monies in each case."[29] Finally, she asked for the extent and sources of gifts, grants, and loans for research on other pest control measures. Records do not indicate whether the university officials complied, although it's worth noting that Wisconsin's Open Records Law was not passed until 1982. If the records had been open, chances are Carla Kruse would have made them widely available.

After graduating from Baraboo High School, Carla attended Sauk County Teachers College and Platteville Teachers College and then taught at rural schools in her home county. She also edited the CNRA newsletter and penned articles marked by perfect prose, spirited activism, and a dedication to making the world a better place, as hinted to in the newsletter masthead, which featured a hemlock seedling growing from a stump.

That desire to improve the world was built on the Kruses' religious background. When Carla died in 2009, her obituary noted her path in life stemmed from her family heritage: her grandfather had founded the Sauk County Free Congregation (*Freie Gemeinde*/Freethinkers). Her belief in the benefits of alternative medicine was fueled by reading about the work of Swiss chemist and physician Paracelsus, who practiced alternative medicine during the Middle Ages.[30]

The German Freethinkers embrace a philosophy that humans rule their own destiny, rejecting the notion that there is any kind of divine intervention in life. Their beliefs center on the idea that nature and natural law guide mankind and that the use of reason, epistemology, and science are the means by which life is validated. Freethinkers usually espouse current liberal ideals of their day, including racial, social, and sexual equality; the abolition of slavery; and the end of political tyranny. Freethought came to Wisconsin with the massive influx of German immigrants in the 1850s, particularly those known as "Forty-eighters" who had fled autocratic German states after the failed revolts of 1848.[31]

Harold Kruse had his own definition of the Freethinkers. "To put it very simply, other religions are trying to get people into heaven, and our religion believes in trying to bring heaven down to earth by improving the earth," he said in a 2010 interview. "Roughly, that's what we believe. Everyone has a right to make up their own mind regarding religious things."[32]

So the Kruses set about bringing heaven down to Earth. They were early CNRA members and were engaged at one of the group's first meetings in 1950. They were pioneering organic farmers and among the founders of the Dane County Farmers' Market in Madison. They worked to preserve fragile areas of the Baraboo Hills well ahead of the development pressure that was to descend on the area years later. Orie Loucks, botanist from the University of Wisconsin, recalled tromping around the Baraboo Hills with Harold Kruse in the early 1960s, identifying areas for future protection. "I was impressed with his botanical knowledge," said Loucks.[33] Harold and Carla both belonged to numerous conservation and civic organizations. Dedicated bird-watchers, they managed the Wisconsin Society for Ornithology's supply room for several years.

As the CNRA's newsletter editor during the DDT hearing, Carla Kruse wrote detailed articles, urged citizen action on legislative bills, kept tabs of donations to the organization, and gave credit to numerous groups that backed the organization's DDT battles. Special editions were printed during the hearing.

The Kruses led by engagement and example. They were honored with the CNRA's Silver Acorn award in 1965, recognized as "active and vocal members of a dozen conservation organizations and moving forces behind Honey Creek and Baraboo Hills Natural Areas projects."[34] The organization also noted that they had set up demonstration areas on their Hickory Hill Farm for good conservation practices, including stream restoration.

The Honey Creek State Natural Area was originally purchased by the Wisconsin Society for Ornithology, and the Kruses managed the 125 acres of diversified habitat for several years. When the WSO presented the Kruses with its Silver Passenger Pigeon Award, it asked a poignant question: "Where in all the state is there a family of farmers who are more ardent conservationists or more deserving of recognition?"[35]

Gretchen Kruse, their daughter, shared this anecdote of family life on Hickory Hill Farm: "Our parents would get the Congressional Records in the mail and we (as kids) would make our dad haul the box up into the tree house and read them to us. So, basically, I was read bedtime stories about the DDT hearings, and it stuck."[36]

Gretchen moved back to the family farm in 2011 after spending nineteen years studying and conducting fisheries research, including a study to determine the effects of contaminants such as organochlorine

CITIZENS NATURAL RESOURCES ASSOCIATION
OF WISCONSIN

(Incorporated under the laws of Wisconsin—1953)
Loganville, Wisconsin
July 21, 1957

JUL 23 1957

Mr. L. P. Voigt, Director
Wisconsin Conservation Department
Madison, Wisconsin

Dear Mr. Voigt:

    Recently I have received a number of letters from members of our
organization expressing grave concern over the effects of the current
Dutch Elm Disease control program on songbirds, particularly in the
Milwaukee area. While I feel that some of the reports of bird mortality
due to DDT spraying may be exaggerated, other reports have come from
reliable people, including experienced ornithologists who have noted a
sharp decline in bird populations in their areas and have had diagnoses
made of some of the dead birds, determining that DDT was the cause of
death. I believe that Mr. Trainor of your Department has made several
such diagnoses.

    I understand that DDT applied at the rate of not more than one pound
per acre provides effective control and is generally not harmful to wildlife, but that most of the current trouble stems from the application of
excessive dosages and from careless use of spray equipment by incompetent
operators. It has also been my understanding that there exists a Wisconsin
Administrative Code which requires that permits be obtained from the Conservation Department for spraying of DDT in excess of one pound per acre,
and that notification be given the Department by anyone wishing to treat
forest or non-crop areas with DDT.

    Is the treatment of elms for Dutch elm disease covered by this Code?
If so, why hasn't the Code been enforced? Since the spraying of elms,
particularly in the cities, presents a serious threat to songbirds, it
would seem to me that the Conservation Department has a clear responsibility
to investigate reports of bird deaths due to DDT, and, if the facts warrant,
to insist upon enforcement of this Code.

    Since Mr. Chambers of the State Department of Agriculture is in charge
of the Dutch elm disease control program in Wisconsin, I recently wrote to
him asking why this spraying has not been more strictly regulated. His
reply was that he feels the answer to the problem lies in "waging an effective
educational campaign" to eliminate the careless use of DDT. I agree with
him that there should be such an educational campaign, but until people
are properly educated in the use of poison sprays, much damage can be done.
Since we are dealing with an emergency program to save the elms, I feel
there should also be emergency regulations to prevent abuses and to protect
birds and other forms of wildlife from the effects of unwise use of spray
materials. If an individual were to kill songbirds, he or she would be
subject to prosecution and a fine (a news item of such a case appeared in
a recent issue of The Capitol Times), but if spray operators destroy large
numbers of birds, nothing is done about it. Why not?

For the Preservation, Management, and Restoration of Wisconsin's Natural Resources

This 1957 letter, penned by Citizens Natural Resources Association president Harold Kruse, a Loganville farmer and nature enthusiast, sought to alert Wisconsin Conservation Department director Lester Voigt to reports of bird deaths caused by DDT spraying. Kruse and his wife, Carla, were longtime members of the CNRA. Harold Kruse is also credited with playing a major role in preserving numerous natural areas in the Baraboo Hills of south-central Wisconsin. *WHi Image ID 73095*

pesticides on reproduction and longevity of the Kootenai River white sturgeon in the northwestern United States and Canada.

Harold Kruse noted in an interview that one of his regrets in life was being unable to take a course from Aldo Leopold. He had enrolled at the University of Wisconsin in the late 1940s, but Leopold died before Kruse could make his way into the professor's classroom.[37] The Kruses did embrace Leopold's land ethic, and they passed it on to their children. They were both pioneers and teachers, and their tireless conservation activities and warm hearts earned the respect of world-renowned ornithologists and fellow farmers alike.

CHAPTER SIX

NATURE LADY OF THE SUBURBS

O NE DAY IN 1964, LORRIE OTTO COLLECTED TWENTY-EIGHT dead robins and dumped them on the desk of the Bayside village manager.

Upscale Bayside, a Milwaukee suburb, seemed an unlikely place to nurture an environmental leader who would step to the forefront of the DDT battles in Wisconsin. But some earlier skirmishes prepared her, including protecting a natural gem in the suburbs from development and defending her right to natural landscaping in her yard.

These early confrontations, stretching back to the 1950s, steeled the woman who referred to herself in her younger days as a shy farm girl. The shy farm girl would go on to help found the natural landscaping movement in the United States. She would engage in a number of environmental causes, but none took so much of her time and energy as the DDT battle.

Several names emerge in the ranks of Wisconsin citizen activists who pushed for a ban on DDT. Foremost among them are Otto and Joseph Hickey. It was still pretty much a man's world in the 1950s and 1960s, but women played key roles in the DDT battle, perhaps influenced by Rachel Carson's *Silent Spring*. In Wisconsin, women took the lead against DDT in several important areas. In addition to Otto, there was the young reporter at the *Capital Times* newspaper, Whitney Gould, who covered the hearing from gavel to gavel. Two of the top four Citizens Natural Resources Association officers at the time of the DNR hearing were women: Carla Kruse and Bertha Pearson. And arguably the most crucial testimony on behalf of the environmentalists' cause would come from Lucille Stickel, a scientist with the US Department of the Interior's Fish and Wildlife Service.

Most of the others on both sides of the DDT fray were men, but this handful of women made a difference. Their growing involvement was a sign of things to come.

x x x

Otto and her husband, Owen, moved to the village of Bayside in 1952. A few feet from the rear windows of their home was a mini-wilder-

Lorrie Otto, shown here outside her Bayside, Wisconsin, home, was a key citizen activist in efforts to ban DDT in the state. Otto was also known nationally for leading the natural landscaping movement. *WHi Image ID 100397*

ness called Fairy Chasm, a ravine cut by Fish Creek and kept moist by chilly fogs off Lake Michigan. It was rich in plant and animal life. The Otto home was one of eighty residences developed by the Fish Creek Park Company. In 1960, road repairs were needed, but the corporation bylaws forbade assessments. Directors had two choices: ask the residents for donations or subdivide part of Fairy Chasm into nineteen lots to be sold to cover the cost of road improvements. "I knew it was wrong to destroy the woods, but I needed the language," she told a reporter years later.[1] So she went in search of the words to make her point. Otto asked her local bookstore operator for every book in the store about identifying flowers, shrubs, and trees. She also asked for books on the environment. One was Aldo Leopold's *A Sand County Almanac*.

She also sought out Alvin Throne, a professor of biology at the University of Wisconsin–Milwaukee. He had studied the rare plants of Fairy Chasm in the 1920s, and he bristled at the thought of their loss. Throne joined the cause. They sought out a *Milwaukee Journal* reporter, and the story ended up on page one. Other media coverage followed, and when it came time to vote, residents opposed subdividing the ravine by thirty-eight to thirty-four. The ravine was saved, and Otto learned an early lesson in environmental activism. The Nature Conservancy bought the property in 1970, making it one of the organization's first Wisconsin holdings. Otto, an early TNC board member, was behind the transfer.

Otto's "weed wars" with the village of Bayside were a good lesson in activism, too, even if she was pretty much alone in that skirmish. In the mid-1950s, she clashed with the village over her landscaping preferences. An early adapter of native plantings, she turned her suburban yard into a rich pastiche bursting with color and variety—a thorough departure from the well-manicured lawns of her neighbors.

Some of those neighbors and village officials saw weeds, not the diverse landscape Otto had created, and one day when she was away, the village mowed down her plants. There was a village weed law, after all. Otto was incensed. She demanded that village officials attend a guided tour of her yard. Using the incident as a teachable moment, she described for them each plant that had been mowed down. They conceded she had a point and reached a settlement with her. The natural landscaping movement took a giant step forward that day. Otto began to spread the word about natural landscaping. After hearing an Otto lecture in 1977, a group of nine women began meeting monthly to share information about natural landscaping. They called themselves the Wild Ones. Otto became their philosophical compass. The organization has chapters throughout North America today.

Lorrie Otto's early life provided few hints that she would become a gutsy citizen activist and environmental leader. Born Mary Stoeber in 1919, she grew up on a Dane County, Wisconsin, dairy farm. By her own accounts, she was "terribly shy."[2] The family was from stoic religious stock. "We were Presbyterians, and it was a sin to be proud," she said.

Still, nature was already tugging at her. The oldest of three daughters, she acquired her love of the land on that farm as she tagged along with her father. "I sort of became the son," she recalled. "I was just his shadow. Loved every minute of it. My dad had such a feeling for the soil."[3]

As a young single woman she began spreading her wings. She saw an ad for the Women Airforce Service Pilots while attending the University of Wisconsin in Madison during World War II and signed up. She was a WASP trainee in Texas near the close of the war, although the program ended before she could claim the official status of WASP pilot.

Stoeber had earlier met her husband-to-be, Owen Otto, in a high school play. They began dating at the University of Wisconsin. He emerged with a degree in medicine; she earned an undergraduate degree in related arts, a major that covered a range of artistic disciplines. They were married in 1944, and it was then she became Lorrie Otto—a sister-in-law already had the name Mary Otto, so Lorrie chose a variation of her middle name, Lorraine.

In 1950, Owen Otto was named medical director at Rogers Memorial Hospital, a psychiatric facility in Waukesha County. Two years later, they moved to Bayside with their two young children, Patricia and George.

Owen struggled with financial challenges at the hospital, and Lorrie raised the children. But seemingly unconnected events were already unfolding, and they would converge a decade later as Milwaukee's seemingly happy days of the 1950s yielded to an altogether different decade.

A few years before the Ottos settled into their suburban home, Aldo Leopold's *A Sand County Almanac* had been published, to little fanfare. Leopold's first and only hire at the University of Wisconsin, Joseph Hickey, helped organize the manuscript and prepare it for publication. Leopold had died fighting a brush fire on a neighbor's property near the family shack in 1948, barely a stone's throw from the Wisconsin River and where he penned many of his essays. Hickey, hired by Leopold just a few months earlier, took over as chair of the Department of Wildlife Management, a small program within the College of Agriculture. It was Leopold's baby, and one of the first in the nation. Hickey, already an ornithologist of international repute, was ready to settle into a career of teaching and research. He didn't yet know Lorrie Otto.

The same year Owen Otto took the position at Rogers Memorial Hospital, the CNRA was forming, ignited by the controversy over tree cutting for a highway project. Early members of the CNRA whose lives would soon touch Lorrie Otto's were already nearby, including Fred Ott, who would play a key role raising funds for the DDT battles, and Owen Gromme, who was on the staff of the Milwaukee Public Museum and a still-undiscovered wildlife artist. She couldn't know it then, but Lorrie Otto would in a few years be working closely with these folks.

Otto was a relative latecomer to the CNRA, her name showing up as a new member—Mrs. Owen Otto—in 1968, the same year the Wisconsin administrative hearing over whether DDT was a water pollutant began. But she had been fighting the village of Bayside and other Milwaukee communities over DDT spraying for Dutch elm disease for several years, as evidenced by her trips to the village offices with the dead robins she had kept in her refrigerator. It was during one of those visits that she was asked the "birds or trees" question by the Bayside village manager. The village had begun helicopter spraying its elms.

It was a tough question, and one that municipal officials were likely asking themselves across much of the East and Midwest in their costly battle to save the elms. With elms dying at an alarming pace, there was pressure to save the trees and do so as cheaply as possible. DDT was less costly than other chemical treatments and considered more effective.

Otto knew there was something wrong when robins and other songbirds twitched, flopped about, and died on suburban lawns. She resolved to end or curtail the spraying. Her Milwaukee-area skirmishes were training for later battles that would mark the early stages of citizen environmental activism in the United States. Her correspondence from that period reflects a growing confidence, if a still-developing understanding of the constraints on people who worked in government. She was dedicated, determined, and impatient.[4]

Latecomer though she was to the CNRA, when Otto did get involved, she almost instantly became a big player.

Otto began her own personal crusade against DDT in the mid-1960s. She joined the Wisconsin chapter of the Nature Conservancy and got to know Hickey, who had already accumulated piles of research on the effects of DDT. On Hickey's advice, Otto initiated contact with Charles Wurster, an Environmental Defense Fund founder and a young biologist/biochemist from the State University of New York at Stony Brook. In a 1965 letter responding to her call for help, Wurster reminded Otto that it was hardly fresh news that DDT was causing bird deaths, and he outlined courses of action that citizens might take. "It is simply a matter of fact that when DDT is used in the quantities customarily employed for Dutch elm disease, birds will be killed—lots of them," he wrote. "This has been known for years, long before our reports, long before Silent Spring. The argument, then, is simply between those who know the facts, and those who don't."[5]

By this time, Wurster had published the findings of his research into bird deaths in the town of Hanover, New Hampshire, where he had been a student and faculty member at Dartmouth University, in the prestigious peer-reviewed publications *Science* and *Ecology*. The *Science* article, copublished with his wife at the time, Doris, and Walter N. Strickland, of the Department of Pathology at Dartmouth Medical School, concluded, "From the number of dead birds found, the many birds observed with tremors, chemical analyses of these birds, and a population decline among certain species, we conclude that DDT caused severe mortality of resident and migrant birds in Hanover during the spring of 1963."[6]

Otto's recollections of the mid- to late 1960s show she was gaining key allies in addition to Hickey and Wurster. She also got to know Walter Scott, who asked her to conduct a survey of DDT use in Milwaukee-area municipalities for possible use by the Wisconsin Conservation Department. She did so, in great detail, her findings carefully recorded by hand on several sheets of paper. Along the way, Otto also collected anecdotal information from people of a variety of backgrounds. Don Johnson, an outdoors reporter at the *Milwaukee Sentinel*, became a confidante.

Armed with this new information, Otto went back to the Bayside Village Board to argue again for a halt to spraying. "The only recollection I have of that evening is of a man slamming his fist on a table

and shouting, 'Young lady, keep your mouth shut or this will reverber-
ate all the way to the halls of Congress,'" she recalled years later, wryly
observing that the man was ultimately right.[7]

By 1968, with the Wisconsin Department of Agriculture sticking
to its guns on the continued use of DDT for Dutch elm disease spraying amid growing citizen discontent, Otto and Hickey became determined to seek the help of the new outfit, the EDF. They headed for
New York and a weekend meeting with Wurster at the EDF headquar-
ters on Long Island.

With curly locks and a firm jaw, the forty-year-old scientist activist cut a dashing figure that didn't go unnoticed by Otto. In a letter to a friend a few days later, she confided, "Charlie stole my heart.
One doesn't know whether to love him as a man or as a son. I plan
to introduce my daughter to him."[8] At their first meeting on August
24, 1968, Wurster told Otto and Hickey it was time to act. "We have
all the marbles," he said. "We just need to roll them out in front of a
judge."[9] Research underscoring the dangers of DDT was piling up. By
this time, Hickey and other researchers had confirmed DDT concentrations in the Lake Michigan ecosystem: everything from chubs to
gulls had concentrations of DDT or its metabolites. Three years earlier, Hickey had convened the conference in Madison on the fate of
peregrine falcons. Scientists from several countries gathered to compare their research. Remarkably similar impacts on wildlife were widespread, and the research found one thing in common: the presence of
DDT. Indeed, they had the marbles.

Otto was breathing rarified air. "That weekend was probably the
most glorious of any in my life. In my memory, I see three Norwe-
gians walking the beach on Long Island. Their ages spanned [20] years.
Charlie Wurster was only 40. I was 50, and Joe Hickey was 60 years
old," she later recalled. "As we walked, the two men called out the
amounts of DDT in the breasts of the birds flying over our heads,
swimming in the ocean or running in the sand ahead of us."[10]

The time for action had come. Little more than a month after the New York rendezvous, the CNRA was ready to move forward with its case. President Frederick Baumgartner wrote a letter "To all Organizations Interested in Conservation," in which he made clear the group's intent. "The CNRA has decided it is time for a test case of this question of water pollution [by DDT]," he wrote.[11] Baumgartner outlined a dual strategy of pursuing a hearing on DDT and calling for various actions in the state Legislature. But there was one big problem: money, or lack of it.

As Hickey and Otto prepared to depart, Wurster let them know what they were up against financially. They needed a lawyer to admit the EDF's attorney, Victor Yannacone, into the Wisconsin legal system and fifteen thousand dollars to pay airfare for EDF board members and witnesses from several states and, it would turn out, one foreign country. "My face fell so quickly it must have distressed Charlie," Otto later recalled, "but he brushed it off with a wave of his hand and said, 'Go to your group.' Group? I didn't have a group, unless it would be the PTA Art Committee, whose husbands in Bayside undoubtedly sprayed with DDT."[12]

Otto knew CNRA had few resources, so she initially looked elsewhere for funds. She got six thousand dollars from a self-described "birding lady" in Oconomowoc. The Milwaukee Audubon Society provided six hundred dollars. The local Izaak Walton League had no money, but said it might be able to provide an attorney.

The CNRA would have to be the group. Though it lacked funds, the CNRA had expressed an early interest in the pesticide issue: the topic of its first conference, in the 1950s, was chemical sprays. Another conference, in 1958, produced a special report on pesticides.[13]

In Sauk County in 1964, CNRA members Harold and Carla Kruse initiated a petition drive on behalf of the group, seeking a halt to the chemical spraying of roadsides. CNRA records later noted it was the first citizen-organized effort in Wisconsin to stop chemical contamination of the environment. In 1966, the group cosponsored the Citizens Conference on Pesticides. The other cosponsor was the botany department at the University of Wisconsin. Hickey, then emerging as a citizen scientist who was growing more willing to stick out his neck, was one of five presenters. He spoke about DDT's detrimental effect on birds and aquatic systems.

A February 26, 1967, statement from the CNRA president was clear about where the group stood:

"Are you about to become poisoned without your consent? This is the feeling many of us have at this time of the year, in spite of the hollow-sounding assurances that the poisons about to engulf us and our properties are well below our tolerance levels and those of the 'desirable' remnants of the natural environment we hope to keep around us. . . . The evidence against DDT seems as strong as that against the use of tobacco. The difference in effect is I abstain from tobacco by personal choice. I'm not allowed to make that same choice regarding DDT."[14]

The CNRA president was Roy Gromme, and he and Lorrie Otto were soon to have an important conversation.

Just after Otto had called the owners of a honey farm who had sent ten dollars because they were concerned about its bees, Otto's daughter, Tricia, came home from Nicolet High School. Hearing her mother's story and accustomed to seeing dead birds in the freezer, she told her mother, "Why don't you call my biology teacher, Mr. Gromme."[15]

Otto later recalled, "I went directly to the phone. He asked me where we lived and said he'd be right over." Roy Gromme would soon be leaving for India with USAID. But when they met that day, Gromme made Otto a promise. She recalled him telling her, "We will give you everything we have: all our money and mailing addresses of our members. We'll open our homes in Madison to house the witnesses. If this destroys CNRA, we will have died for a good cause."[16]

The Gromme family had deep connections with old-Milwaukee

wealth. Soon, Lorrie Otto would learn just how "old Milwaukee" would respond to the cause.

⊠   ⊠   ⊠

Lorrie Otto is known for many accomplishments. In the end, maybe it was her willingness to stand up and fight something she felt to be wrong that earned her the most praise. As Don Johnson of the *Milwaukee Sentinel* wrote to Otto in 1969, after the DDT hearing had ended, "Your energy, enthusiasm, and interest have wrought much. Things have happened which I don't believe would have without your involvement."[17]

When she was inducted into the Wisconsin Conservation Hall of Fame in 1999, she wore slacks and bright-colored tennis shoes, reminding the audience that she was one of the "little ladies in tennis shoes" derided by a municipal official in battles over the spraying of DDT.[18]

CHAPTER SEVEN

OLD MILWAUKEE

REMINISCING ABOUT THE DDT DAYS FROM HIS CONDOMIN-
ium in Oconomowoc in 2011, Roy Gromme talked about how his
brother-in-law, Fred Ott, was able to raise tens of thousands of dollars
for the Wisconsin administrative hearing.

"The Otts were old family money," Gromme said.[1] So when Ott set
about to raise the money needed to bring the Environmental Defense
Fund to Wisconsin and cover a variety of expenses for witnesses and the
EDF's lawyer, he reached out to the wealthy Milwaukeeans he knew.

Tracing the Ott bloodline leads directly to that old Milwaukee
money. Ott's grandfather, Emil, had married Ida Steinmeyer in 1886.[2]
She was the daughter of William Steinmeyer, who had established the
Steinmeyer Company, a successful carriage trade grocery business in
Milwaukee.[3] It employed a staff of order takers that would dispatch
groceries to private homes via a fleet of delivery wagons serving all
parts of the city. Upon William Steinmeyer's death in 1894, Emil Ott
and his brother, Charles, assumed control of the business. The Ott
family fortune was tied to that company, which operated until 1940
when personalized grocery service became uneconomical.

Raised among the Milwaukee upper crust, Fred Ott might have
taken any number of career paths. He became a salesman for Leslie
Paper Company, a printing and industrial paper distribution company
based in Minneapolis. But, as his daughter, Riki, an environmental

activist, told the *Milwaukee Journal Sentinel* after his death in 2008, "His real job was his many causes."[4]

Ott's Grandpa Emil took him birding as a child. "That sparked a lifelong love of birds and conservation," read his obituary.[5]

"Freddie," as many knew him, was also fascinated with natural history. As a teenager, he began hanging out at the Milwaukee Public Museum with Charles "Chappie" Fox, the Oconomowoc author, circus aficionado, and conservationist, and Walter Pelzer, a young man from Fort Atkinson who would become chief of taxidermy at the museum. There, these "museum rats," as Roy Gromme called them, met up with his father, Owen Gromme. Thus began an enduring friendship between Ott and Owen Gromme.

Both were strong conservationists. Owen Gromme was fiery and quick to rise to the fight once he took to a cause. Allowing that he had some of his father's "go sic 'em dog" tendencies, Roy Gromme remembered Ott as "a little more reserved. He'd hold you on the leash and go for the jugular."[6]

But there was no doubting Ott's dedication to conservation. He would prove it time and again. He was also, "one of those guys, he could con you into anything. He had that goofy personality that worked, and he was a hard worker," recalled Roy Gromme. It was Ott "who conned me into joining CNRA," he added.

That ability to be convincing came in handy at a crucial moment for the CNRA and the EDF.

Citizen movements are built on guts and tenacity. They are propelled by commitment and belief in purpose. But big or small, they are fed by money. Ott brought all of these to the CNRA. He was not solely responsible for raising the money necessary to bring the EDF and scientists from near and far to Madison in 1968 and 1969. But he clearly opened more wallets than anyone else.

The National Audubon Society was funneling money to the CNRA for the Wisconsin DDT fight through its Rachel Carson Trust for the Living Environment, established for this purpose. Donations Ott solicited were directed to Audubon for legal and tax purposes, affording people the opportunity for a tax deduction.

Despite Ott's fund-raising successes, as the DDT hearing continued longer than anyone anticipated, there was concern about whether the funds raised would be sufficient. The urgency of the situation was underscored in a February 13, 1969, letter from CNRA president Frederick Baumgartner to Dr. Elvis Stahr, president of the National Audubon Society, in which Baumgartner wrote: "In its broad context I am not convinced that we can raise sufficient funds to insure that the DDT issue can be carried to a definite conclusion. It is difficult to anticipate the length of the DDT hearing in Madison, and the costs involved. We also have no assurance that the Wisconsin Department of Natural Resources will order a strict ban on the use of DDT for agricultural purposes. Court action against such a ban is a distinct possibility, perhaps a probability."[7]

The CNRA president went on to emphasize the need to prepare for a "long and costly battle on this issue." He stressed the need for advance commitment of funds to see the matter through. Baumgartner added: "To date we have employed many different approaches to raise monies. Mr. Ott has had outstanding success through his personal contacts with influential people and several foundations. The response of small conservation clubs to our bulletins and news releases has also been very good. Now we are in the process of approaching many national and regional conservation organizations asking them for financial support and more specifically for help in explaining the vital significance of this issue to foundations and individuals who are in a position to make significant financial contributions."

Later that year, Roland C. Clement, vice president of the National Audubon Society, wrote to Baumgartner, praising Ott's efforts: "We are particularly appreciative of the fact that CNRA and, in particular, Fred Ott, are continuing to solicit help for EDF operations, and thus helping us meet the budget we undertook to support earlier this year."[8]

The list of people who gave to the cause reads like a who's who of business and philanthropic activity in Milwaukee and beyond during the height of the fight.

Ott shared his recollections in *CNRA—The First 50 Years*, published by the group in 2001 and dedicated to him. "The DDT hearings cost plenty, mostly travel expenses for scientists and lawyers. We had $200, a typewriter and a list of names. Sent out letters, people sent back money. But not enough. . . . We were scratching for money from anyone and everyone. I even went to a floating crap game and broke the damn pot: came out with $1,200 to $1,500. Told everyone I was doing it for your feathered and furry friends."[9]

Despite going to such lengths, Ott felt his efforts fell short. "I always thought I should ask for more," he said. But a tally sheet showing income and expenses from the Rachel Carson Trust through June 30, 1969, tells another story, one of Ott's hard work and many connections.[10] Harry J. Nunnemacher, from a Milwaukee industrial family, gave $1,000. David Uihlein, from the Schlitz beer family, gave $100. The W. Uihlein Family gave $500. Dorothy Vallier, another Uihlein descendant, also gave $100, and her husband, Jacque Vallier, donated $473.

David Pabst contributed fifteen shares of Skelly Oil Company, valued at $940.67. The Puehlicher Foundation gave $1,000. Jack Puehlicher was president of Milwaukee's M&I Bank.

Businesses or their foundations also donated. The Schlitz Foundation gave $1,000, the Harnischfeger Foundation $500, and the Maytag Foundation donated $100.

Not all the donations came from well-heeled Milwaukeeans. The estate of Harry Steenbock, a biochemist from the University of Wisconsin in Madison, gave $5,000. Steenbock had patented the irradiation process for producing vitamin D and conceived the idea of the Wisconsin Alumni Research Foundation, a nonprofit foundation that invests the proceeds from patents to support research in the natural sciences at the University of Wisconsin. WARF would have a role in the DDT hearing.

Donations came from near and far. Some were small, others large. Some people didn't want their names attached to the cause, but they still gave. Audubon chapters and other bird clubs chipped in. Total income on the tally sheet: $52,519.

At some point, the Godfrey Foundation provided $250. Fred Ott had reached out to Arthur Godfrey, the radio and TV personality. Godfrey had become an advocate for the environment. In a January 19, 1969, address to the Advertising Council, he had said, "Nowadays, I question any value that does not take into account the total ecology of our planet. Any personal deed, any business transaction . . . that does not carry with it all precautions against injuring the environment . . . must be promptly and vigorously challenged."[11]

Lorrie Otto corresponded with Godfrey, who answered her on February 6, 1969: "Thank you very much for your letter of 1/17. I am very much aware of the DDT hearings in Wis. Mr. Fred Ott is keeping me in touch. Thanks for your interest and more power to you, Wurster and Yannacone."[12]

Accounts vary about how much money was raised for the Wisconsin administrative hearing and related activities. While Gromme recalled it to be more than $250,000, Ott put the number raised through the Rachel Carson Trust at $100,000.[13]

When the DDT battles were over, Ott stayed engaged in an array of causes. He gave of his own wealth, too. Shortly before his death, he donated $500,000 to help keep a struggling Milwaukee Public Museum afloat. Little wonder, for Ott had his environmental awakening at the museum.

CHAPTER EIGHT

A SCIENTIST SPREADS HIS WINGS

JOSEPH HICKEY WOULD PROBABLY SCOFF AT THE NOTION, but his life seemed to be marked by synchronicity, or meaningful coincidences.

Hickey the scientist would say there's no proof these coincidences had meaning. But still they existed for this man of so many loves: of family and science and birds and teaching and song.

There was the Bronx County Bird Club, the spirited but serious group of teens prowling the Bronx and beyond for notable bird species, including the herring gull, which would have a part in the DDT battles. Its members included Allan Cruickshank and Hickey, and latecomer to the group, Roger Tory Peterson. Some would say they were chasing birds. History would show that several were chasing their passions and careers.

There was the American Museum of Natural History, where the teenagers were challenged by a young but authoritative German ornithologist and environmental biologist, Ernst Mayr. Through Mayr, they met men like Konrad Lorenz, the renowned and multitalented German scholar who pioneered ethology, the study of animal behavior.

As a young man trying to make his living during the Great Depression, Hickey would fortify himself with birding in the 1930s, especially the development of a list of peregrine falcon aeries, or nests—275 in all—across eastern North America. These nesting sites would play a pivotal role in the DDT battles decades later. He published the findings in 1942, likely satisfied that his work would provide a baseline for future population biology studies but not anticipating it would be fodder for an environmental debate. Two decades later, as evidence built indicating the peregrine falcon population decline, he would arrange for a resurvey of the sites. Finding them empty set him in motion to figure out why.

A chance meeting with Aldo Leopold at a cocktail party at the Yale Club in New York City in 1940 would lead to an invitation from Leopold to join him for a research project in Wisconsin and earn a master's degree to boot. He did so, working on a study of potential wildlife habitat on submarginal farmland in southwestern Wisconsin.[1] Hickey would move on to Patuxent Wildlife Research Center in Maryland. The work done by researchers there would also have an impact on later DDT battles.

Leopold would call on Hickey again in 1947, inviting him to become his first assistant in the Department of Wildlife Management at Madison. Hickey accepted. Leopold would die a year later, but his legacy at Madison would help foster an enhanced ecological understanding of the world that would be embraced by talented young scientists, including botanists Orie Loucks and Hugh Iltis. Some of the young turks were more willing to jump into the public arena and nudged the older and more reserved Hickey.

Indeed, the life of Joseph Hickey would involve other moments when the stars seemed to line up. But Professor Joseph J. Hickey was a scientist first, and nothing about his evolution into a citizen scientist was coincidental. He plotted his steps one at a time, one careful move after the next, the latter building on the former.

🗵   🗵   🗵

Born in New York City in 1907, Hickey's lifelong interest in birds was first ignited by a scoutmaster, Reverend Basil Hall. That led him to the Bronx County Bird Club. How a group of nine teenagers who held a common passion for birding found each other was the stuff of synchronicity, too. In any case, there they were, the BCBC, a group of young bird-watchers remarkable for what they would accomplish in life.

Years later, Hickey and Roger Tory Peterson would reflect on their BCBC days. Early on, they encountered Ludlow Griscom, author of *Birds of the New York City Region*, who pushed them to build their bird lists. When Ernst Mayr took a position at the American Museum of Natural History, "He wanted to learn something about American birds," Hickey recalled.[2] "The best way to know American birds was to pal around with the Bronx County Bird Club." Peterson added, "He quickly got educated, and then he educated us. And he said, 'Everybody's got to have a problem.'" Hickey recalled, "We laughed at first," but the concept of having a problem to be worked on systematically and thoroughly would stick with him for life, whether pioneering studies of bird mortality rates or chasing down the mystery of DDT.

Fame struck early for Peterson. His *A Field Guide to the Birds* was published in 1934, making bird-watching accessible to the masses by concentrating on quick identification focused on field marks. He was in his mid-twenties. "I'm often given the credit for this great explosion [in birding], but simply because I was an artist to put it all down. I couldn't have written my field guide without the BCBC and Griscom."[3]

Peterson's would be a more direct career path than his pal Hickey, whose early adulthood included earning a bachelor's degree in history from New York University, where he was also a track champion mile runner. Upon graduating during the Great Depression, Hickey took jobs as a track coach at NYU and businessman at Consolidated Edison. But he didn't abandon birding. Mayr encouraged Hickey to obtain scientific training and turn his hobby into a professional career, and Hickey responded by heading off to night school, where he pursued undergraduate studies in biology.

Then came the encounter with Leopold and the invitation to introduce himself to Wisconsin and graduate work in wildlife management at the university in Madison. Leopold's protégé soon proved worthy. Noting that there was no American equivalent for the British book *The Art of Bird-Watching*, by E. M. Nicholson, Hickey chose to fill that niche as his master's thesis. He undertook work on what would become a classic in its own right. "A Guide to Bird Watching" was submitted as his master's thesis and published immediately, in 1943, by Oxford University Press. It endures on library shelves today by reason of its distinctive focus. In it, Hickey encouraged going beyond finding and identifying birds to truly studying them and their lives. In the preface Hickey noted he was writing for both the novice and the veteran.

Hickey then earned a doctorate at the University of Michigan, where his dissertation, "Survival Studies of Banded Birds," uncovered a gold mine of unexploited bird banding data accumulated by the US Fish and Wildlife Service. The dissertation was later published in 1952. Hickey's two publications and the science behind them would have been a career's worth of accomplishment, and they had already earned him recognition as a top-notch ecologist and ornithologist. But other tasks awaited Hickey.

While working at the Patuxent Wildlife Research Center in 1947, Hickey accepted Leopold's invitation to join him as second professor in the Department of Wildlife Management. Leopold's letter of January 8 noted, "I am writing at this early date in order to anticipate offers from elsewhere. I am hoping you may wind up your present undertaking by January 1, 1948."[4]

Hickey went about his work in Madison with vigor, satisfied in his role as a scientist, not a conservationist. But within a decade, evidence of a pending disaster would begin to emerge. "I picked up rumors of DDT affecting songbird populations in something called the Bulletin of the Illinois Audubon Society . . . and here were people in Winnetka and suburbs of the city [of Chicago] reporting wholesale die-offs of robins," Hickey recalled.[5] "Now, no scientist had ever looked at these things," he added.

His experience at the funeral in Kenilworth, where he noted an absence of robins from a mulberry tree, got under his skin. "I really wasn't connecting DDT with anything like this," Hickey recalled. He asked the minister about the robins and was told, "They were here in the spring, but I think they all went north." Hickey remembered thinking, "That almost sounds like the passenger pigeon stories that you heard."[6]

Hickey went back to Madison to try to determine if the rumors were fact. The year was 1958. That produced his earliest research on DDT, which led to his tearful encounter with Gene Roark.

Hickey began laboratory work in autumn 1958. Years later, he recalled: "And so we captured robins and we fed them DDT. It was a horrible experiment. But we did find out that DDT was quite lethal, particularly with respect to methoxychlor—another pesticide used to control Dutch elm disease—which in one case might have made the robin sick, but it did not die."[7]

With the help of students, he followed up in spring 1959 with a census of two twenty-five-acre plots in three communities that did not spray DDT and the same number of plots in three communities that had been sprayed. "In the wealthier communities, where they'd been spraying quite a while, everything was way down. *Silent Spring* was there: let's say 90 percent of the whole bird population was wiped out."[8] That same spring, the Madison campus was sprayed with DDT, as was the upscale village of Maple Bluff nearby. Of the latter, Hickey recalled, "Everything was dying over there, and those women were calling me up."

In fact, Hickey liked to say it was women who got him going on his DDT research. There was Rachel Carson, of course, but also the suburban housewives who kept calling him and sending dead birds they found when their communities were sprayed in the 1950s and 1960s. "The suburbs of our big cities—Chicago, Milwaukee, Madison—these are populated mostly by college graduates, and this is one of the best-educated groups of women in the world," he recalled in a 1982 magazine article. "When they began to report that these birds had died, the scientific community paid no attention to them."[9]

Hickey had also been cautious about stepping out too far. But Hickey the scientist activist was emerging as the 1960s approached.

In addition to his other research in 1959, Hickey and some of his students did a careful survey on campus that spring and estimated that 86 to 88 percent of the campus robins had died. Yellow warblers were wiped out, as was the only pair of screech owls on campus.

The mystery of DDT was only just emerging. Research was showing DDT's connection to the lethal effects on songbirds, but, as Hickey recalled, "We had no idea of the insidious effect of DDT in a sub-lethal sense."[10] Hickey would encounter pressure to keep what he knew under his hat. He was in the College of Agriculture, where DDT use was being recommended for use in the battle against insect pests, whether in agricultural fields or stately elm trees.

Attending the 1962 International Ornithological Conference at Cornell University in Ithaca, New York, Hickey heard something new. "I picked up the rumor that not a single peregrine falcon in the northeastern part of the United States had raised any young that year. I picked this up as a rumor, and I didn't necessarily believe it," he recalled.[11]

The peregrine falcon was known as a resilient member of the land community, despite the fact that the birds had some strikes against them: they were often sought after by falconers; their hunting skills led them into the crosshairs of pigeon racers who saw them as foes; collectors prized their eggs. Despite these pressures, records from Europe indicated that some aeries had been in use continuously for centuries, and nesting histories in the United States date back to the mid-1800s.[12] Challenges of life among humans aside, peregrines were cosmopolitan in their nesting and eating habits, and their population stability was built on that.

"Ah, but the following June my copy of *Bird Study* [The Journal of the British Trust for Ornithology] came in, I think it was *Bird Study*, and there was Derek Ratcliffe's report of the decline of the peregrine falcon in Britain and I thought, my God, this may be going right on in the United States and we are not even aware of it!"[13] Ratcliffe was chief scientist for the Nature Conservancy Council.

Hickey immediately recognized what he must do. "I had a personal responsibility to run this down right away. This was my job! It was something I couldn't duck."

And the BCBC helped him. Among his earliest friends, going back to second grade, was Dick Herbert, a charter member of the club of youthful birders. A few years after Herbert's death, one more contribution to the cause would be made on his behalf. Hickey explained: "I organized a research project which my good friend, Kathleen Herbert, financed as a memorial to her late husband, Dick, who was one of my oldest and best friends. We put two men to work to census the peregrine falcons that I had mapped in the 1930s."[14]

Research assistants Dan Berger and Charles Sindelar had been sent off for the eastern United States and Canada in 1964. Hickey asked them to seek out aeries in wilderness areas when possible. "They covered 14,000 miles looking at peregrine falcons at the time they would have young in the nests, but they did not see a single bird! They found some whitewash on one [aerie], indicating recent occupancy." Berger and Sindelar traveled from Georgia to Nova Scotia, reaching 133 known nesting sites, some that had been occupied for a hundred years.

Hickey, meanwhile, was doing some of his own investigative work. On a seven-month swing through Europe, he interviewed colleagues in Finland, Switzerland, France, England, and Germany, learning that their peregrine falcon populations had also plummeted.

"This looked like something that had happened on two continents," he recalled. "It therefore seemed absolutely imperative that we call an international symposium to bring all these population stories into focus and plan the research that was needed to explain exactly what was taking place," he told the National Audubon Society years later, when he was honored with the Audubon Medal.[15]

But the conference needed funding. "I did get immediate encouragement from the U.S. Public Health Service, but the U.S. Departments of Agriculture and Interior turned me down cold. It was at this point, when I was becoming very discouraged, that Audubon's President [Carl William] Buchheister phoned me, right out of the blue, to say that his Board of Directors had just voted me some $8,500 to help make the Madison international peregrine conference a reality. I never had communicated with Audubon about such a symposium, and I never did learn how they reached a figure like $8,500."[16]

Again, the BCBC was with him. "I was told that the whole idea was the brainchild of board member Roger Tory Peterson. It seems to be absolutely certain that this [grant from Audubon to support the conference] was the critical decision that brought scientists and naturalists together from seven countries and led to the extraordinary discovery that on two continents parent peregrine falcons were breaking and eating their own eggs."

In 1965, with the help of the National Institutes of Health, the Wisconsin Society for Ornithology, the American Museum of Natural History, and the National Audubon Society, Hickey held the peregrine falcon conference in Madison. "We brought people in from Europe and from Africa, our own colleagues and institutions around the United States and Canada, and had about 50 people. We tried to discuss what research we needed to find out what was going on.

"Well, the British had done their homework, and when they came, it was a magnificent meeting. They came with their facts, and their facts were that the peregrine falcon population crash in Britain was due to a reproductive failure and this reproductive failure was due to the fact that the birds were eating their own eggs. And, wow, did that hit us like a bombshell, because nobody in this country had ever suspected this thing. . . . But the British at this meeting convinced us that we were dealing with broken egg shells and this peculiar behavior."[17]

The conference was loaded with accomplished ornithologists and ecological scientists. Ratcliffe was there, as were husband and wife

William and Lucille Stickel of the US Fish and Wildlife Service. Hickey's old friend Peterson was on hand, as were Wisconsin researchers and Citizens Natural Resource Association members Frederick and Frances Hamerstrom, who were making names for themselves with research on raptors and prairie chickens in central Wisconsin. Frances Hamerstrom presented "A Harrier Population Study in Central Wisconsin," in which she told of steep declines in the number of migrating harriers through the area from 1960 to 1965. Nests had decreased 84 percent from a high of twenty-five in 1963 to four in 1965. "The cause of the harrier decline is unknown, but there is suggestive evidence that pesticides, acting through the avian component of the harrier's diet, may be involved," she speculated.[18]

Hickey's conference proceedings capture understandable scientific reticence from William Stickel. Allowing that pesticides might have a role in bird declines, he said, "There is also a tendency, now a habit, to blame pesticides for all avian declines, even where evidence does not support the belief."[19] Many other factors, including disease and depredation might be at work, he said. Through their research at the Patuxent Wildlife Research Center, William and Lucille Stickel would both end up making major contributions to the study of the influence of pesticides and other contaminants on wildlife. Lucille Stickel's work on eggshell thinning—brought on by dichlorodiphenyldichloroethylene (DDE), a breakdown product of DDT—would be a major contribution to the body of knowledge and would engage Hickey in another key research effort.

When the conference concluded, Hickey had the task of summarizing the findings. "Then, this was a long process of translating the spoken English at this conference into the written English which are two different languages," he later recalled. "It was an experience that I had never had before and never hope to have again."[20]

Hickey labored over the work. Four years later the nearly six-hundred-page *Peregrine Falcon Populations: Their Biology and Decline [Proceedings of an International Conference Sponsored by the Univer-*

sity of Wisconsin, 1965] was published in 1969. James E. Roelle, a colleague in the Department of Wildlife Ecology, assisted him in the effort.

In its conclusion, Hickey wrote that a new life history phenomenon had emerged. The ability to mobilize large amounts of calcium for production of eggs "has long been an evolutionary triumph of [birds]." But DDT and its metabolites had caused "a failure to lay eggs (or eggs that would persist), decreased numbers of eggs, egg breakage and egg-eating, inability to re-nest and decreased viability of their young.

"The ecological case against the chlorinated hydrocarbon insecticides as the pervasive factor in these phenomena is essentially complete."

As though to anticipate criticism, he added, "There is no doubt that these compounds have been of enormous benefit to mankind. But they are persisting chemicals, and they tend to be progressively concentrated in wild animals at the tops of certain food webs and ecosystems."[21]

The peregrine falcon wasn't alone. Also affected, Hickey concluded, were Scottish golden eagles, sparrow hawks, American ospreys, and bald eagles, all victims of "a new process of physiological deterioration. Many other species are almost certainly involved—and in regions far from the original ports of environmental contamination."

The findings were stunning. But perhaps as important, the conference had served to bring together researchers who looked at scientific problems from an ecological perspective. Work on pesticides had, until DDT, been primarily limited to research by economic entomologists who toiled for industry or universities, and a few chemical-friendly agencies of the federal government.

Joseph Hickey's transformation was complete. He was, after all, a scientist who had believed Rachel Carson's *Silent Spring* was a book "full of truths, half-truths and untruths."[22] The same year in which he published the proceedings, 1969, Hickey was already deeply engaged

in efforts to call DDT on the carpet in the DNR's administrative hearing. He was no longer just a scientist; he had become a citizen activist.

Hickey and other citizen scientists were laying the groundwork for
assessing human actions based on their impacts on other members of
the land community. Aldo Leopold, who had laid out these interwo-
ven relationships in *A Sand County Almanac*, would have been proud.

But Hickey and others would run into powerful opposition.

Despite his early concerns about DDT's impacts, Hickey was an
unlikely protagonist in this public-policy debate.

Hickey put it this way: "And one of the dilemmas of the time was
that as much as one wanted to be a conservationist, it was impossible for a research worker to come out against DDT because we didn't
have the research and if you were conducting research in this field, you
were then conducting research to prove that you were right, and that is
something you cannot do. So, my wife Peggy would say, Joe, why can't
you come out against DDT the way Roger Peterson is. Well I would
say Peggy, Roger Peterson isn't conducting research. My contribution
is to test hypotheses and one hypothesis is that DDT may be causing
this thing but I cannot afford to . . . make a flat statement and then try
to prove I am right."[23]

Hickey also had doubts about whether scientists should engage
in messy public debates, where decisions aren't made on the basis of
science alone. But the Madison peregrine conference had thrust him
onto a new trajectory.

Still, he needed science to back him up. "Finally, I sent Ratcliffe 10
hypotheses having to do with why the birds were breaking and eating
their own eggs. And two of the 10 hypotheses included the possibility
that the eggshells had become thinner, and at this point he wrote me
and he said, 'Yes, it is an eggshell change, and I have been testing this
for about three months,' and he had been going to private egg collections in Britain and finding that the eggshells there were thinner than
those in the museums. And so he broke this story to me in February,

and I immediately . . . had to write him and say, 'Can I make this public?'"[24] Hickey was asking permission to share the information with other ornithologists and ecologists, the Stickels among them.

Events were coalescing. Hickey was soon to enter the public arena. But before he did so, he needed some hard data on eggshell thinning in North America. He turned to Dan Anderson, the graduate student who had worked with him on herring gull response to chemicals in Lake Michigan.

CHAPTER NINE

FALCON WANDERER

IT'S NO SURPRISE THAT THE SIGHT OF ROBINS DYING ON CITY lawns got people's attention once the DDT sprayers had passed. Robins are ubiquitous and easy to love, a harbinger of spring, and about as close to nature as some city dwellers get.

But what about the peregrine falcon? It is not so easily embraced, except by those who know it well, and even some of them are conflicted. The peregrine's colors are not spectacular. Adults are slate black and barred on the chest. Most Americans in 1968 had probably never heard of this solitary raptor. Those who had fell into several disparate categories: Bird-watchers who appreciated its dramatic aerial displays. Pigeon racers and duck hunters who despised it for taking their birds on the wing. Falconers who sought to tame it. Egg hunters who robbed its aeries.

Early editions of Roger Tory Peterson's *A Field Guide to the Birds* carried this message in its index: "Peregrine. See Hawk, Duck." The peregrine, was, of course, not a hawk at all, and the reference struck a pejorative note among some populations, duck hunters among them.

Authors who opposed a ban on DDT treated it with disdain. In the 1973 book *DDT Myth: Triumph of the Amateurs*, journalist Rita Gray Beatty made the case that the DDT battles were unduly influenced by uninformed citizen activists. She found it necessary to disparage the peregrine falcon, too, writing, "The unpleasant ecological fact remains that the peregrine falcon, throughout 90 percent of its worldwide range, is a weed species commonly called the duck hawk."[1]

Her point: Even if DDT did impact some species, they weren't worth the worry.

People like Frederick Ott, the Milwaukeean who used his connections to raise funds for the DDT hearing in Madison, had a different view of the bird. The peregrine had come within a whisper of extinction, but a few determined people sought to bring it back, and Ott was among them. By the time he died in 2008, the peregrine had been removed from the endangered species list. Greg Septon, founder of the Wisconsin Peregrine Society, credited Ott for the bird's revival. "He loved peregrines and he loved being around when I was banding the birds," Septon said. "He helped me get started early on and cut through the red tape."[2] The birds had been absent from the state for more than twenty years, but Ott died knowing that dozens of nesting pairs had been reintroduced in his home state, producing young each year.

Joseph Hickey's affinity for the bird is well documented. Little wonder: what the bird lacks in good looks, it makes up for with aerial ability. About the same size as a crow, peregrines are recognized as the fastest-flying bird in the world, capable of diving speeds up to two hundred miles per hour.

It is a cosmopolitan bird species, one of the most widely distributed in the world. Its Latin name, *Falco peregrinus*, means "falcon wanderer," and it is a good fit for a bird that is found on every continent except Antarctica. But despite this wide distribution, the falcon wanderer's worldwide population has never been high. When its numbers began to tumble, the bird quickly edged near extinction. Hickey's peregrine conference in 1965 drew attention to this imminent threat.

In earlier times, Hickey had reveled in the bird's wild behavior. Having adapted well to the tall buildings that humans erected in their twentieth-century cities, the birds found new nesting sites but didn't change their behavior. This, for a boy from the Bronx, provided some storytelling fodder.

Upon receiving the Audubon Medal in 1984, he regaled the crowd at the Grand Hyatt hotel in New York with peregrine stories.

Recalling his days with the Bronx County Bird Club, Hickey said, "The high point of New York's birding in the late 1930s and early 1940s was the nesting of the peregrine falcon on Manhattan Island. About 20 different individuals overwintered each year in the city. In 1938 a pair took up year-round residence in mid-Manhattan. . . . Their main [aerie] was the Hotel St. Regis on Fifth Avenue where they nested in 1943, 1946 and 1947. The sight of the male peregrine racing down the avenue over the taxicabs and after a pigeon was one of the great spectacles of Atlantic Coast birding."[3]

Then came an encounter with a movie star. "The excitement reached a peak in 1947, when a motion picture actress, Miss Olivia de Havilland, decided to take a sun bath on a balcony within a few feet of the peregrine nest full of half-grown young. You can readily visualize the pandemonium that followed. Our female peregrine falcon began to scream and attack Miss de Havilland, who retreated in panic and bewilderment. The management was called. The N.Y. Police Department followed. The Society for Prevention of Cruelty to Animals was next brought in. Rosie Edge of Hawk Mountain Sanctuary was consulted. In the end, our Fifth Avenue babies were removed from the St. Regis, sent to Lehigh University and raised on top of the biology building there."

Things took a drastic turn for the worse for the world's peregrine populations about the time of de Havilland's unfortunate sun bath.

While Hickey, Derek Ratcliffe, Lucille Stickel, and Dan Anderson helped solve the mystery of the bird's rapid and nearly total decline, another name merits mention: Joseph Hagar. A Massachusetts ornithologist and longtime peregrine admirer and protector, he might well have been the first person on Earth to notice peregrine mating problems. At the time, though, he blamed predators.[4]

As a young man in the 1930s, Hagar organized a sanctuary system to protect Massachusetts birds of prey from egg collectors, hunters,

falconers, and other humans. He kept a close eye on the Common-
wealth of Massachusetts's fourteen peregrine aeries, witnessing the
male peregrine's spectacular mating flights and other antics of the falcon wanderers under his watch.

Three decades later, Hagar was in Madison, at Hickey's peregrine
conference, telling scientists that no peregrines were to be found anywhere in Massachusetts. He had first noticed something was wrong
in 1947.

Seeking to capture a photograph of a falcon family, he set up in a
blind near an aerie that had produced four young hawks the previous
year. He recalled watching the female scrape an indentation in the
rocks on the rock ledge (peregrines are notoriously sloppy nest build-
ers) and lay three eggs. One afternoon when he returned to the cliff, he
saw that two of the three eggs were broken. The falcons courted again,
and the female laid four more eggs. Only one hatched, and it died a
nestling. The birds tried again in 1950, failing. In 1951, they returned
once more, but did not mate. That was the last he saw of the pair.

Hagar had seen raccoon tracks near the broken eggs and decided
they were the cause of the birds' failure to reproduce. It would be
another fifteen years before DDT was found to be the cause. By that
time, peregrines had virtually vanished in many of the places they had
inhabited for centuries.

The species' low population numbers in the best of times and its
preference for inaccessible nesting sites helped keep its decline a secret.
Migrant falcons traveling routes from the Arctic tundra to the tropics
also served to mask the decline, as did the adult birds' relatively long
life span, which was a buffer to an immediate population crash even if
the birds weren't reproducing.

As researchers from the United States and several European countries compared their findings at Hickey's Madison conference, the
truth about the thinning eggshells sought out Hagar. "I was more
impressed [in 1947–1950] with the significance of the raccoons than

I am now; it is wholly unlikely that they could have been the whole story, even in Massachusetts."[5]

In a paper delivered at the 1965 Madison peregrine conference, Derek Ratcliffe—who later would play a major role in sorting out the cause of the decline—speculated on causes of the birds' population decline, ruling out dwindling food supply, persecution (at the hands of humans), and other possibilities and focusing on what he considered two likely causes: "increase in radioactive fallout and in use of agricultural pesticides."[6] But he didn't know how to compare eggshell thickness in the DDT era to that of earlier years. That's when illegal collectors of eggs became part of the story.

In a 1970 *New York Times Magazine* article on peregrines, David Zimmerman wrote: "Nest robbing, for the purpose of building large collections of blown-out eggs, had long been a popular subcult of ornithology, and a persistent—and destructive—non-ornithological hobby. Immense numbers of eggs, of all species, were preserved in private and museum collections. An obsessive breed, many egg collectors carefully recorded the place and date they stole each egg. Now, one could compare the weight, size and shell thickness of eggs taken before 1946 with eggshells taken from current, unproductive English peregrine [aeries]."[7]

Following up on his hypothesis about agricultural pesticides, Ratcliffe traveled across England, from museum to museum, collector to collector, weighing and measuring blown-out eggs. He found a direct link between eggshell thinning and the use of DDT. Learning of this, Hickey quickly arranged to duplicate the study in the United States. That's when he sent Dan Anderson on the great egg hunt.

CHAPTER TEN

THE GREAT EGG HUNT

J OSEPH HICKEY'S OBITUARY LISTED DAN ANDERSON AMONG his survivors. There was no blood tie between the two, but there was a rare personal closeness between the likable graduate student who hailed from North Dakota and the Hickey family. Anderson called himself Hickey's "academic son."[1] They shared an affinity for bird research, Manhattans, and the Green Bay Packers.

The two got along famously, except, as it happened, when Hickey asked Anderson to go on the great egg hunt. It ended up being the experience of a lifetime for Anderson, even if it nearly cost him his life.

Having sent his set of hypotheses about the cause of steep declines in peregrine falcon populations along to British scientist Derek Ratcliffe, Hickey soon knew what had to be done to confirm the growing understanding that eggshell thinning was at the heart of the matter.

Hickey got the OK from Ratcliffe to share the eggshell hypothesis with other researchers. "So I got on the telephone, and I called Lucille Stickel in Maryland, and had Tony Keith from the Canadian Wildlife Service on the phone, and the three of us talked together, and they knew about it but they didn't attach as much importance to this as I did," he recalled. "I immediately got some money from Patuxent to start measuring egg shells . . . and I selected a fellow named Dan Anderson who was one of my graduate students, who was working with me on herring gulls. In [earlier research], we found that Lake

Dan Anderson clutches a herring gull while doing research on DDT concentrations in gulls and other wildlife on Sister Islands, off Door County in Lake Michigan's Green Bay, in 1967. As a graduate student, Anderson worked closely with Joseph Hickey, a professor of wildlife management at the University of Wisconsin in Madison, and played a key role in providing the link between DDT and the reproductive problems of certain bird species. *Photo by Jim Evrard*

Michigan was loaded with DDT or what we thought was DDT. And the herring gulls were loaded. . . . Actually, it was loaded with something besides DDT, it was [also] loaded with a group of compounds called PCBs [polychlorinated biphenyls], which on the gas chromatograph have the same peaks as . . . DDT."[2]

This clouded the picture. There was a need to find eggshells in other settings, where concentrations of PCBs were absent, and where DDT and its toxic metabolite DDE could be correlated with eggshell thinning. Complicating matters was the fact that eggshell collecting—once a popular hobby—had been banned for half a century in the United States. So museum collections had plenty of eggs from pre-DDT days, some dating to the 1860s, but not many from years coinciding with DDT's use. There was a need to find eggs that had been illegally collected during the years of DDT exposure.

Hickey turned to Anderson, who had come to Madison straight out of the army specifically to do graduate work under the man who would become his mentor. "I was just a graduate student at the time, and Hickey literally grabbed my hand one day and dragged me over to the engineering department where we talked to an engineer/technician. Joe said we need this and this and that. Several weeks later, our engineer had a perfect little device ready for us to take and measure those tiny holes our peculiar egg collectors made."

The device was a micrometer, capable of measuring eggshell thickness to a high degree of accuracy. Hickey obtained funding, from a grant in the form of a contract, for Anderson's travels from Patuxent after speaking with Lucille Stickel. Everything was set. But Anderson was a field guy. He wasn't excited about the assignment.

"Then Joe and I argued about what I was to do, go to the museums and measure thousands of eggs [Hickey's plan] or go into the field and sample eggs from populations with different exposure levels of insecticide [Anderson's wish]. Actually, Joe ended-up letting me do both things, with a lot of help from his extensive network in the ornithological world," Anderson recalled. "He basically put me on the case, with the advantage of the many, many good ornithological colleagues he had developed over the years. And Joe let me freely snoop around for data and expand our network of contacts, doing all of the traveling and sleuthing myself."[3]

The travels were to last for six months straight, and on and off for several more years. "One travel agent in Madison bragged to Joe and me once that the largest ticket ever written by his agency was written for my 'eggshell travels,'" Anderson recalled.

So Anderson set off for the great museums across the country and some less inviting environs, where egg collectors held their clutches. The year was 1967. Communities across the eastern United States were spraying DDT in futile efforts to control the spread of Dutch elm disease. In Wisconsin, where DDT spraying for the disease was recommended by the Department of Agriculture, citizens in several communities were challenging local authorities over the practice and the results of DDT's acute toxicity. Anderson's job was to track down one of the impacts on wildlife stemming from sublethal dosages of DDT.

Years later, Hickey remembered it this way: "What Anderson did was go around to all the museums in the United States [and some in Canada]—to all the major museums—and measure their peregrine eggs as well as the eggs of about 10 other species. I think in the course of that study he measured about 40,000 egg shells. . . . The one thing that Anderson had that I didn't realize was, I knew that he was a very likeable guy, but Anderson proved to be almost a confidence man. He could charm an egg collector into selling him all his illegal treasures.

"In the course of that tour, he found over 80 sets of bald eagle eggs illegally collected. . . . One or two of them by some very prominent ornithologists. Hmmm. . . . And so, what Anderson found, with the help of these egg collectors was that in 1947, the same year as the change had taken place in Britain [and when widespread use of DDT as a commercial pesticide began], we had an eggshell change in peregrine falcons in Massachusetts and in California, Southern California. So here we had our evidence of a startling change unprecedented in the history of the species."[4]

Anderson learned a few other things, too. "I found out through experience that egg collectors were a very curious bunch. I had to gain their confidence, among other things, because many of them had collected eggs illegally. I made sure it was clear we weren't going to betray their confidence. I made sure that was clear before we got too far."[5]

The trick for Anderson was to find the "new stuff," as he put it. "There was a lot of old stuff in the museums. The new stuff was with guys still out there collecting." These were the illegal collectors. "I went into some neighborhoods that were a little scary at the time. I'd go knock on the door, and I didn't know who was going to answer. A lot of them had collected eagle eggs illegally, I remember one guy pulling drawers open. He didn't want me to open this one door. Well, I opened the door and said, 'My God, here's a 1951 bald eagle egg.'"

He found a thin-shelled egg in another private collection. Anderson could tell it was dated incorrectly. "I asked him about the date. 'Are you sure?' Finally he said, no, he had collected it in 1958."

In addition to measuring eggs, Anderson was collecting them for Hickey. Once he gained their confidence, he found the egg collectors to be cooperative. "They kind of liked to brag about their stuff. There were only two guys who refused. They didn't trust me or anybody. They thought I was a government guy."[6]

Anderson's museum and collection tour reached a high point in Camarillo, California. There, he met Ed Harrison, a wealthy man who had established the Western Foundation of Vertebrate Zoology. "He was collecting a lot of stuff, consolidating it," Anderson recalled. "He had a huge building and a huge office on top of that and was very accommodating. He was an old egg and specimen collector from way back. He had the money to be able to consolidate everything and had probably one of the biggest collections in the world. He gave me his car and truck and turned me loose [in search of egg collectors]. I spent two or three weeks there. That's where it really started to come together."[7]

It's also where it almost came apart for Anderson.

The California visit was early in his travels, but he had found clear evidence of peregrine falcon eggshell thinning. "I called Joe with the good news, put my data away, and then went out for a drink to celebrate in one of the local bars near UCLA. That night, some crazy SOB that I was drinking with pulled a loaded .45 out and began to wave it about, threatening everybody in the bar.

"For a brief moment, I thought that our monumental discovery and data were going to die right there on the barroom floor. That's all

I could think about, the data. Fortunately, the bartender and I talked this lunatic down. Somehow he had grown to trust me over the evening as I listened to his lamentations about the wife he had tracked from Michigan west to California to kill—perhaps he had trusted me in the same way that those egg collectors with illegal eggs had. The police finally came and took him away sobbing. I am sure that I never told this story to Joe, although I told him nearly everything else from my trips. I didn't want him to get worried and cut my trips short."[8]

Anderson lived, and so did his contributions to the eggshell thinning mystery.

CHAPTER ELEVEN

IN THE COURT OF PUBLIC OPINION

A S JOSEPH HICKEY AND OTHER RESEARCHERS SOUGHT TO make the link between sublethal exposure to DDT and the decimation of some wildlife populations, citizens and local officials in Wisconsin clashed over the chemical's use in futile efforts to halt the spread of Dutch elm disease.

Some newspaper editorials and opinion columns questioned continued use of DDT in the face of songbird deaths and concerns about human health. Others pointed out the value of elm trees and the costs of removal. Frequently, newspapers carried stories and letters to the editor about DDT dangers in their news columns while advertising DDT products for home and garden use in the same edition.

By 1968, the tide was already turning against DDT, but not based on science alone.

Newspaper clippings of clashes between citizens and elected officials bear out the fact that DDT had already been tried in the court of public opinion. As early as 1957, citizens like Dixie Larkin of Milwaukee had raised concerns about DDT. Larkin was an early environmental activist and a founding member of the Citizens Natural Resources Association.

Bird-watcher Ernstine Brehmer expressed concerns in a letter to the *Sheboygan Press* in 1960. "Now I am told by the park commis-

Letter sent out with our 7 recommendations

JUL 29 1957

Dear Sir :

It has been found that for the past few years the D.D.T. spraying for controlling the Dutch Elm Disease has caused an increasingly heavy toll of birds. The mortality not only affect the migrant species, that are with us in the spring and fall, but also the familiar summer residents.

Because of this, a group of interested citizens have made a detailed study of the situation to see if there is a way to reduce the excessive destruction of our bird and animal life.

The seriousness of the Dutch Elm Disease, and the economic and civic considerations involved are fully appreciated. To find some approach that would be practical, and at the same time be less destructive to our birds and animals, we have consulted numerous authorities. As a result of our study, we have developed the recommendations in the attached report.

It is our aim to acquaint as many people as possible with these recommendations, including municipal and state authorities. We believe the recommendations represent a most practical manner in which to fight the Dutch Elm Disease and at the same time to give some measure of consideration to other living things. It has been established by scientific research that many harmful insects build up resistance to poison sprays, including D.D.T. If in the process nature's balance is upset by the destruction of birds and parasitic insects and other natural enemies, then the man-made means of control will have to be so lethal as to destroy their master.

It is the hope of this group of interested citizens who see a threat to wildlife and humans alike in the widespread use of poison spraying in our communities that you will use your influence to see that the seven steps outlined in the attached material are adopted as soon as possible. Please let us have your views on this important matter.

Sincerely yours,

Mrs. F. L. Larkin
5333 N. Idlewild Ave.   The Committee of a Thousand*
Milwaukee 17, Wisconsin

Dixie Larkin
Chairman

*Seeking the support of a thousand organizations to oppose the widespread use of poison.

we now have over 60.000 members

Dixie Larkin of Milwaukee was an early citizen activist in efforts to curtail the use of DDT. This letter, written by Larkin in 1957, seeks to raise awareness about DDT's harm to wildlife and asks recipients to follow steps to reduce the pesticide's impacts. Larkin was an early member of the Citizens Natural Resources Association. *WHi Image ID 73092*

sion here that my fears are ungrounded, only emotional. But the first year of elm spraying left us with numerous vibrating, painfully dying birds," Brehmer wrote, calling on other bird-watchers to speak up.[1] "For, if this situation is as serious as we suspect, a unified public protest is necessary."

Clashes between municipal officials and concerned citizens heated up in the mid-1960s, no doubt in response to *Silent Spring* and, in no small part, to the deaths of songbirds in populated areas.

Cities like Whitewater, Wisconsin, had been using DDT to control mosquitoes almost since its introduction for general use, but the city's elm-spraying program is what opened citizens' eyes.[2] Mrs. E. Skindingsrude's letter to the editor that ran in the *Whitewater Register* on March 28, 1963, was representative of many that would make their way into that popular newspaper forum of the day. "Drenching the soil with deadly poisons is highly destructive to our bird life, which are the natural predators of insects, and how many birds do we see except starlings and some sparrows and pigeons. I haven't had any chickadees, red or white breasted nuthatches, downy woodpeckers for the last two years. How silent shall our spring be?"[3]

The city's officials weren't convinced that either Mrs. Skindingsrude or Rachel Carson might be right until several years later. DDT use was halted in 1967, as the Whitewater City Council switched to a more expensive but less toxic alternative, methoxychlor.

Overall DDT use was already on the decline by the time these local battles heated up. The *La Crosse Tribune* editorialized on this topic in 1969: "It is interesting to note that, while the furor is growing over the threat that the pesticide DDT may pose to fish and to mammals including man, its use is steadily declining in some states, including Wisconsin."[4]

While DDT's death knell was eventually sounded based on its overall impact on ecosystems, it's not likely that city folks would have paid much attention had it not been for Dutch elm disease.

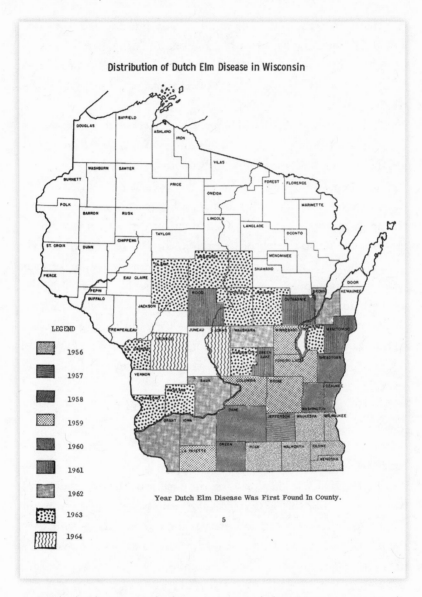

As Dutch elm disease marched across states including Wisconsin, municipalities faced burgeoning costs for the removal and disposal of dead trees. They turned to DDT in an effort to kill the beetles that spread the disease. *WHi Image ID 100309*

The origin of the Dutch elm disease is unclear. Some sources believe it was native to Asia. Most historical accounts trace its introduction to Europe from the Dutch East Indies in the late 1800s. It is believed to have arrived in the United States in the 1930s on wooden crates made with infected elm wood, but no one knows for sure.[5]

A fungus spread by both European and native elm bark beetles and also through transmission from one tree to another via their roots, the disease quickly spread across the eastern United States, devastating tree populations.

The American elm had long been considered the ideal street tree. It grew quickly and gracefully, forming canopies that shaded city streets, sidewalks, and yards. Elms tolerated soil compaction and air pollution and were fairly easy to maintain. Because of these traits, an urban monoculture of planted elms existed in many cities. If nothing else, Dutch elm disease pointed out the folly of monoculture planting and helped give birth to a new form of urban forestry that recognized the importance of diversity.

But in the 1960s, the disease decimated tree populations and walloped municipal budgets. Rapid removal of diseased trees that served as incubators for huge beetle populations was one of the best ways to control the disease. It was costly and labor-intensive work.

DDT spraying, on the other hand, offered some success in limiting the disease's spread by wiping out the beetles. And it was cheap. But even in the best of scenarios, it served only to delay the inevitable.

"I think we were doomed to failure no matter what we did," recalled Tim Lang, who became city forester in Green Bay in 1961, the year before Dutch elm disease arrived in that city.[6] At first, there was no choice but to use DDT. "I'd have been run out of town if I didn't," Lang said. "All these people were recommending it." Like many other municipal officials, Lang was soon caught in the cross fire. DDT's impact on songbirds caused a vocal backlash. "The Audubon Society was mad. It was quite controversial in the end," Lang recalled. "There were letters to the editor against what we were doing."

Those recommending DDT's use included James Kuntz, a respected plant pathologist at the University of Wisconsin in Madison who was known for developing the popular Wisconsin 55 hybrid tomato, and George Hafstad, plant pathologist with the Department of Agriculture, who "was passionate about saving elms," Lang recalled.

In a 1966 Wisconsin Department of Agriculture "Dutch Elm Disease Report," that recommended the use of DDT in fall spraying, Hafstad waxed sentimental: "The Christmas card of President and Mrs. Johnson this year featured 'the White House on a winter evening with an elm tree in the foreground symbolizing peace and serenity.' The American elm is intimately associated with the past and typifies much of that which is best in America."[7]

By 1966, Dutch elm disease had spread across much of the southern and central counties of Wisconsin, reaching as far west as Eau Claire and Chippewa Counties.

People who were alive during the era of DDT spraying have vivid recollections. Baby boomers remember trailing the mist sprayers on their bikes in a DDT-laden fog in the early days of spraying. Cities often used mist blowers to spray a DDT solution up to one hundred feet into the air to reach treetops. The next day, it was common to find dead and dying birds in the wake of the sprayer. When birds began to die, concerns about possible impacts on human health grew. People were warned to go inside as spraying crews passed by.

Soon, helicopters were incorporated. They were purported to be more effective, directing their payloads more precisely and quickly. But the specter of a helicopter swooping down to drop pesticides was overwhelming for some.

Howard Mead, a retired magazine publisher in Madison, remembered what alarmed him and his wife, Nancy. "The first thing that got us indignant was when our daughter, who was five or six at the time, and other kids were walking to Spring Harbor School along Lake Mendota Drive and helicopters came over and sprayed for Dutch elm and got the kids."[8]

Soon, west-side Madison residents were raising a ruckus about DDT. They were vocal and effective, but they were by no means the only protesters in the state.

Milwaukee Sentinel reporter Bill Janz was on hand in October 1965 when Lorrie Otto sprang into action. In a story headlined, "Birds, Bees, Butterflies Case Rests on a Robin," Janz wrote, "The Bayside village board was offered a frozen robin Thursday night. There was some indication it might accept."[9]

Otto told the board the village's spraying program was killing birds, butterflies, and bees in the village. To determine the exact cause of death, Janz wrote, she told the board, "You're welcome to one of my frozen robins." The cost for an autopsy was $60, she added.

Otto had collected dead or dying robins every day for a month the previous summer and had frozen some. She had help, too. Janz reported that "during the summer, she said children brought her convulsing robins, wrens and seagulls in shoe boxes, doll buggies and bushel baskets." The village president said a committee would likely be appointed to investigate the situation.

The determined Otto would be named to that committee. A few months later, she would be quoted in the *Milwaukee Journal* saying that, while DDT was saving some elm trees, "in the process of doing it, we're killing so many other things. In nature, diversity and beauty are synonymous. We're taking all of this from our lives for elm trees— or for money."[10]

Otto wasn't alone in making alarming claims. Dixie Larkin and others were up in arms in Whitefish Bay. "Several irate Whitefish Bay residents Monday accused the village board of 'spraying poison on helpless people' without the people's consent," read a February 8, 1966, *Milwaukee Sentinel* story.[11] The *Whitefish Bay Herald*'s report was a bit more colorful: "Animated protests by alarmed women caused the Whitefish Bay village board, Monday night, to halt its program for helicopter spraying of elm trees."[12]

Larkin, a longtime activist, proclaimed to the village board, "The health of my grandchildren or my dog is of much more importance than every elm in this village." Physician Alice Watts agreed, claiming that "DDT is toxic to the liver."[13]

Larkin claimed a friend had to be hospitalized every time the village sprayed its elms.

In response, the board temporarily suspended spraying while the village manager considered Dutch elm disease control options. A week later, Hafstad and University of Wisconsin entomologist Charles Kovalt were on hand to assure the board it was innocent of "spraying poison on helpless people."[14]

Not to be outdone by the over-the-top claims from some village residents, Kovalt "pointed out that the death of birds at about the time of DDT spraying also could be caused by the highly toxic chemicals used privately in combating quack grass."[15]

As for the residents, Hafstad said his only advice about DDT was, "Don't drink it."[16]

Hafstad's and Kovalt's reassurances aside, the skirmishes continued. Bayside put a one-year moratorium on its DDT spraying program for 1966, and Gordon Ruggaber, chair of the citizens' committee, told a reporter, "We hope some of the birds, fish and cold-blooded amphibians come back."[17] In her files, Otto penned the word "Success!" across the top of the article.[18]

"At last!" was what she wrote on a copy of a February 22, 1966, *Milwaukee Journal* editorial that questioned the decisions by three Milwaukee suburbs to use DDT despite disturbing questions raised by reputable scientists and researchers.

A growing sense of discomfort and fear of the unknown was reflected in the editorial: "The worrisome thing about such chemicals as DDT is how little we know of their cumulative effects on wildlife and even on human beings. What little we do know is unsettling. DDT has an awesome ability to persist in toxic form."[19]

Despite growing public opposition, twenty-eight municipalities filed notices with the Wisconsin Conservation Department, declar-

ing they would spray DDT in 1966–1967. Some communities, after
suspending DDT use in 1966 in favor of the less toxic but more expensive methoxychlor, reversed themselves in 1967 in the wake of heavy
elm losses. Some cited concerns about declines in property values due
to the loss of trees.[20]

The city of Milwaukee was among those returning to DDT use.
This decision would set the stage for a 1968 lawsuit that would ultimately lead to the DNR administrative hearing.

As cities struggled to control Dutch elm disease they encountered
an increasingly agitated public. One news account recalled an uprising in Neenah. The city was scheduled to use DDT in 1966, "but
an aroused public jammed city council chambers, signed petitions
and waved copies of 'Silent Spring,' in a successful attempt to stop
the spraying. Some 1970 persons, including 18 Twin Cities [Neenah
and Menasha] physicians, signed a petition against the use of DDT in
October of 1966."[21]

Similar citizen uprisings prompted Janesville to halt DDT use in
1968. "Public Concern Cited as Reason for DDT Reversal," read a
headline in the December 17 *Janesville Gazette*.

But citizens were getting mixed messages. In a classic clash of state
agencies, the Wisconsin Conservation Department had suspended
most uses of DDT on state lands years earlier, while the Wisconsin
Department of Agriculture and the University of Wisconsin continued to advocate its use in certain settings, including elm-lined city
streets.

The Wisconsin Conservation Department became the Department
of Natural Resources under a reorganization completed in July 1968.
But the old controversy lingered. As the DNR administrative hearing on DDT got under way in December 1968, the *Janesville Gazette*
reported that the Department of Agriculture and the university had
reversed themselves and stopped recommending DDT for Dutch elm
disease control. However, the decision didn't affect use of DDT in
other settings, such as agriculture.

Clearly, the policy change was a reaction to public concerns. "The effectiveness of DDT in the control program has not been the primary question," the joint statement said.[22] It cited "the significance of persisting DDT residues in the total environment," and also "public concern and unrest among scientists." The statement seemed to seek to differentiate between use of DDT for Dutch elm disease and for agricultural and other applications, citing "the general lack of appreciation by the public for the continued need of pesticides in the production of food, fiber and the protection of public health."

And not all citizens were opposed to DDT. Joseph Wachtel of Wauwatosa took the *Milwaukee Sentinel* to task for telling the Federal Communications Commission to halt attempts to ban cigarette advertising on radio and TV while calling for a ban on DDT. In a letter to the editor, he wrote, "Now comes along a very respected and mature study on the human body. It shows that smoking and air pollution do severe provable damage to man and his environment. This cannot be said about DDT yet. So here we have your paper calling for the ban of one product condemned on some pretty flimsy evidence and another product far more deadly is OK because a ban would be interfering with commerce."[23]

In Madison, Betty Chapman, wife of respected University of Wisconsin entomologist R. Keith Chapman, sought to defend DDT in letters to the editor and, eventually, as executive secretary of a citizens' group called Sponsors of Science, which fought the ban on DDT. She earned plaudits from Nobel Prize–winning agronomist Norman Borlaug, father of the Green Revolution, who expressed disdain for pesticide foes. As DDT's fate was sealed in several states and the federal government was moving toward a ban, Borlaug took the time to pen a letter to Chapman, "Thank God some courageous volunteers are getting into the act of fighting back against the propaganda campaign against pesticides and fertilizers, which is based on emotion, minitruths, maybe truths and downright falsehoods and launched by full-bellied philosophers, environmentalists and pseudo-ecologists."[24]

Borlaug's backing notwithstanding, Betty Chapman was in the minority in Madison.

An aggressive and vocal group of citizens pushed for a halt to DDT spraying of the city's elms in 1967. Howard and Nancy Mead, whose daughter and her friends had been sprayed with DDT by a helicopter, and the DNR's Walter Scott were among those who led the effort.

Also involved were writer George Vukelich; University of Wisconsin botanist Hugh Iltis, who would play an important role in the DNR administrative hearing; and Karl Schmidt, whose reading of *Silent Spring* on WHA public radio's "Chapter A Day" caused such a stir.[25]

Perhaps James Zimmerman, a naturalist at the University of Wisconsin Arboretum, summed up the citizens' concerns best in a March 9, 1967, letter to Mayor Otto Festge. Earlier, Zimmerman had voted in favor of DDT use as a member of the Madison Parks Commission. But he had changed his mind, believing DDT caused too much harm. He wrote: "The birds, bird-watchers, and eventually fishermen, are not the only ones to suffer from present policies, although this is valid reason enough. I do not like to see children, on picking up dying birds, having to be told that (a) nothing can be done for a bird displaying tremors, and (b) the birds must die because we parents are lazy and inept in managing our environment."[26]

Festge would recommend the city halt the use of DDT, but the matter was in the hands of the city council. With spraying scheduled to begin soon, City Forester George Behrnd relented, announcing that DDT spraying was being abandoned for 1967. "Behrnd said the decision not to use DDT was not related to the storm of protests that followed his original announcement. He said weather conditions between now and April 1 will not permit use of DDT," read a newspaper account.[27] Despite his announcement, the city council went on with a hearing on whether to ban the use of DDT.

A lot of turf was covered during that March 21, 1967, hearing of the Madison City Council Committee of the Whole, held to allow discussion and debate on the use of DDT, and it was a lively setting.

Howard Mead recounted for the city council the story of his daughter's dousing. Iltis, recalled Mead, "had quite a bit of scientific knowledge. He was colorful, too."[28] Newspaper accounts confirm that. Iltis told the councilmen that the substance would affect all forms of life. He used a comic turn to remind them that DDT accumulated in fat glands. The *Capital Times* reporter captured it this way: "'As you sit here tonight on your gluteus maximus you all have some DDT in you right now,' he told the startled aldermen."[29]

Behrnd assured the crowd he was aware of DDT's hazards but didn't think his program would cause much harm. The city's forestry department had fifty barrels of DDT on hand, and using it in Madison's fifty-square-mile area wouldn't have much effect, he said. "By next summer, housewives and gardeners will throw out more than that in aerosol bombs in gardens and at picnics," he said.[30]

Bringing the Wisconsin Conservation Department[31] into the picture, Walter Scott said findings by department scientists and numerous others supported Festge's recommendation. He identified himself as assistant to the director of the department, and he also represented a group called Mendota Beach Homes. "It is significant that on this first day of spring concerned citizens come before you with a plea to preserve the quality of life this season usually brings."[32]

Behrnd's spraying regime had its supporters. George Hafstad was on hand from the Department of Agriculture, along with two colleagues, department entomologist W. E. Simmons, who also served on the Dane County Board of Supervisors, and John F. Reynolds, also of the Department of Agriculture.

They told the council that until it appropriated enough money for a complete Dutch elm disease program, DDT was the only sensible way to keep the disease under control.

The council was divided on the matter, and the controversy lingered for months. The *Wisconsin State Journal* recommended continuing DDT's use. The city was making progress on managing Dutch elm disease, "but a total program to curb the destruction of the elm must include spraying of DDT, according to experts. There is no cure, but DDT will stop the beetles which transmit the disease," read an August 10, 1967, editorial.[33] Answering the lingering question that activists had been asked, the newspaper asserted: "The argument that DDT is dangerous to bird life must be viewed in light of what it would be like for birds if 50,000 elms are destroyed."

The Madison Audubon Society went on record in opposition to DDT. The Dane County Conservation League also called for a halt to spraying.[34] Many of the group's thousand-plus members were hunters and fishers. Gene Roark, who years earlier had interviewed a tearful Hickey, was its secretary. The Yahara Fishermen's Club also opposed spraying. As the DDT debate continued, in later years more traditional hook-and-bullet groups took similar positions, in no small part due to findings that fish in Wisconsin rivers and lakes were bearing DDT concentrations.

As the autumn of 1967 arrived, the Madison City Council again faced the question of whether DDT should be used for scheduled fall treatments. After reaching a deadlock a couple of nights earlier, several votes changed on October 26, 1967, when the council voted fourteen to eight to ban DDT use on trees. Zimmerman's testimony that night, in which he told of changing his mind, was credited with helping sway the vote.[35] An expert on plants and especially sedges, he would be inducted into the Wisconsin Conservation Hall of Fame in 2003.

The Madison battles were well covered by the city's newspapers. But the same story was playing out in communities wherever DDT was used to control Dutch elm disease. The local battles pitted citizens concerned about the pesticide's impacts against embattled local officials who were dealing with a devastating and costly disease that was mowing down beloved elms.

The DNR hearing and state and national bans on DDT were still down the road. But the story was unfolding rapidly, and news media across the state and nation was finding the plotline of wonder-chemical-turned-culprit irresistible. DDT was a hot story. Whitney Gould, one of the first female reporters hired at the *Capital Times*, was interested in the story. She would have her day when the hearing began a year later.

Other events that year would underscore deep divides that remained in the scientific community and turn the spotlight on the impact of DDT on Wisconsin's precious and valuable fisheries.

CHAPTER TWELVE

SWIMMING IN DDT WATERS

I F THE DDT STORY WAS WARMING UP DUE TO SPARKS OF PRO-
test around the state over spraying elm trees with DDT, it went white
hot in early 1966.

Don Johnson, an outdoors writer for the *Milwaukee Sentinel*, shook
things up with a series of articles on DDT concentrations in Wisconsin's lakes and streams. "State Fish Swimming in DDT Waters" read
one front-page story.[1] Johnson's lead was an eye-catcher: "If the same
analytical yardstick were applied as it is used on red meat, fish in many
Wisconsin waters could be classed unfit for human consumption—
because of high pesticide content. However, the meat yardstick does
not apply to fish, and authorities say there is no evidence of an acute
health hazard."

Johnson had been dogging the story for months, combing through
data from a variety of sources. "State and federal agencies have been
collecting mounting evidence of the situation in recent months, but
have been reluctant to publicize their findings. Most plead that the
results thus far are incomplete, and are inconclusive," Johnson wrote.

Indeed, findings of several studies released in 1966 and 1967
showed DDT was present in virtually every water body in Wisconsin,
with the highest concentrations near populated areas. It was explosive
data, considering the potential impact on the billion-dollar Wisconsin fishing and tourism industries.

Johnson had been determined in his efforts to get at the information, and officials had resisted its release. He wasn't the only one in pursuit of the information. Just days before his stories went to press, Lorrie Otto learned of the reports. Her advocacy efforts had become the equivalent of a full-time job by then. She was no longer the shy farm girl or timid housewife.

"One gray day, [Joseph] Hickey gave me an ink-wet report on DDT in Lake Michigan. I went from his office to the Shade Tree Conference [in Madison], where the Agriculture Department continued to recommend the use of DDT on elm trees," she recalled. "When the meeting adjourned, and I was lifting my coat from a hanger in the hall, I noticed the nametag on the man next to me." The man was a representative of the Wisconsin Conservation Department. "I looked directly at him and asked how could they continue to use DDT after the recent fish report?

"Surprised, he responded, 'How do you know about that report?' Then he told me every lake and river in our state contains DDT. At the time I didn't know anything about the other lakes and rivers. I only knew about our 22,400-square-mile Lake Michigan."[2]

Otto recalled his next comment: "Keep quiet about this. It will destroy our tourist industry. Do you realize how many fishing licenses we sell?" Otto baited him with a question about whether fishers would play musical chairs and rush to another state to fish. His reply: "Other states are just as bad as we are."

She hustled back to Milwaukee, drove to the *Sentinel* office, and looked up Johnson, who she knew was following the issue. "He begged me not to mention this for at least another 24 hours," she said, adding that Johnson had confided that the story took a long time to crack. It took him a while to pry the Conservation Department apart from the Department of Agriculture, he told her. While the Conservation Department had been moving steadily toward restricting DDT use, the impact of the fish findings was a tender matter given the amount of revenue generated for conservation activities by license sales.

Years later, Johnson recalled how the story unfolded. "The truth is, I could not have accomplished much without the complicity of some who literally put their jobs and careers on the line to help me tell the public what was happening," he recounted in a guest editorial he penned for the *Dunn County News* in 2000.[3] He had waited more than thirty years to tell that part of the story for a reason. "I have protected the identities for years, but it will do no harm to name some of them now," he wrote. In fact, they deserved recognition, he added.

Johnson's investigative work started after a conversation over a drink in Rice Lake with Ed "Doc" Schneberger, then fisheries chief of the Wisconsin Conservation Department. Johnson was concerned about the impact DDT was having on songbirds in communities trying to control Dutch elm disease. "It seemed evident that it [DDT] was killing songbirds and doing other environmental damage, but there was no solid proof," Johnson explained.

"Doc Schneberger quietly confided that he was scared. He told me that state fish hatchery crews were no longer collecting musky eggs from fish in certain lakes because the eggs from those lakes were no longer viable. I pressed him for more information. He answered, 'It's up to you to find out why. You haven't heard anything from me,'" Johnson would later recall.

So Johnson set out to do some sleuthing. He learned of research that had already been done on DDT contamination in fish and wildlife and "also that the frightening findings were in the possession of certain individuals at the University of Wisconsin–Madison, the Conservation Department, and the Wisconsin Department of Agriculture."

But no one was talking. "There appeared to be a conspiracy of silence. If the truth got out, agency heads feared the consequences to the tourism industry, sportfishing, and the already failing commercial fishing industry. As for the university, I suspected that research grants from chemical companies might be having some influence," Johnson recalled.

Soon, he learned that musky eggs weren't the only evidence of

DDT contamination. Seagulls on Green Bay were no longer reproducing, Hickey's research had showed, and, Johnson later wrote, "chubs laced with big doses of DDT were still being netted from Lake Michigan, smoked and sold for human consumption. But the public wasn't being told."

Johnson was getting closer, but he needed more. He pondered collecting and analyzing samples himself, but didn't have the money to pay for the gas chromatograph tests that would have been needed.

Still, he persisted. "Without revealing details which could still embarrass someone, I can reveal that it was the late Walter Scott, assistant to the director of the Conservation Department, who saw to it that I finally found what I was looking for. (Walter had often been called 'the conscience' of the old WCD, and with good reason.) And back at the university, it was the late Prof. Joe Hickey, bless him, who confirmed that I had broken the code," Johnson recalled.

Lorrie Otto's recollections of the events are also on record. She noted that Lester Voigt, director of the Conservation Department, stonewalled Johnson, telling him that a joint release was planned and that all the states around the lake planned to release it at the same time. Her recollections of Johnson's visit to Scott are also on record. She noted that Scott first told Johnson he couldn't give him anything but that Johnson persisted. Scott stood up, opened a drawer, pulled out a stack of papers, slammed them on his desk, and walked out of his office.[4]

Otto acquiesced in Johnson's *Sentinel* office the day he asked her to wait twenty-four hours. She was rewarded with major coverage in the paper. "The next morning, the Sentinel had the entire story from robins to mink to fish to worms," she recalled. "At last—a big audience!"[5] The story detailed a number of angles to the new findings. "Of hundreds of fish collected from 30 bodies of water around the state all were found to contain DDT," Johnson reported at the time.[6]

He continued to hammer away at the DDT story, despite threats of lawsuits and demands by chemical companies that he be fired.[7] "Fishermen Upset by Lake Pesticides," was the headline on a January 29, 1966, Johnson story. The Department of Agriculture, Conservation Department, and University of Wisconsin researchers had released their findings after Johnson's original exposé. Their research showed that significant amounts of DDT had been found in the tissues of fish taken from several inland lakes and outlying waters—including Lake Michigan and Lake Superior.[8]

"There were some attempts to discredit and intimidate me," Johnson recalled in the *Dunn County News*.[9] "Some editors worried about the accuracy of my reports and the consequences of printing them. And there were threats of lawsuits for astronomical sums, claimed as damages by the chemical makers.

"But, as he did a number of other times, Harvey Schwandner, executive editor of *The Milwaukee Sentinel*, backed me all the way. Harvey was a real newspaperman, of the old school."

Johnson and the *Sentinel* went on to cover and, in his words, "campaign against" other environmental poisons and contaminants.

His early DDT reports in the *Sentinel* weren't exactly new information. Concentrations of what appeared to be DDT had been identified in Lake Michigan fish several years earlier, and questions had been raised about the chemical's impact on fish reproduction.[10] But Johnson's stories came at a time when Wisconsin was moving closer to a confrontation over DDT. They served to stir up the hunting and fishing community, broadening public support for a ban on DDT. In addition to the Izaak Walton League, several mainline hunting and fishing organizations jumped on the bandwagon, as did the fish and game industry. In 1969, the American Fishing Tackle Manufacturers Association would donate ten thousand dollars to help fund the Citizens Natural Resources Association's efforts in Wisconsin. A check for five thousand dollars went directly to the CNRA. Another five thousand dollars, raised by individual members of the association, was presented to the Rachel Carson Trust for the Living Environment, a fund established by the National Audubon Society, with instructions that the funds be used in Wisconsin for the Department of Natural Resources hearing.

For the citizen activists, the findings provided new fodder. CNRA president Frederick Baumgartner sought to link the findings to their potential economic impacts. In a letter from the CNRA to "all organizations interested in conservation," he warned of the potential threats DDT had on the health of fish, water quality, and the local economy. "The level of DDT and similar related persistent pesticides has risen to the point where scientists report the coho salmon fry can't even grow in our hatcheries. . . . Also, the flesh is questionable as human or animal food," he wrote. "The lake trout, steelhead and other fine game fish (even in our inland lakes) and our bald eagle, osprey and other fish-eating birds are suffering nesting losses. It's time for action!"[11]

A full report issued by the Conservation Department just prior to the opening of the Wisconsin inland lake sportfishing season in 1967 added fuel to the fire. Researchers found DDT residues in fish from thirty-two lakes and thirty-one streams. Residues in some lakes may have reached levels harmful to fish, the department said, hastening to add that the Wisconsin Department of Agriculture and the Board of Health didn't believe there was a hazard to people who ate the fish.[12]

The findings also correlated DDT residues in fish with use of the pesticide in the watersheds. Higher residues were found in "various urbanized, outdoor recreation and agricultural locations known or suspected to be areas of frequent pesticide use," a 1967 *Milwaukee Journal* article noted.[13] In addition to the normal suspects—household, lawn, farm, and forest insect control, and Dutch elm disease treatment—a finger was pointed at "bug bombs," aerosol cans or foggers, used to kill mosquitoes in cottage and camp areas.

DDT wasn't the only pesticide found in the fish. Dieldrin, a related but more toxic insecticide introduced as an alternative to DDT, was also detected.

The news on DDT concentrations in fish continued to roll out. Indeed, it would become a subplot throughout the course of the next two years and beyond, both at the state and local levels. In 1967, there were no federal standards for DDT concentrations in fish, although efforts to establish a threshold were underway.

Not much more than a year after Johnson broke the story about DDT residues in fish, a *Sentinel* headline read, "Lake Pesticides Reported Nearing 'Lethal Level.'" Reporter Quincy Dadisman, who would cover the DDT hearing for Milwaukee's morning newspaper, was quoting W. F. Carbine, regional director of the Bureau of Commercial Fisheries, who issued that dire warning.

"Pesticides, herbicides and related chemicals represent an area of water quality change of major importance to fish and aquatic life," said Carbine. He spoke at a Lake Michigan water quality conference called by Secretary of the Interior Stewart Udall. "A continuation at high levels or an upsurge in pesticide application anywhere in the Lake Michigan basin could increase the pesticide concentration prevailing in the open lake from the present nonlethal level to a lethal level."[14]

The fishery had undergone a number of other changes over the years, Carbine noted. The sea lamprey had devastated native lake trout populations, and nonnative alewives had a significant impact. With declining native populations, states sought to bolster sportfish opportunities in the lake by introducing species like the nonnative coho salmon. Perhaps anticipating a future problem, Carbine noted that pesticides especially impacted lake-dwelling fish such as coho that also spend part of their lives in streams, where higher concentrations of pesticides accumulated.

In August 1968, natural resource officials from the four Great Lakes states—Illinois, Indiana, Michigan, and Wisconsin—issued a warning: "We believe that unless timely steps are taken to control persistent pesticides and other economic poisons, Lake Michigan's usefulness will shrink to a fraction of its potential—indeed to the point of disaster."[15]

The officials noted that DDT was likely responsible for the deaths of nearly one million coho salmon fry in Michigan and Wisconsin hatcheries that year, and that "irreparable contamination is imminent."

The warning urged a series of steps to address the problem, including the passage of new laws, citing examples of pending bills to create pesticide review councils in Wisconsin and Michigan. But the report did not expressly recommend banning DDT.

In step with the four-state warning, Wisconsin's top conservation agency was becoming more vocal on the subject. In November 1969, just a couple weeks before the DNR's administrative hearing on DDT began, the Wisconsin Board of Agriculture and the DNR's Natural Resources Board—both of which are comprised of appointed citizens who oversee department operations—met jointly in Madison. The DNR was a new configuration, having inherited responsibilities from the former Conservation Department, Public Service Commission, Board of Health, and Board of Resource Development.

Walter Scott, whose new title was assistant to the deputy secretary of the DNR, spoke to the boards, noting their meeting was the first time conservation and agriculture boards had gathered jointly.

He reviewed some basic conservation history and then went on to speak about DDT and other persistent pesticides. Knowledge had grown over the course of twenty years of DDT use, he said. This included a better understanding of how pesticides like DDT persisted in the environment. "They also build up in the food chain of animals so the best predatory game fish are most vulnerable to these poisons as also are many desirable fish-eating and flesh-eating birds," Scott noted.[16] He also tied water quality to the state's Public Trust Doctrine, established by the Wisconsin Supreme Court: "The right of the citizens of the state to enjoy our navigable streams for recreational purposes, including the enjoyment of scenic beauty, is a legal right that is entitled to all the protection which is given financial rights."

This concept of "navigable waters" included, Scott asserted, "such things as fishing, swimming and wading, and so the preservation of water quality, as well as quality of the fishery and the total water-related environment, is of utmost concern."

He went on to point out that research on lake trout reproduction in New York State in 1964 revealed that eggs would not hatch properly if they contained too much DDT or its residues. That was the year the Wisconsin Conservation Department had stopped all use of DDT on forest pest control.

Scott explained that in 1965 the Conservation Department began detailed studies to determine the levels of pesticide residue in fish taken from state lakes and streams. He cited the coho salmon fry dieoff of 1968, the published results of DDT and dieldrin residues in fish, and the joint statement issued by the conservation leaders of the Lake Michigan states. He also noted that of the fifty tons of DDT shipped into Wisconsin that year, thirty tons went for Dutch elm disease control efforts.

Scott even worked religion into his remarks while noting that Lake Michigan had historically yielded huge quantities of fish. "About 10,000 fishermen using thousands of boats harvested this crop from the Great Lakes in a type of farming which yields food very nutritious and desirable," he said. "In fact, when Jesus fed the multitude he used only two fishes to go along with the five loaves that were available. The plea here is that every possible effort be made to restore the quality and maintain the quantity of fishery production in the Great Lakes." Scott made no mention of commercial fishing methods that had depleted the fishery or of the impacts of nonnative species such as lampreys and alewives.

He did, however, cite a statement from a 1967 department publication: "The results of laboratory tests conducted over a period of years leads inescapably to the conclusion that the persistent chlorinated hydrocarbon pesticides (particularly DDT) are progressively accumulating in our environment and in consequence are threatening fish and game interests." He added: "This in turn affects the quality of our outdoor recreation resources and the tourist industry which generates a billion dollar annual value for the state."

Scott went on to reference the upcoming DNR hearing, closing this way: "We are here today in a good cause with a promise of future meetings in the interest of the people's welfare. Nothing should concern them more than their fish and wildlife and their public waters—except possibly the quantity and quality of their next meal. We need to assure them of both."

Lorrie Otto remained impatient and unsatisfied with the slow-moving bureaucracy and those who tended it. In a September 1968 letter to Environmental Defense Fund attorney Victor Yannacone, she wrote: "It's not all sheer terror or naïve glee out here, Vic. There are long plateaus when I think that those colorless, weak sneaks in the Wisconsin Conservation [Department] are going to defeat us. There isn't a one of them who has enough guts to support you in a lawsuit."[17]

There's no record of whether Otto was present at that joint meeting of the state's DNR and Department of Agriculture boards. If she was, perhaps her feelings about Scott and his colleagues were about to change. Viewed in the prism of history, Scott's speech was anything but colorless or weak. As the studies on DDT concentrations in fish emerged in Wisconsin and other states, the DNR had a hook to hang its hat on: fishing was a big business in Wisconsin, and sportsmen's licenses helped fund an array of other DNR duties, including environmental enforcement.

The DDT hearing would begin in December 1968. As the hearing continued into 1969, word came of an explosive new finding. "FDA Cites Pesticide, Asks Seizure of Coho," read the page-one headline in the March 27, 1969, *Milwaukee Sentinel.* Reporter Richard Bradee in the newspaper's Washington bureau reported that the Food and Drug Administration had requested seizure orders for 21,000 pounds of frozen coho salmon from Lake Michigan that tests indicated contained hazardous amounts of DDT and dieldrin. The fish had been caught near the eastern shore of the lake and processed by a Grand Rapids, Michigan, company.

Tests showed the coho contained up to nineteen parts per million of DDT and a smaller amount of the more toxic dieldrin. "The tolerance for DDT and Dieldrin in fish is zero, meaning that fish cannot be sold if they show any trace of either pesticide," Bradee wrote. US senator Gaylord Nelson of Wisconsin, who had been pushing for a DDT ban for several years, called the need for the seizure orders "a tragedy." Bradee quoted him as saying, "This is the first case where the concentration of DDT has traveled hundreds of miles and gone through the food chain of a half dozen organisms and ended up in hazardous residues of coho salmon."

It seems that the coho had raised quite a stir. A series of stories cascaded from that original report.

Robert Finch, secretary of the Department of Health, Education and Welfare, called a high-level meeting to deal with a growing political controversy over the tainted coho, reported the *Milwaukee Sentinel* on April 9, 1969. He summoned representatives of federal and state agencies, along with US congressmen and conservation and health officials from Wisconsin, Illinois, and Michigan. One of those congressmen, Representative Gerald Ford of Michigan, charged the FDA with "pure speculation" about the health hazard caused by DDT in coho.[18] The FDA did not, the future president noted, raise the same doubts about canned salmon from other parts of the country. "I can imagine the hue and cry from people all over the United States if all fish that have any residue in them were prohibited from being caught or consumed," Ford said in a speech before the US House of Representatives.

The FDA moved quickly, establishing on April 22 a temporary tolerance standard of five parts per million in commercially sold fish. Permanent guidelines would be set after a six-month study, the FDA said.[19] Almost immediately, the temporary standard drew complaints. The Michigan Natural Resources Department predicted the state's commercial fishing industry faced a $2.5 million annual loss under the new tolerance level.[20] Michigan's sports and commercial fishing industry was said to have a $60 million annual economic impact.

Meanwhile, with the DDT hearing underway in Wisconsin, the first witness called by the Task Force for DDT of the National Agricultural Chemicals Association said fish caught in Wisconsin were safe to eat, despite fears of DDT contamination. Testifying on April 29, 1969, Dr. Wayland J. Hayes Jr., former chief of the toxicology laboratory of the US Public Health Service, pointed to a frequently cited piece of research in which measured doses were fed to convict volunteers at federal correctional institutes. They received doses of 0.05 to 0.5 milligrams daily, which Hayes said was about two hundred times the amount of DDT ingested from the environment by an average person.[21] At the end of the experiment, from twelve to twenty-one months after they started, no deleterious effects from eating DDT could be found in the men, Hayes said.

Other newspaper reports speculated that inland waters might be closed to fishing, since stream species had higher concentrations of DDT than Lake Michigan fish. By September, Wisconsin governor Warren Knowles and his counterparts in four other midwestern states asked the FDA to establish "realistic tolerance levels for DDT in fish."[22] In November 1969, a committee of Upper Great Lakes state health officials filed a petition asking for a fifteen parts per million tolerance in edible parts of coho salmon and ten parts per million in other fish.

By that time, another story had played out in Wisconsin. While the DNR hearing had proceeded in early 1969, the Wisconsin Legislature began its own hearings on a bill to ban DDT. That's when a northern Wisconsin conservation activist decided to stir things up in a big way.

CHAPTER THIRTEEN

WARNING: CONTROVERSY AHEAD

W HEN MARTIN HANSON PRINTED THOUSANDS OF HAND-
bills warning "Fish Eaten from Wisconsin Waters Could be
Dangerous to Human Health," he really got under the skin of the
Wisconsin tourism industry and state lawmakers from the northern
counties.

As lawmakers attacked him for the scheme, hatched just prior to the
start of the 1969 open water fishing season in Wisconsin, the bachelor
who lived most of his adult life in a backwoods retreat didn't flinch.
He wanted DDT banned, and he was going to do whatever it took to
accomplish that goal.

If it's possible to be both reclusive and an engaged citizen, that
would describe Hanson. He also had a mischievous streak to go along
with a strong conservation ethic. He was known for bringing a squirt
gun to meetings, sitting in the back of the room and launching a spray
on those toward the front.

But the handbill campaign wasn't a prank. It was intended to stir
up the public and add an exclamation point to findings of DDT concentrations in popular game fish. The research provided environmentalists with a powerful weapon in their efforts to ban the pesticide, and
Hanson took advantage of it.

Heir to a Chicago furniture-making fortune, he and his siblings,
including fellow bachelor brother Louis, moved in 1961 onto a 1,240-

Conservation activist Martin Hanson caused a stir in 1969 when he spearheaded an effort to distribute fliers across the state warning people that consuming fish from state waters might be a health hazard because of DDT concentrations in fish. He's pictured on his property near Mellen. *Courtesy of Tia Nelson*

acre family-owned retreat west of Mellen. With the freedom that wealth can afford, they became engaged in their personal passions: politics and conservation.

Soon the Hanson retreat, which included a string of cottages for guests, became a popular haunt for Democratic politicians. Gaylord Nelson, himself from the north, was a frequent visitor and friend. Young David Obey of Wausau, who would be elected to the House of Representatives in 1969, often took his rest at the Hansons' place. Both men and an array of other politicians benefited from the brothers' time, talent, and 'treasured getaway.

Cocktails and dinner parties gave way to political discussions that lasted into the wee hours as bears, illuminated by outdoor lighting, chomped on roadkill deer hauled to the retreat by Martin.[1]

The discussions weren't without results, the *Milwaukee Journal* would note in a 1994 story: "The strategy for supporting the St. Croix and Namekagon as national scenic rivers took form at the Hansons.' Opposition to nuclear power plants jelled [there]. Part of the campaign that led to a ban on the pesticide DDT in Wisconsin was fashioned here. The strategy for saving the Apostle Islands in Lake Superior was hatched at the Hanson table."[2]

In September 1963, President John F. Kennedy had visited northern Wisconsin as part of a conservation tour. Kennedy boarded a
military helicopter for an aerial view of the Apostle Islands. He was
joined by Senator Gaylord Nelson, Wisconsin governor John Reynolds, Secretary of the Interior Stewart Udall, and Secretary of Agriculture Orville Freeman. Hanson, an expert on the islands, was also
aboard the helicopter, acting as the president's guide.

Years later, Hanson would recall the helicopter ride in an interview
with the *Milwaukee Journal*. "On the helicopter, I was lecturing the
president about the Apostles. I said you could get them cheap, but he
didn't seem too interested. Then he saw a big group of sailing boats
and his eyes lit up. Here was the Massachusetts sailor seeing some of
the best sailing water around," Hanson said.[3]

Two months later, Kennedy was assassinated in Dallas. But his support gave the Apostle Islands project a needed boost. Kennedy was
impressed, but he stopped short of endorsing an idea gaining steam
in northern Wisconsin to place the Apostle Islands under federal protection, possibly as a national park. Nelson was among those cham-
pioning the islands, and he had arranged Kennedy's visit, part of a
multistate conservation tour in 1963. After his helicopter tour, Kennedy would say, "Lake Superior, the Apostle Islands and the Bad River
area are all unique. They are worth improving for the benefit of sportsmen and tourists. . . . In fact, the entire Great Lakes area is a central
and significant part of the fresh water assets of this country, and we
must act to preserve these assets."[4] Kennedy's comments served to raise
the project's profile, and, as Nelson noted, Kennedy's remarks "would
be noticed by the park service and everybody else."[5]

Nelson guided the project to success, but not without many twists
and turns. Rather than a national park or wilderness area that would
preclude or restrict hunting, trapping, commercial fishing, and wild
rice gathering, Nelson proposed a national recreation area. Finally,
in 1970, President Richard Nixon signed a bill protecting 22 islands,

39,500 acres, and 11 miles of Lake Superior shoreline. The Bad River area was excluded after two Ojibwe Indian bands, the Bad River and Red Cliff, objected to the project. Wisconsin had a national seashore, and Hanson was credited for years afterward with playing a major role.[6]

There can be little doubt that DDT came up regularly as a topic when the friends gathered at the Hansons' retreat. Whether the hand-bill scheme was concocted with Nelson at the table is left to speculation. But there can be little doubt that Nelson had at least been apprised of Hanson's plans. In fact, Nelson had already empowered Hanson to participate in the public fray. He was named the first council chair of the Wisconsin Council for Resource Development and Conservation and served on the group from 1962 to 1972. It had been formed at the behest of Nelson when he was governor to provide a unified statewide voice speaking on key conservation issues. Historian Thomas Huffman described the group this way: "In many ways, this group proved a forerunner of the Wisconsin environmental organizations of the 1970s. It . . . established an intellectual perspective involving the issues of the 'new conservation,' an approach considerably broader than the hunting, fishing and forestry concerns of the traditional state conservation community."[7]

The council's membership of thirty-five organizations was indeed broad, ranging from the CNRA and the Sierra Club to the Wisconsin Federation of Women's Clubs, the Wisconsin Federation of Lake Property Owners, the Wisconsin Bowhunters Association, and even Humble Oil Company. It was in his capacity as council secretary that Hanson appeared before the Wisconsin Assembly Agriculture Committee, which was considering Bill 163-A to ban the use of DDT. The Department of Natural Resources' DDT hearing was yet to be completed and the hearing examiner's decision still six months off, but lawmakers in Wisconsin, Michigan, and other states were seeking to enact state bans in the absence of federal action.

Hanson appeared before the committee to tell lawmakers the Wisconsin Council for Resource Development and Conservation wasn't going to wait for passage of a bill and planned to distribute the handbills.

"I have not come here to offer testimony on the scientific aspect of a DDT ban. The council feels there already has been an overwhelming amount of scientific testimony given to warrant passage of Bill 163-A.

"I am here, rather, to inform this committee that we already have had thousands of handbills printed warning of the possible health hazard caused by the level of DDT found in fish taken in Wisconsin waters. We intend to distribute these warnings to the people of this state and to out-of-state tourists."[8]

He went on to tell the committee, "We intend to make up in manpower what we lack in financial power in the fight against the giant pesticide industry. We hope our efforts will help convince you that the ban is needed."

Hanson's announcement drew immediate scorn from a variety of sources. Representative Norman Nuttelman of West Salem, chair of the committee Hanson addressed, told Hanson the campaign "could create mass hysteria."[9] He added that there was no proof that DDT would cause human health problems if it was present in fish.

Assembly Majority Leader Paul Alfonsi of Minocqua, a popular North Woods destination, didn't waste time. The day after Hanson's dramatic announcement, he told his assembly colleagues the distribution of leaflets was objectionable. "Such efforts by Hanson can only hurt the tourist industry in the state," he said.[10] "I'm as much against pollution, which apparently is caused by DDT, as anyone else."

The next day, Hanson fired back at Alfonsi. "The truth, and it may hurt, is that the Wisconsin Legislature by its failure to come to grips with the pesticide problem is to blame for any harm that may be done to our great tourist industry as a result of the level of pesticide residue found in fish taken from Wisconsin waters."[11]

The Vilas County Board voted to send a letter of objection to the council for its "asinine" publicity.[12] Representative Gordon Bradley of Oshkosh chastised Hanson for "blackmailing the Legislature at the expense of the tourist industry."[13]

The handbills were "without any basis in fact" said the *Wausau Record-Herald* in an April 17 editorial. "There is no reason to be alarmed about the 1969 fishing season in inland waters. However, this does not mean that we can overlook the DDT problem. It could, conceivably, result in unsafe levels in Wisconsin fish five or ten or fifty years from now."[14]

Other newspapers took on the legislature for failing to act.

"All this, of course, is likely to bring screams from Wisconsin resort operators and related business that depend on the tourism trade," said the *Janesville Gazette* on April 9. "The outrage, however, should be directed at the Legislature, not the conservation council. You do not curse a sunbeam because it illuminates a pigsty."[15]

The *Waukesha Daily Freeman* slammed Alfonsi on April 11: "Assemblyman Alfonsi, like so many of his fellows in the legislature, has a penchant for brushing problems under the cloakroom rug of the capitol in Madison. So it comes naturally for him to concede DDT is a threat to human as well as animal life, but he'd just as soon keep it quiet." This, the newspaper said, "is another example of attempting to protect special interests at the cost of not defending the public interest."[16]

Were the handbills distributed? The *Vilas County News-Review* answered that question on April 10, writing, "To dramatize its conclusion, the Resource Council began this week to distribute 20,000 warning posters."[17] On April 14, the *Capital Times* of Madison ran an article by *Vilas County News-Review* editor Dan Satran, which reported that the handbills would also be "passed out by students in various university communities, such as La Crosse and Stevens Point."[18] The latter, of course, was home to the president of the Citizens Natural Resources Association, Frederick Baumgartner.

Art Oeluneke, a fishery expert for the DNR in Woodruff, said in the same article that while he favored a DDT ban, there was no reason for sportfishermen to worry about fish in northern Wisconsin. DDT concentrations in northern fish were below FDA standards for other types of food, he said. The highest concentrations of DDT were in downstate waters, he added. The source of DDT contamination in the north likely came from insect bombs and fogging for mosquitoes and other nuisance species, Oeluneke said.

Governor Knowles, a dedicated sportsman, was compelled to issue a statement in advance of the open-water fishing opener about the safety of Wisconsin fish taken from inland waters. "The Department of Natural Resources has given assurances that fish taken from our inland waters are completely safe and wholesome," Knowles said in a statement issued prior to the Great Lakes governors meeting in Chicago concerning pesticide poisoning in Lake Michigan.[19] "Although the presence of DDT poses a serious threat to commercial and sportfishing in the Great Lakes, Wisconsin's inland lakes are not similarly threatened."

Knowles didn't tell people not to eat Great Lakes fish, but he didn't give them the same endorsement as fish in inland waters. On the same day Knowles issued his statement, Michigan governor William Milliken asked merchants and residents in his state to cease using and selling DDT.

Did Martin Hanson's handbill scheme work? It obviously garnered public attention, and politics—to a much greater degree than science—was highly sensitive to public opinion.

CHAPTER FOURTEEN

"SUE THE BASTARDS"

D DT had been on trial in the court of public opinion for several years prior to the Wisconsin hearing.

Federal and state agencies sparred over the pesticide's use, and some,
such as Wisconsin's Department of Natural Resources, had already
eliminated it from their arsenals or dramatically restricted its use. Gaylord Nelson, the US senator from Wisconsin, had introduced a bill to
ban its use nationally in 1966.

Sometimes heated local skirmishes in communities where Dutch
elm disease spraying led to bird deaths garnered the attention of local
media, and citizen awareness grew. One such local fight—in this case
over the use of DDT to control mosquitoes—took place in New York
and led to the founding, in 1967, of the Environmental Defense Fund.
Comprised of a small group of citizens intent on using legal action to
fight environmental degradation, the group's unofficial but frequently
mentioned motto was "sue the bastards."[1] The EDF also tried to initi-
ate an action in Michigan but failed. But after Joseph Hickey and Lorrie Otto visited Charles Wurster and his EDF colleagues in August
1968, the wheels began to turn. The EDF's goal was to put DDT on
trial, and it found a venue in Wisconsin.

The first round came that year in Milwaukee, as autumn settled over
the Midwest. The EDF agreed to join the Citizens Natural Resources
Association in seeking an injunction to prevent the city of Milwau-

kee and Buckley Tree Service from spraying DDT on elm trees until a
DNR hearing could be held. Citizens signing the petition seeking an
injunction included the CNRA's Frederick Baumgartner of Stevens
Point; George C. Becker of Stevens Point, a colleague of Baumgartner's at Wisconsin State University–Stevens Point; Louise W. Erick-
son of Racine; Harold Kruse, CNRA member from Loganville;
Russell Rill, CNRA member from Clintonville; and Roy Gromme,
CNRA member from River Hills. They sought to prevent spraying
that was scheduled to begin October 15.[2]

Their petition was based on the belief that DDT was a harmful and
persistent biocide that was degrading the entire environment of Lake
Michigan, according to a notice released by Baumgartner, who had
succeeded Gromme as president of the CNRA.

A DNR hearing got underway on October 18, 1968, at a state
office building in Milwaukee in what DNR hearing examiner Maurice Van Susteren called a "roomful of very agitated people."[3] The
hearing, wrote historian Thomas Dunlap, "was a fiasco."[4] The defen-
dants agreed they would not use DDT and said there was no contract
between them for such spraying. Van Susteren dismissed the petition
and declared the hearing "moot."[5]

But what seemed like the end was only the beginning. The CNRA
and the EDF had secured an empty victory in Milwaukee, but in the
process found Van Susteren, a hearing examiner with a firm grasp of
the law and an independent streak that earned him a reputation as a
bit of a gadfly. Van Susteren steered the citizens to a new possibility,
one that would have far-reaching ramifications.

Dunlap put it this way: "Van Susteren was curious, however, why
the winners of the suit were so dejected. He confronted [EDF counsel
Victor] Yannacone, who explained that EDF wanted a forum in which
to present the scientific evidence against DDT and to get a judgment.
If that was the case, Judge Van Susteren told him, he should use a
different approach. Section 227.06 of the Wisconsin statutes allowed

citizens to ask any state agency for a declaratory ruling on the applicability of a law enforced by that department to any particular situation or set of facts."[6] The DDT foes could, Van Susteren informed Yannacone, ask the DNR for a declaratory ruling on whether DDT was a water pollutant under Wisconsin water quality standards. The DNR, which oversaw the state's natural resources, could then hold a hearing and permit interested parties to present their evidence. This is exactly what the EDF had been pursuing. In effect, the EDF and the CNRA could put DDT on trial in a quasi-judicial setting. Witnesses would be under oath and subject to cross-examination.

The DDT foes wasted little time. On October 28, the CNRA petitioned the Department of Natural Resources "requesting a declaratory ruling on whether DDT was an environmental pollutant within the definitions of section 144.01(11) and 144.30(9) of the Wisconsin Statutes."[7] The Wisconsin division of the Izaak Walton League of America would soon join the CNRA in the action. Though they had disagreed about the founding of the CNRA almost two decades earlier, the two groups were now joint petitioners in a hearing of immense importance. The Wisconsin Department of Justice and its public intervenor Robert McConnell later entered on behalf of the citizens of the state. The stage was set for a showdown. Well, not quite. The CNRA had almost no resources. The EDF wasn't much better off. It planned to call scientific experts from around the country and beyond in a carefully orchestrated attempt to show that DDT was causing irreparable harm to the environment. The witnesses would not be paid, but there were travel costs and related expenses. Yannacone would initially work for free, but later there would be a need to support his law practice. Witnesses had to be housed and fed.

Who would raise the tens of thousands of dollars needed for the hearing? Baumgartner did some of the fund-raising, as did Orie Loucks, the botanist from the University of Wisconsin in Madison, Peg Watrous, a key Madison activist, and Bertha Pearson, the Wausau businesswoman and conservationist. The biggest part of the task fell to Lorrie Otto and, especially, Frederick Ott.[8]

But for all their efforts, funding still fell short. As the administrative hearing dragged on longer than anyone anticipated, the CNRA was forced to make public appeals for more donations. Newspapers across the state accommodated them, running CNRA press releases about their needs.

Loucks was the public voice in some of those releases, along with William Reeder, a professor of zoology at the University of Wisconsin in Madison. They issued a request for more funds in early 1969 and another in May. In the May release, Reeder said a group of science students was planning a fund drive among university staff and students on behalf of the anti-DDT forces. In another news release, Loucks said that the National Agricultural Chemicals Association, which represented the chemical industry, "has sent in well-organized public relations people and has enlarged its legal staff in an all-out effort to defeat the request for a ban on the pesticide in Wisconsin."[9]

But what the anti-DDT folks lacked in funds, they made up for in organization and volunteer action. Much has been written about the DDT hearing and its consequences, but less about the volunteers who pulled it off.

An orderly plan was in place by the time the hearings began. Lorrie Otto's files contain a neatly typed one-page list of dozens of volunteers who had tasks ranging from providing lodging and transportation to serving as hearing room assistants, bibliographic search assistants, and transcription and publicity assistants.[10] Fund-raisers were listed as Mrs. Charles Carpenter and Mrs. Owen Otto. "Accommodations for Visitors" was chaired by Mrs. James Crow. Its members included Mrs. Emily H. Earley and Dr. and Mrs. (Peg) Watrous and fourteen others, including several university professors and their wives. Mrs. John Marshall chaired the group of "Hearing Room Assistants," who included Peg Watrous and 154 other individuals, all but one of them women. The list of "Bibliographical Search Assistants" named eight people "and many others." "Transcription and Publicity" was handled by Mrs. Dorothy Camper, Mrs. Bernard Kline, and Mrs. Gloria Rytting.

Then there was the corps of graduate students that provided support. Reeder, who still can be found holding office hours at Birge Hall in Madison, recalled their contributions: "My long-term responsibility was information gathering, and I had organized a group of graduate students. There were at least a dozen—maybe more—so during the time of the hearings at Hill Farms we had a student in the ag library, the medical library, and the biology library. Any time something was mentioned on the other side or we needed background information on, I got up and made a phone call to these guys who within a half hour to 45 minutes would send back a Xerox of findings, usually from journals."[11]

Fund-raising had allowed the DDT foes to rent a ground-floor apartment across the street from the Hill Farms offices where much of the hearing was held. A phone line there was used to communicate with the students. "We got to be very good at that, and this was a piece of the activity that the other side was never able to develop," Reeder recalled.

In addition to organizing graduate students, Reeder served as a sounding board for Loucks, who would end up being a crucial summary witness for the environmentalists. "I was very influenced by Bill. He was a good guy to talk with," Loucks recalled. "He had been at Wisconsin longer than I had and knew the insects, birds, and small mammals. He was always busy with graduate students, but he would make time for me to talk to him about what went on."[12]

Newspapers and other media from around the country covered the Madison hearings, putting DDT on trial before the public. Network news occasionally covered the story, although the level of complexity didn't lend itself to TV news.

Seeking to gain the attention of the *New Yorker* magazine in a February 8, 1969, letter, Otto wrote: "A letter just arrived from Dr. Robert Rudd [a University of California, Davis, scientist], the summation witness. A part of it reads, 'It is difficult to express sufficiently my admiration for the citizens of Wisconsin in this campaign. I think that you are thoroughly splendid. My faith has been restored.'"[13]

Otto went on to detail the work of volunteers. "When EDF decided to come to Madison, 60 volunteers came forth to drive cars, run to the printers and the library, and find places to eat and do whatever else anyone wanted them to do. There were 43 homes of strangers opened up to them within three hours of having such an idea. Money was needed for plane fares, transcripts, recordings and to operate Yannacone's office while he was gone. One man in the Milwaukee area [Frederick Ott] quietly raised $221,000. A notice in the Madison paper brought 5 and 10 dollar bills to add up to $1200. A professor's wife [likely Watrous] did the laundry for the men and darned their socks. The chairman of the Art History department [Peg Watrous's husband, James] cut Charlie Wurster's hair while he talked on the phone to his witnesses."

What went on outside the hearing rooms, first in the Wisconsin Assembly Chamber, then the Hill Farms State Office Building, had been carefully orchestrated ahead of time. Nightly discussions were held at one of the volunteer's homes, where the next day's testimony was prepared. Yannacone often held forth at these gatherings, hammering away at key points and running the scientists slated to testify the next day through the ringer so they wouldn't be overwhelmed in cross-examination.

Early sessions were held at Reeder's home. "We had a large living room and, downstairs, a large recreation room, so we could divide equally into discussion groups," he recalled.[14] Sometimes a dozen or more people were on hand. As the hearing progressed, meetings were sometimes held in other homes, or in the rented apartment across from Hill Farms.

Whitney Gould, the young *Capital Times* reporter who covered every session of the hearings, sometimes attended these evening meetings, garnering valuable background material.

"Of the people behind the scenes, Emily Earley and Peg Watrous were real foot soldiers. They worked behind the scenes and did as much as anybody," Gould recalled.[15] Earley and Watrous were tireless volunteers for an array of causes, many of them related to the environment. Both were active for decades with the Wisconsin chapter of the Nature Conservancy. Both were well connected in the community and unafraid to pick up the phone and goad others into action.

"They kept the wheels moving. They would make food for everyone, and people were coming in from everywhere to testify. CNRA didn't have any money. It was all up to the volunteers to take care of these people," Gould added.

The volunteers left a deep impression on Gould. "When you saw these people, they were not a bunch of hippies. It was a mix of distinguished scientists, homemakers, retired people, environmental activists, young folks from the university. This group of environmentalists had organizing capability and numbers behind them, and they believed an environmental tragedy was unfolding.

Emily Earley of Madison was among the citizen activists who served in a variety of volunteer roles during the DDT hearing in Madison. Volunteers housed and fed scientists who testified at the hearing and provided support in a number of other ways. One observer termed the effort "the anatomy of a perfect citizens movement." Earley was a tireless organizer for conservation causes for several decades. *Courtesy of Howard Moon*

"The DDT hearing, I think, was sort of the first burst, at least in Wisconsin, of modern-day activism. It showed what a group of citizens could do without any money."

Loucks recalled the exchange of ideas at those evening sessions. "We spent long evenings preparing for testimony. But if there weren't big issues for the next day, we would try to sit down and talk about how to tie this all together. I had friends in engineering who used systems models. I was using this in some of my work. The group got very animated at times. There were some very creative thoughts."[16]

Most nights, Peg Watrous, Earley, and other volunteers sat in on the sessions, listening quietly, soaking up the knowledge shared by the scientists.

Watrous, her husband, James, and Earley were among the Madison residents who served as hosts. The Watrous and Earley homes on Sylvan Avenue were side by side, in an area that was something of a "faculty enclave," as recalled by Lynne Eich, the Watrouses' daughter. "She was very taken with what they were doing," Eich said of her mother. "She worked very much behind the scenes."[17]

University of Wisconsin law professor James MacDonald, whose area of expertise was environmental law, and his wife, Betty, turned over their home for a week or more at a time to be used as a command post and site of the nightly sessions devoted to tactics and strategy. Betty characterized this outpouring of volunteer support for the hearing as "the anatomy of a perfect citizens movement."[18]

The EDF's Wurster, the biochemist who helped plan and orchestrate the environmentalists' strategy for the hearing, noted that the organization was far from sophisticated in those early days. "We had no bylaws, no treasurer, no letterhead, no anything. We were just a handful of ruffians who migrated from Long Island to Wisconsin," he recalled.[19] "But when we came to Wisconsin, a whole bunch of Wisconsinites came out of the woodwork. I came away thinking, 'What a wonderful group of people there.' Fred Ott raised money. Big money never came our way, but the expenses were paid, and they were paid by people in Wisconsin."

Wurster described Lorrie Otto, who would attend every session of the hearing, as "exceedingly dedicated and smart. . . . She had a good personality, and she fired people up."

x   x   x

During a recess in the DDT hearing, on February 19, 1969, Peg Watrous had sat down to pen a letter to Lorrie Otto. "It's hard here to think about anything but the riots and marching, etc. Everyone is too upset to do much; kids can't study, etc," she wrote.[20] Her earnest comments capture the mood in Madison at the time. The university had emerged as one of the hotbeds of opposition to the Vietnam War. The so-called counterculture was alive in Madison, too. Something was always in the air, be it tear gas or marijuana.

Dan Anderson, Joe Hickey's graduate student who played a key role in helping solve the mystery of why raptors and other birds were disappearing during the DDT era, remembered, "We graduate students felt like we were just as much rebels as the demonstrators were, but we were in the lab doing things our way."[21] Anderson chuckled when recalling one wild spring day on campus. "I remember sitting up in a lab at Russell Laboratories and looking out, and this big mob of students comes roaring across this big field, and there were a couple of topless women out in front, their breasts waving in the wind. We got a big laugh out of that."

On the surface, few students seemed interested in the story that had been playing itself out since 1968 in the Assembly Chamber and later the Hill Farms State Office Building. Vietnam and other causes had their attention. The only media record of student activism came on December 12, 1968, when about twenty students armed with squirt guns and signs proclaiming "Ban the Bug-Bomb" conducted what the

Wisconsin State Journal called a "friendly march" on the capitol to protest the use of DDT. The group called itself the DDT Commandos and was primarily comprised of representatives of the UW Science Students Union.

"After a merry frolic around the huge Capitol building and onto the grounds, squirting their guns at trees, bushes and vegetation to the chant of, 'We hate bugs,' the group marched peacefully inside where they attended a hearing being conducted on a proposal to ban the use of DDT in the state," wrote the paper's reporter Richard W. Jaeger.[22] The demonstration, said spokesman David Lipsky, was intended to "characterize the callousness of the industry that manufactures DDT. It was to show the harm of such chemicals."

Inside the capitol, students were greeted not by police but by the imposing figure of EDF attorney Victor Yannacone, who informed them "no disruptions would be permitted."[23] He made the students check their "weapons" at the door, and guards instructed them to file into the Assembly Chamber gallery five at a time.

Anderson and other students were sometimes on hand for evening strategy sessions at homes in the city where volunteers hosted the EDF entourage throughout the hearing. And during the day, they served as runners at the hearing.

Yannacone recalled that the students interested in the DDT hearing played important roles as volunteers. "What was interesting was the students who came out and supported us, who ran to the library, ran errands, all kinds of stuff for us. Most of them hung in and most of those chose careers that had a public service component," he said.[24]

University of Wisconsin botanist Hugh Iltis and other scientists credited the students, many of them in graduate school, with a key role in chasing down the research Yannacone needed as the hearing proceeded.

There was an air of intensity during those hearing days, Wurster recalled. "It was very exciting. I barely could keep my wits about me.

Things were happening all the time, and important things, not trivial. It was a very dynamic time. I remember my armpits were always seemingly wet. I was wearing a suit, and I couldn't keep dry, especially when I was cross-examined by the opposing attorney. That was very intense."[25]

Wurster and the other scientists gave freely of their time. "That's one of the really interesting things," he recalled. "Everybody was voluntary. Nobody got paid for banning DDT, or trying to."

CHAPTER FIFTEEN

IN THE HEARING ROOMS

O N A DAMP AND CLOUDY DECEMBER DAY IN MADISON, A young reporter walked a few blocks from the Capital Times Building on Carroll Street to the state capitol.

Little did Whitney Gould know what she was in for when she entered the Assembly Chamber that day. It was December 2, 1968, and a major story was about to unfold before her eyes. The Wisconsin Department of Natural Resources administrative hearing on whether DDT was a water pollutant was about to get under way.

Gaylord Nelson, the state's junior US senator, was first to speak on behalf of the petitioners who brought the action—the Citizens Natural Resources Association and the Wisconsin division of the Izaak Walton League of America.

The *Capital Times* was an afternoon newspaper, and Gould was able to beat most of the competition and get out the first story on that opening day. She hustled back to the paper's tired, old building and hammered out a story on an Underwood typewriter. From there, the story went past city editor Elliott Maraniss, then to typesetters who cast the stories on Linotype machines fed by cauldrons of hot lead. When the presses began to rumble, reporters and editors could put their feet up and catch a breath. Not Gould.

By that time, she was running back to the capitol to catch the unfolding drama. When the *Capital Times* hit the streets that day,

US senator Gaylord Nelson of Wisconsin was the first person to testify at the DDT hearing. The *Capital Times* newspaper of Madison, which covered the hearing from start to finish, ran a banner headline on the day the hearing began, December 2, 1968. Nelson led efforts nationally to ban DDT.

there was a front-page picture of Nelson, along with a large all-caps headline, "NELSON URGES BAN ON DDT."

Gould's lead sentence read: "The first of what promises to be a long series of hearings into the use of pesticide DDT opened today in the State Capitol with the stern warning from U.S. Sen. Gaylord Nelson that 'we are literally heading toward environmental disaster.'"

Nelson had already been working to ban DDT at the federal level, and he likely knew quite well what the DDT hearing would mean to the effort. Gould, a twenty-five-year-old Madison native who had earned an undergraduate degree at the University of Wisconsin in Madison, grew to understand the hearing's importance as it unfolded.

Her editor, Maraniss, grasped the significance before many others. "Elliott, above all, was the real stalwart. He saw ahead of a lot of other people how important this was. He said Wisconsin was in the spotlight, and we had to stay on it. He sent me out to cover what we thought would be a couple days' worth of hearings. Lo and behold, it turned out to be a six-month process," Gould recalled.[1]

Gould was on hand for the whole show, including twenty-seven days of testimony from thirty-two witnesses. During the sometimes lengthy adjournments, she focused on analytical stories related to the issues presented at the hearing.

When the hearing shifted from the capitol to the Hill Farms State Office Building more than a mile from the newspaper offices, Gould was constantly on the move. Her daily routine was to drive to the hearing, get enough of the morning testimony for a same-day story, jump in her car and head downtown to the newsroom, by then clouded in cigarette smoke, sort through the complicated information in her notebook, file the story, hop back in her car, and return to the hearing room for the afternoon testimony.

She was a general assignment reporter at the time. "That was my baptism by fire as an environmental reporter, which I became," she said. Her stories were picked up by wire services and were soon gaining national attention.

No other newspaper devoted gavel-to-gavel coverage to the hearing, although the hearing drew attention from state and national newspapers, magazines, network television, and other sources. The *Milwaukee Sentinel* was on hand often, with reporter Quincy Dadisman filing most of the stories. Editors at the *Milwaukee Journal*, Gould

Whitney Gould was a young reporter at the *Capital Times* of Madison when she was assigned to cover the DDT hearing. She went on to cover other environmental issues for the newspaper before moving on to the editorial staff of the *Milwaukee Journal. Wisconsin State Journal Library*

recalled, seemed not to grasp the importance of the hearing in its early phases, but they caught on as it began drawing attention across the country and beyond. The *Journal*'s Madison bureau reporter, Richard Kienitz, covered the story for that paper.

If some news sources failed to understand the importance of the hearing at the outset, they weren't alone. The chemical industry was caught off guard, too. After filing for the administrative hearing, the environmentalists quickly organized their strategy, secured witnesses, and lined up volunteers, money, and housing. Meanwhile, DDT's defenders were unaware that there was any challenge underway and that environmentalists were actively preparing a case. The National Agricultural Chemicals Association, the primary defender of DDT, "did not learn about the hearing until a few days before it started," wrote author Thomas Dunlap.[2]

Louis McLean, a retired Illinois lawyer and former counsel for Velsicol Chemical Corporation, read about the hearing in a newspaper article. He alerted the Washington, DC–based NACA only days before the hearing began and offered to represent the association in Madison.[3] A longtime DDT supporter, McLean would be outmatched by the fiery Victor Yannacone, the lawyer from the Environmental Defense Fund who represented the CNRA and the Wisconsin division of the Izaak Walton League of America. In January, the

NACA brought in a well-known Madison attorney, Willard Stafford, and Frederick S. Waiss, an attorney for Stauffer Chemical Company. By the time they arrived, the environmentalists had effectively put DDT's supporters—known as intervenors, in hearing parlance—on the defense, both in the hearing room and, perhaps more importantly, in the court of public opinion. Stafford is said to have remarked, "They would have stoned John the Baptist on State Street [in Madison] if he had come out for DDT."[4]

The NACA had clearly underestimated the importance of the Wisconsin hearing, and by the time it beefed up its efforts, it was too late. It was up against an underfunded but determined group of citizens and scientists anxious to have their say about DDT. The NACA, too, lacked funds for the effort. Some sources speculate the industry had already given up on DDT. Domestic production had peaked by 1963, according to a 1975 US Environmental Protection Agency report. By the time of the Wisconsin hearings, domestic usage in the United States had declined by about a third. Agricultural and forestry uses were dropping, but communities persisted in efforts to employ DDT for Dutch elm disease control and other uses. But even though agriculture and forestry uses had declined, those interests were generally opposed to a ban.

Environmental law was in its infancy at the time. The Wisconsin hearing was like a child's first steps. In addition, more than DDT was on trial. Also under the microscope was humankind's impact on the environment in the modern era.

The world was definitely watching. Nationally syndicated columnist James J. Kilpatrick visited Wisconsin that December in 1968. The column he filed started this way: "It seems an odd place for the trial of mankind—a small midwestern city, whipped by the driving winds of December, sidewalks nearly empty, the grass of Capitol Square mouse-gray beneath the patchy snow. And perhaps it is merely fantasy that sees within Wisconsin's marbled capitol a trial of godlike dimensions."[5]

Recounting the early days of the trial, in which the environmentalists sought to build their argument while McLean "scoffs at the petitioners' case," Kilpatrick concluded: "Enormous sums may hang on the
Wisconsin decision, once it is made final in the courts. While Wisconsin consumes only 100,000 pounds of DDT a year, 58 percent of it in
treating Dutch elm disease in cities, the precedent set here will have
large significance elsewhere. The outcome will affect food supplies, disease control, and the conflicting economic interests of farmers, fishermen and sportsmen. Both sides are contending that they represent
generations yet unborn. The probabilities are that they do."

The hearing produced its share of startling headlines, but its daily
routine was more like a chess game. "A lot of the testimony was very
dry," Gould recalled. "The scientists were not used to being in the spotlight, in the public arena, and here they were testifying at a public
hearing, and it was going in the newspaper. I tried to be as faithful as
possible to what was going on, and so my editors would see it and say,
'This is very dry.' They wanted to pump this up."[6]

Maraniss got what he wanted one day in January 1969 when Dr.
Richard M. Welch, a biochemical pharmacologist from New York, testified. He had worked with laboratory animals and testified that the
pesticide lowered hormone levels in rats, including testosterone. Yannacone pressed him, seeking to "impress on the public the possibility
of DDT's danger to man. He asked Welch if testosterone in rats was
the same compound as the male sex hormone in humans." Welch confirmed this.[7]

Gould dutifully reported the testimony: "If the pesticide DDT is
playing havoc with the sex hormones of rats, rabbits, pigeons and Japanese quail, what is it doing to man? At this point, no one can be sure.
But that troubling question was raised repeatedly today at the continuing hearing on a petition to stop the use of DDT in Wisconsin."[8]

Readers of the January 14, 1969, *Capital Times* were greeted with
Maraniss's headline on Gould's article: "Scientist Warns of DDT Peril

to Sex Life." Even the EDF's Charles Wurster thought the headline was a reach. "This is really hitting ag below the belt," Wurster whispered to Lorrie Otto, according to her notes.[9]

"I went back to the hearing, and the scientists were mortified. I tried to explain that I didn't write the headlines," Gould recalled in an interview. "Later, I told Elliott about their reaction. Elliott's response was, 'It got their attention didn't it?'"

A *Milwaukee Journal* headline that ran as the hearing neared its end also caused a stir, even though it appeared on page twenty-eight. "DDT Found in Mother's Milk, Hearing Told," read the headline.[10] The *Capital Times* headline the same day read, "Claim Babies Get Too Much of DDT."[11]

The scientist whose testimony generated the headlines was S. Goran Lofroth of the University of Stockholm in Sweden. His appearance was a story in itself. Lofroth, who had conducted a review of DDT's toxicity to humans, was not a witness for the environmentalists. Instead, he was called by the Wisconsin Department of Justice, which had intervened in the hearing. Technically, the Wisconsin Department of Justice had the same intervenor status as did the NACA. Wurster had asked the department's public intervenor, Robert McConnell, to sponsor Lofroth's appearance, since the hearing had by then moved on to the NACA's defense of DDT and hearing proceedings did not allow the environmentalists to call any additional witnesses. But since McConnell's budget provided no funds for travel, Lofroth's travel from Stockholm to Madison was financed by the EDF. Stafford objected vociferously on behalf of the NACA, but Hearing Examiner Maurice Van Susteren ruled that the witness could appear, allowing Stafford to cross-examine him as if Lofroth were an EDF witness.

"Here's this guy, minding his own business in Stockholm, and some character he'd never heard of in Madison, Wisconsin, calls, wanting to know if he'd come and testify. I told him we could cover his airfare and expenses. We could have been selling gold bricks," Wurster recalled years later of his phone call to Lofroth. "The amazing thing was I called out of blue, and he accepted and came. That was true of a lot of people. There was a lot of dedication by scientists in many categories who wanted to talk about this, because they were upset about the entire situation."[12]

The eye-catching headlines related to Lofroth's testimony happened to be tied to one of the environmentalists' goals: establishing DDT's potential hazard to humans. His testimony also generated national and international publicity. For the average person, DDT in fish or birds was one thing; DDT in mother's milk was something completely different. In organizing the case, the EDF's Wurster and Yannacone, working with Wisconsin scientists and others, had made that issue one of five major contentions the environmentalists sought to prove. Dunlap summarized them: "First, that there was an ecosystem—an interrelated system of air, water, soil, and biological organisms. Second, that DDT unavoidably—because of its physical and chemical properties—contaminated the entire ecosystem when released into it at any point. Third, that residues of DDT had adverse effects on wildlife. Fourth, that they were a potential hazard for humans; their safety was not established. Finally, EDF argued that it was possible to replace DDT with safer insect controls."[13]

The scientists were well aware that media coverage was an important component of their ultimate goal: a national ban on DDT for most uses.

Did the young *Capital Times* reporter understand the significance of what she was covering? "Not at first, but after a couple of months, I began to realize the importance. I started to see how all the pieces fit together. . . . About midstream, I realized how significant it was, in some ways it was of worldwide significance," Gould said years later.

The environmentalists saw to it that reporters like Gould got the stories they wanted. "Victor Yannacone, in particular, was determined to try the case before the public as well as the hearing examiner," wrote author Dunlap. "He provided interviews and information for the press; each day some interesting testimony was produced well before the Madison Capital Times' midday deadline. The EDF opened its strategy sessions to selected reporters, asking only that they respect confidences. Charles Wurster also talked to reporters, and the scientists checked stories and headlines for accuracy."[14]

Gould was among those reporters, Wurster recalled in an interview. And by ensuring she had time to file a story of significance on deadline, the environmentalists were guaranteed wide coverage. Once Gould's stories appeared in the hometown paper, they were sent on to the wire services that served newspapers across the country.

The reporter's growing understanding of the hearing's complexities is reflected in the newspaper clippings Lorrie Otto collected.

x   x   x

Day two of the hearing was memorable, and Gould was on hand to report. On that day, the environmentalists called Ellsworth Fisher, a DDT proponent and a professor of entomology at the University of Wisconsin in Madison. "Yannacone, a contentious, aggressive man with the bobbing, bouncing movement of a boxer, eventually succeeded in getting his own witness declared 'hostile,'" she wrote. Indeed, only the threat of a subpoena had brought Fisher to the hearing.

Fisher testified that he had advised many communities to discontinue the use of DDT for mosquito control, but stressed that the US Public Health Service "still recognizes DDT as very useful as a larvacide and fog treatment in mosquito control." Yannacone pressed him, seeking to solicit testimony that research on DDT's effects on humans was insufficient. Fisher was upset, and he let it be known. Gould was there to record it. "Fisher later complained to listeners on the sidelines during a recess: 'They're trying to indict us for contaminating the landscape when we're just trying to do our job as entomologists in Wisconsin.'"[15]

Fisher wasn't the only scientist to express discomfort over the

Ellsworth Fisher, an entomologist at the University of Wisconsin in Madison, defended the use of DDT. He believed the benefits of pest controls outweighed the risks. Fisher testified at the DDT hearing. *Wisconsin State Journal Library*

quasi-judicial setting that put them on the hot seat. Lucille Stickel of the US Fish and Wildlife Service would provide crucial testimony on eggshell thinning. "Lucille was very reluctant to testify," Wurster recalled. "But she did come and testify." Dan Anderson, Joseph Hickey's graduate student at the time, noticed her discomfort. "I was helping to shuttle experts around, and I got to spend a nice afternoon out in the field with Lucille Stickel, who went out bird watching after her testimony, which had her quite shaken."[16]

The attorneys on each side were at times aggressive in their questioning, but Yannacone's style especially often left witnesses upset—even his own. "Yannacone was a brilliant lawyer, but he made people so mad. He would goad people into saying what they didn't want to say," Gould recalled.

Early witnesses for the environmentalists included University of Wisconsin botanists Hugh Iltis and Orie Loucks, along with Wurster. Iltis was cut from a new cloth of scientists. He felt it his duty to stir the pot in order to get results.

Witnesses had come from far and wide to Madison, but none had endured the travails that Iltis had to reach America years earlier. His father, Hugo Iltis, was a Jew and a social democrat in the family's native Moravia, in the Czech Republic. Hugo publicly criticized the Nazis for their position on eugenics. A botanist, he was also the biographer for Gregor Mendel, the Austrian friar and scientist whose experiments with garden peas gave birth to the science of genetics.[17]

The Mendel connection helped save the family just before the Nazis invaded the Czech Republic in 1939. The family knew it had to leave. Hugo Iltis was giving lectures on Mendel in England, and the family fled on a harrowing train trip through Nazi Germany to join him. The family ended up settling in Virginia. Like his father, Hugh became a botanist. He came to Madison from the University of Arkansas.

"Hugh was rabble-rouser from day one," Gould recalled years later. "He was head of the herbarium at UW and collected plants. Way ahead of his time, he saw that plant species were endangered by pesticides. . . . He was very explosive and would get very ticked off at people who were just doing their thing and not getting involved. But he was very respected in his field and saw the whole picture. He was a good scientist, and you had to take him seriously."[18]

Iltis's style contrasted with Hickey's, who for years had resisted stepping into the public arena. "Joe was reluctant to get involved because he didn't think it was a scientist's job. Their job was to do the research. It was for others to take action," Gould recalled.

Loucks, she said, "was sort of the connector between these different factions. He was very scholarly and intellectual on one hand, but also very shrewd about the politics of this whole episode." Wurster and Yannacone would return to Loucks as the hearing drew to a close. "They chose him for their final witness, the one who would provide a summary of the case."

Wurster was on the stand for two days in the early part of the hearing, and the NACA attorney Louis McLean did his best to bring the scientist's credentials into question. Gould took advantage of Wurster's willingness to speak directly to the press. She caught him outside the hearing room for an interview. "DDT," he said, "is the relic of another age. The agro-chemical people like to say they need it for their crops. But that's a worthless argument. There are other alternatives. The pesticide must be gotten rid of, and the 'absolute authority' of the agriculture Establishment must be challenged. The new breed is the ecologist."[19]

Botanist Hugh Iltis of the University of Wisconsin in Madison was one of a new breed of scientists who emerged in the modern environmental era: men and women who willingly stepped into the public arena on controversial topics. Iltis testified at the DDT hearing. *Wisconsin State Journal Library*

McLean countered the second day. "Today McLean accused
Wurster of operating from an 'ivory tower' in his research on pesticides, and charged that the biologist was trying to set himself up as the
'Supreme Court' in judgment of studies in related disciplines," Gould
wrote. McLean asked the young scientist if he thought federal authorities weren't competent to judge human tolerance levels for pesticides.
"Our tolerance levels are out of date," Wurster replied.

Gould's coverage of the day's events also focused on a decision of
a circuit court judge to allow Public Intervenor McConnell to participate in the hearing, ending a dispute between the Department
of Natural Resources and attorney general's office. McConnell was
granted the power to cross-examine and subpoena witnesses, acting as
an ombudsman representing the public's interest.

As the hearing moved along, the news coverage was introducing
the public to a whole new understanding of science. Reporting for
the *Milwaukee Sentinel* early in the proceeding, Dadisman explained
the meanings of terms like "ecosystem" and "genetic effects." Readers
learned that DDT could actually increase the population of certain
insects by eliminating their predators.

Hickey was called as a witness on December 10. "Residues of DDT
have made Lake Michigan one of the most pesticide-polluted lakes
in the world, a University of Wisconsin ecologist said today," Gould
reported. "And the same pesticide, he warned, is contaminating fish
and wildlife in and around Wisconsin's lakes."[20] His statistics were "dry
and punctuated with decimal points," she wrote, but he "offered telling evidence."

Hickey, Gould later recalled, underwent a major transformation
during the DDT battles. "You've got to give that guy credit. He was
an older scientist by then, but he really grew. He showed this capacity
for intellectual growth and the ability to be open-minded and to see
the connections between disciplines."

His December testimony was bolstered, Gould noted in print, by
that of Robert Risebrough, a molecular biologist with the Institute

of Marine Resources at the University of California, Berkeley, who
had done pioneering research on DDT's impact on brown pelicans.
The media didn't give much play to Risebrough's testimony, but Dunlap later said he was a key witness. Risebrough testified about the biochemical mechanism through which DDE, the DDT metabolite, was
believed to affect birds' reproductive systems. He also explained the
analytical work that had determined the level of DDT in animal tissues. His testimony, Dunlap noted, showed that DDE's effects were
not confined to the central nervous system. This cast doubt on the
DDT supporters' claims that there was no danger to humans because
there were no symptoms of central nervous system effects from environmental levels of the chemical. "No one had looked for this other
type of action," Dunlap wrote, "and, as Risebrough pointed out, 'there
was no mechanism in the establishment of (pesticide residue) tolerance levels to consider this enzyme-induced phenomenon.'"[21] Risebrough's research opened new doors of understanding and raised new
questions, some of which are still being sorted out today when considering the impacts of pesticides on human health.

Risebrough, it turns out, played an important role in the hearing
room beyond testifying. Along with Wurster and sometimes University of Wisconsin zoology professor William Reeder, Risebrough sat
near Yannacone throughout the hearing, providing him with valuable insights and scientific information. "He was a great scientist and
a great man," Yannacone said years later.[22]

Risebrough's appearance on December 10 ended testimony for
1968, as Van Susteren recessed the hearing until January.

Lorrie Otto had attended every day of testimony. As Christmas
1968 approached, her card to Carol Yannacone, the attorney's wife,
sounded a weary note. She had taken on some of the fund-raising work
in addition to coordinating volunteer activities and other duties.

"This money thing has become a monkey on my back, and I detest
it!! It eats at me and does ugly things to my spirit. I seldom ask any-

Attorney Victor Yannacone (right) confers with Robert Risebrough, a molecular biologist with the Institute of Marine Resources at the University of California, Berkeley. Yannacone represented Wisconsin citizens who petitioned the Department of Natural Resources for a declaratory ruling on the use of DDT in the state. Risebrough offered key testimony. *WHi Image ID 100409, Madison Newspapers Inc.*

one for anything, but now to have to ask many for MONEY is so distasteful that it is destructive.

"On top of this, I've had to drive to Madison and spark up our gal who offered to find homes (and save hotel bill fund raising) for our men. I told her, 'no food, no females and no weekends'; that I would

grab up Vic and Charlie and any other hangover, and take them home
to Milwaukee for Friday and Saturday nights and return them on Sunday evening," she wrote.[23]

Attorney Yannacone had been enforcing a "no eating" rule at the
nightly briefings held in Madison private homes. "It seems to me that
some eating could be done in private homes," Otto wrote, "but Vic
says not, because they need to talk together at these times, and it gets
everyone to bed on time."

By then, Gould had come to know Otto. "She was an amazing person, just amazing, an elegant person. She made a huge contribution,
no question about it," Gould recalled. "It was her energy, spirit and
drive that kept a lot of these people going."[24]

x   x   x

As the environmentalists prepared to continue their case, the NACA
roused from its slow start, a move signaled by the act of beefing up its
legal team. Willard Stafford, especially, brought a skilled if swagger-
ing presence to the hearing room, which had been shifted to the Hill
Farms site. McLean's role was diminished, though he would conduct
the NACA's cross-examination of the remaining witnesses for the petitioners. Orie Loucks recalled how McLean's demotion became clear
to him outside the state office building. "When we resumed the hearings, we had been used to hearing McLean. All of a sudden, this hot-
shot lawyer Stafford came up and threw the keys to McLean and told
him to go park the car. That told me and everyone else how much this
was stepping up."[25]

One reason: the environmentalists' goal of trying DDT in media
was working. Coverage of the hearing's early days had been heavy. The
New York Times had been keeping an eye on the hearing from the outset, proclaiming in one editorial, "If DDT is ruled unsafe for use by
farmers in Wisconsin, its further use anywhere will be hard to jus-

tify."[26] The *Milwaukee Sentinel* on January 6 called for a moratorium on the pesticide's use pending the outcome of the hearing. "Although the hearings have not been concluded, evidence submitted so far has produced sufficient reason to believe that DDT has been killing fish and some birds, interfering with the reproduction of other birds and possibly affecting the sexual chemistry of mammals, including man."

The same day, the *Sentinel* began running a six-part series of articles, "DDT on Trial," written by Dadisman.

It was probably no coincidence that as the hearing recessed at the end of 1968, the Wisconsin Department of Agriculture announced it was dropping its recommendation for the use of DDT in Dutch elm disease control. It will be left to speculation as to whether the hearing would have taken place at all if the department had come to that decision earlier.

For her part, Gould also had been focusing on analysis pieces during the recess. The headline on her December 16, 1968, story read "The DDT Fight: David vs. Goliath." She noted that the early portion of the hearing had been held in the Assembly Chamber "where four sentimental murals from Wisconsin's past look down on the combatants. . . . Those were the days before we had made cesspools of our waterways, befouled our air, and raped our landscape."[27] In the story, Wurster laid out the stakes, saying, "There's no doubt about it. Wisconsin is the showdown. We can't afford to lose."

More than just DDT was on the line for the pesticide industry, Gould added. "What is at stake for the pesticide industry, besides millions of dollars in DDT sales, is the chance that if DDT is banned here, a host of other related pesticides, all in the 'chlorinated hydrocarbon' family, may also eventually be lost."

Gould included comments from McLean in the story, and they underlined his failure to read the importance of the hearing: "This is not a matter of environmental pollution. (The hearings) are important only in a publicity sense, not in a real sense." Indeed, the hearing was drawing publicity—and the publicity itself would lead to real action on other levels. Gould also cited McLean's references to DDT foes in some publications. "In magazine articles on the subject of the pesticide controversy, McLean has sought to characterize the critics of pesticides as 'purposeful' types who subscribe to medical quackery and food fads, and 'compulsive' types, who reject most man-made endeavors and are 'preoccupied' with the subject of sexual potency.

"The irony of his stereotypes," she continued, "was not lost on many who heard the past two weeks of testimony from respected national scientists and U.S. Sen. Gaylord Nelson."

On January 13, Gould was preparing to condense the morning's testimony and file a story in time for the afternoon newspaper. The environmentalists pressed their case by citing dangers to fisheries. Kenneth Macek, a zoologist with the US Bureau of Sport Fisheries and Wildlife, testified that DDT was found to impair brook trout reproduction and to increase their susceptibility to stresses such as starvation and temperature changes. His findings showed that trout mortality followed the same pattern as the deaths of a million coho salmon in Wisconsin and Michigan hatcheries in 1968.[28]

Then came Lucille Stickel, the pesticide research coordinator at the US Department of Interior's Patuxent Wildlife Research Center in Maryland. Her testimony was considered pivotal, as she told about experiments establishing DDT's link to egg breakage and unhealthy mallard ducklings. Gould took note of the significance: "Her revelations on DDT's effect on waterfowl in laboratory experiments were important because they came on top of the earlier testimony that the chemical has also contributed to the decline in population of birds of prey throughout the world."[29]

Lorrie Otto's handwritten note on a copy of Gould's story observed: "Lucy Stickel was the only woman witness, and she was a real surprise. She had brown eyes with arched eyebrows and a funny mouth which looked like a third brow except during her quick smiles. She had her testimony written out, and wouldn't tell Yannacone what it was.

She made our case so tight that after she left the stand, witnesses were rearranged or cancelled until rebuttal time. . . . You should have seen the men Queen her! The results of this research had only been gathered together hours before her plane took off."[30]

Hickey testified again on January 15, 16, and 17 as the environmentalists moved toward closing their case. He sought to link the decline of a number of bird species to DDT and its metabolite, DDE. He said DDT, not disease, was responsible for the radical decline in bald eagle, osprey, and peregrine falcon populations. Disease had been one of the hypotheses considered by ornithologists after the declines had been detected, but research clearly pointed to another cause: DDT. In just a few days, the environmentalists had made the case for DDT's harm to everything from robins, mallard ducks, and birds of prey to fish.

The key witness on January 17 was Robert Rudd, a zoology professor at the University of California, Davis, who made the ecological hazard argument for the petitioners. Rudd had linked DDT to the deaths of mallard ducks and pheasants that had consumed sprayed rice crops in California. He had also linked DDD, a near relative of DDT, to the deaths of western grebes at Clear Lake, California, in the 1950s and early 1960s. The Clear Lake research was considered pioneering.

DDT, Rudd testified, was an ecological hazard because it was insoluble in water; tended to stick to particles in water and air; was dispersed widely and easily in the environment; and was stored in the fat tissues of organisms and built up in larger organisms as they fed on smaller ones.

Rudd was treated gingerly by the NACA's attorneys. Lorrie Otto's handwritten notes on copies of newspaper clippings from the day included this: "Rudd was an older man with a beautiful speaking voice, and such an ideal summation that McLean gave up and didn't ask him a single question. A lawyer from Calif. asked a few, but then he quit!!! And so to everyone's great surprise the case rested at 11:45, and everyone flew home in the afternoon."[31]

Rudd was widely considered an expert on the effects of pesticides on the environment, and his 1964 book, *Pesticides and the Living Landscape*, was published by the University of Wisconsin Press. The book came to many of the same conclusions as did Carson's *Silent Spring*, and Rudd is said to have consulted with her frequently, with his findings helping formulate some of Carson's book.

Hearing Examiner Van Susteren adjourned the hearing to permit the preparation of a transcript. It ran 1,363 pages by that point.

The NACA would use the time to prepare its case. Other intervenors would have their opportunity to present information, too, and the environmentalists would have an opportunity for rebuttal. Otto's handwritten notes on a photocopy of Gould's story that day also included this: "Fresh set of witnesses panting to come next spring for the rebuttal. (89 to choose from!)"

◼   ◼   ◼

The hearing didn't resume until April, but the DDT story continued to swirl in state and national publications. As the new Wisconsin legislative session began, State Senators Martin Schreiber of Milwaukee and Fred Risser of Madison introduced a bill to ban DDT in Wisconsin. The bill would run into opposition from groups including the Wisconsin Farm Bureau and the Wisconsin Farmers Union, and even the DNR, which favored a more comprehensive federal ban, much to the disgust of Otto, who was anxious for the state to take action. The legislative maneuvering was gaining its own share of attention during the adjournment.

Gould wrote a two-part series on the impact of the hearing on public opinion. The hearing proceedings "have already caught the interest of conservation-minded citizens throughout the country, through coverage in the New York Times, the Wall Street Journal, Sports Illustrated, The Nation, assorted scientific journals, and national television," she wrote on March 25.

The DNR had stiffened its regulation of DDT for 1969, temporarily banning its use even during periods when no DNR permit was
required, she wrote. Previously, municipalities had been allowed to
spray DDT without a DNR permit in the so-called "dormant period"
from autumn to early spring. Meanwhile, she noted, "the agricultural
chemical manufacturers launched an expensive public relations blitz
to salvage their much-maligned money-maker."[32]

The PR materials, produced by the NACA, were sent to newspapers around the country, Gould noted. "DDT, we are told, contrib-
utes to increased food production, reduction of wildlife parasites and
diseases, and improved health conditions, among other things."[33] The
materials also claimed that "all species of animals, insects, fish, amphibians, birds and mammals that have been studied are able to degrade
and excrete DDT residues they have acquired in their fat." That con-
tradicted testimony in the hearing, she added.

While the media may have portrayed the NACA as Goliath, author
Dunlap later claimed the group was short on funds and scientific
advice, and thus "the lawyers could do little more than present a suc-
cession of unrelated witnesses."[34]

The hearing resumed on April 29, 1969, sharing front-page bill-
ing with reports of protests by black students, some of them bearing
weapons, at Voorhees College in South Carolina. Protests at Memphis State University and Saint Louis University also were reported,
as were black uprisings in communities in Illinois, Iowa, and North
and South Carolina. Newspapers that day also reported that Defense
Secretary Melvin Laird proclaimed the Pentagon was backing off on
its military recruitment efforts on university campuses in response to
student protests in places including Madison.

The action at the Hill Farms State Office Building didn't carry
that level of drama, but its opening salvos produced their share of
headlines. Wayland J. Hayes Jr., professor of toxicology at Vanderbilt
University, was a key witness for the NACA. A former chief of the

Toxicology Section, Technical Branch, Communicable Disease Center of the US Public Health Service, Hayes had overseen the only extensive body of evidence on the effects of human exposure to DDT or ingesting large doses of the chemical over an extended period. "Poised, confident, and with the prestige of degrees, awards and extensive publications, Hayes was an impressive figure as well as a scientific expert," wrote Dunlap.[35] Stafford put Hayes's qualifications on the record and reviewed his studies, helping Hayes conclude that DDT was of no harm to humans.

Hayes also tossed cold water on the action of federal officials who had seized Lake Michigan coho salmon containing from thirteen to nineteen parts per million of DDT, testifying that they would have been safe to eat. The same was true for fish in Wisconsin lakes and streams, he said. He punctuated his remarks skillfully, noting that a person who ate nothing but coho salmon with DDT levels of nineteen parts per million for the next nineteen years would have the same amount of DDT as workers in a DDT plant used for a long-term study of toxicity.

When asked what effect a world ban on DDT would have, Hayes replied, "It would have a very disastrous effect. DDT still remains the most important single tool for control of malaria. There undoubtedly would be a revival in many parts of the world."[36] This argument, which became one of the central points made by those who opposed the DDT ban, lingers to this day.

In cross-examination, Yannacone sought to establish that a resurgence of malaria could be due as much to resistance to DDT by malaria-bearing mosquitoes as to a ban on DDT. He also sought to raise doubts about the research on humans, contending that the research had focused only on healthy males and failed to address whether the enzyme-producing function of the human liver had been tested.

During cross-examination, the US Department of Agriculture intervened with its own witness, Harry Hays, director of pesticide

Among those present during testimony in the Wisconsin DNR's administrative hearing on DDT were: Samuel Rotrosen, president of Montrose Chemical (1); Hearing Examiner Maurice Van Susteren (2); Victor Yannacone, attorney for the Wisconsin citizens who brought the action (3); Lorrie Otto, the Bayside citizen who attended every session of the prolonged hearing (4); Louis McLean, representative for the National Agricultural Chemicals Association at the hearing (5); and Willard Stafford, attorney for the National Agricultural Chemicals Association (far right). *WHi Image ID 100393*

registration at the department. He claimed the USDA was regulating pesticides effectively, but then admitted, when pressed by Yannacone, that the department didn't evaluate pesticides itself; rather, it reviewed information submitted by manufacturers.

Newspapers jumped on this angle, and Hays earned headlines in the press and scorn from the NACA's attorneys. Dunlap noted that McLean later called Hays the "world's worst" witness. He was "easily led, quickly flustered and short-tempered."[37]

University of Wisconsin entomologist R. Keith Chapman, a longtime DDT proponent, testified that DDT was the safest, most economical, and most effective pesticide for many vegetable crops. He predicted Wisconsin farmers would lose two to three million dollars annually if the pesticide was banned.[38]

He said the compound produced "miraculous results" in controlling plant diseases, the potato leafhopper, and the cabbage looper. A ban would most seriously affect carrot growers, he added. Still, University of Wisconsin pesticide experts had reduced their DDT recommendations by half "as a compromise with the clamor in the public over DDT," testified Chapman.

The NACA's biggest success could have come in testimony that threw some doubt on whether DDT residues in fish may have been confused with polychlorinated biphenyl (PCB), an industrial compound. Francis Coon, head of the chemistry department at the Wisconsin Alumni Research Foundation, was a witness for the NACA. Coon noted that the department had done up to thirty thousand pesticide residue analyses on fish and wildlife and first became aware of the possible role of PCBs in 1967. "We found evidence that PCBs were undoubtedly present in some of our analyses," he testified.

Stafford called Robert Risebrough back as an adverse witness, attempting to poke holes in his work. But Risebrough stood by his findings. He acknowledged that PCBs are found in large amounts in many marine birds, but noted he had found only a few in which there were more PCBs than DDT or its metabolites.[39] Risebrough also testified that computer analysis showed "no significant statistical relationship" between PCB content in white pelican eggs and the thickness of their shells. As DDE content increased, "the shells became thinner" in pelicans and another seabird, the double-crested cormorant.

Reflecting on that moment, Risebrough noted, "Those hearings took up a lifetime supply of adrenaline. Tension was very high."[40] He called the testimony that day his best moment of the hearing. He admitted having erred in his December testimony, saying that North American pelicans were extinct. "I should have said they weren't reproducing," he noted.

But when called by Stafford, he was ready. Stafford had hoped to get Risebrough to say that PCBs were responsible for eggshell thinning. Risebrough didn't, and he had a research paper to prove his point that DDE was responsible. "While in Madison, I was staying with Dan Anderson. He was completing research on cormorants and white pelicans. We went over the chromatograms [the patterns formed by substances that have been separated by chromatography] at that time, and we were able to get good relative measures of their amounts and correlate that with DDE and shell thinning. . . . In white pelicans, there was a significant correlation between thinning and DDE and not PCBs."[41]

But there was the matter of getting that research published. "Ted Mosquin was editor of the *Canadian Field-Naturalist*, and I had dinner with him and his family in early 1969. He offered to give the manuscript high priority," Risebrough recalled. "So we wrote up the manuscript, and by the time the hearings resumed, it was already in print. So when Stafford asked the question, I was able to pull out this manuscript, and by that time we had also found out about [DDT's impact on] brown pelicans."[42]

Stafford apparently harbored no grudge over the matter. "We met in the washroom, and, well, he said, 'Congratulations, you're not a bad lawyer.' He was a professional," Risebrough recalled.

Still, the environmentalists needed to dispel doubts cast by Coon's testimony as a NACA witness. In cross-examination, Yannacone got Coon to admit his laboratory had no difficulty identifying the traces left by DDE, the DDT metabolite. He acknowledged he had left out that information earlier. This was significant, since WARF had done the analyses for Hickey's studies of the Lake Michigan ecosystem that showed the lake, as Hickey recalled years later in an interview, "was loaded with DDT or what we thought was DDT."[43] Hickey and Dan Anderson were conducting research on herring gulls at the time. Their research found DDT in the gulls, and also in arthropods, which were eaten by fish that the gulls ate. But the lake was also loaded with PCBs, Hickey recalled.

Yannacone needed to clear up the confusion. Gould reported the cross-examination this way: "Yannacone pursued Coon's laboratory techniques doggedly until he got from the chemist the admission that there was not enough PCB interference with his residue detections to warrant sending out a standard disclaimer to clients who had submitted samples for analysis." She added, "Coon acknowledged that WARF Institute would be paid a fee for his appearance at the hearings by the National Agricultural Chemicals Association, which is financing DDT's defense here."[44]

Another NACA witness, Paul E. Porter of the Shell Development Company, was also called to testify about problems involved with chemical analysis. Questioned by NACA attorney Waiss about the petitioners' analytical work, Porter said both WARF and Risebrough had excellent reputations. His testimony on DDT's breakdown was considered more positive for the environmentalists than the NACA, which had called him. "DDT Defendant Delights Pesticide's Foes with Testimony on Residues," was the headline on Gould's May 8 story.[45] DDT breaks down fastest in the absence of oxygen, Porter testified. As Gould noted parenthetically, "The world environment is full of oxygen, however, and it is this fact which disturbs anti-DDT scientists. They acknowledge that DDT is degraded but not fast enough to prevent harm to fish and birds." Porter noted that DDT is partly converted to DDE in the fat of mammals and eventually excreted. The pesticide is stored in the fat of birds, too, he said, but added, "I don't know what is exactly excreted."

While PCBs can interfere with DDT detection, Porter noted, the PCBs can be separated out under further analysis. "The techniques are time-consuming, and are rarely used by commercial labs, because that would make them non-competitive," Porter testified.

Feeling no need for cross-examination, Yannacone simply thanked Porter for appearing.[46]

The environmentalists were thrilled. Otto, in another of her series of notes scribbled on copies of news reports, wrote, "Porter said DDT

was insoluble in water. (Yes! One reason it is such a problem.) He gave
the breakdown story. . . . He did the PCB's so well that we don't need
to rebut on this. . . . The Shell man, Porter, was competent and honest.
Vic just thanked him. Stafford was stunned." Her notes were not so
kind to Coon: "In January, when Stickel, Hickey, Anderson, Wurster
and Risebrough visited him at WARF, he was most eager to be one
of the 'good guys,' so it came as quite a shock when Coon appeared
as a paid witness for Ag-chem! He cast doubts on his own analysis of
our scientist's work. He shaded and cheated, so Vic fried him in public. . . . Really a great week! It is supposed to be Ag-chem's show, but
most of the time it is ours because of Victor Yannacone."[47]

Despite Stafford's skills, the NACA's case wasn't going well. Testimony a few days before Porter's appearance underscores this. Francis
Cherms, a professor of poultry science at the University of Wisconsin, was called in an attempt to refute the eggshell thinning testimony
that had been entered earlier. His experiments with Japanese quail that
were fed DDT showed no effects on their reproductive capacity. He
disputed research showing that DDT upset the calcium function in
birds of prey, causing them to produce thin-shelled eggs. "What, then,
caused thin-shelled eggs?" Stafford asked.[48] "A host of things," Cherms
replied, ranging from selection of breeding stock, age, family and species differences, and diet. Fear could also be a factor, he said. "When
you frighten birds, you can expect thin shells. The disturbance of wild
birds can result in failure of reproduction," testified Cherms. Stafford, reported Ray Pagel of the *Green Bay Press-Gazette*, couldn't pass
that up. "You scare the shell out of them," he said. A grinning Cherms
agreed. "Environmental factors, including fear and fright which we
call hysteria in chickens, can result in thin shells."[49]

Gould's May 5 report showed that her ongoing coverage had helped
her understand the complexities of the hearing. "The central question this morning was whether experiments in which DDT was fed to
Japanese quail, with no apparent effects on their reproductive capacity, have any relevance to the effects of DDT in the environment of

wild birds like the peregrine falcon," she wrote. Of the poultry professor pressed by Yannacone to speculate on aspects of the physiology in
raptors, she noted, "Cherms himself insisted several times that he was
not a wildlife expert."[50] Under Yannacone's cross-examination, Cherms
had admitted he wasn't qualified to discuss the biochemical processes
of eggshell formation.

Shell Chemical Company wildlife specialist William Gusey denied
DDT was a threat to wildlife and pointed to increases in populations
of various birds and mammals throughout the United States, Gould
reported on May 13. But under cross-examination, he admitted he
was not an expert on peregrine falcons or other raptors. Still, Gusey
took some swings at the petitioners. Gould captured this: "The lanky
game manager also took a few potshots at what he called 'the wildlife and environmental interests' who, he said, 'have literally pounded
knots into the heads of chemical companies for reported effects on the
environment that may have resulted from the use of some chemical.'"[51]

"It's very easy to criticize," Gusey said. "But criticism is of little value
if some sort of remedial action is not offered." Pesticide critics had
failed to provide advice or guidance to the chemical companies, "other
than casually. About the only thing they (the industry) ever heard was
'stop,' or 'ban,' and in a sense this wasn't particularly helpful."

▣   ▣   ▣

It was becoming obvious that the NACA wasn't going to score any
major victories. Yannacone's grasp of the science and his badgering
style of cross-examination were holding the petitioners' case together.
He was also getting under Stafford's skin, as would become apparent
when the petitioners began their rebuttal.

Plus, in the midst of the NACA's case came the curveball tossed
by Wurster and Public Intervenor Robert McConnell, who called the
bearded Swedish scientist S. Goran Lofroth.

The timing couldn't have been worse for the NACA, and it was becoming apparent that the environmentalists were winning this early environmental legal skirmish at least in the public's eyes. It had already been reported in US media that Sweden had become the first country in the world to ban DDT on a two-year trial basis to determine whether a local prohibition would reduce the amount of the compound finding its way into plants and animals. The decision had come after an international conference was held in Stockholm to discuss DDT's dangers. Reports on Sweden's ban noted that officials were especially concerned about increasing concentrations in humans and the fact that no scientist was able to say for certain that DDT was harmless to higher forms of life.[52]

The NACA limped to the conclusion of its case on May 14, when the president of the Montrose Chemical Corporation of California, the nation's largest manufacturer of DDT, was called. Samuel Rotrosen added little to the scientific case, focusing instead on the impact of Rachel Carson's *Silent Spring* on DDT sales. By 1969, Montrose was producing about 50 percent of all the DDT made in the United States. The compound was also made in Europe, Mexico, and Japan, he testified. Earlier witnesses had told of factories in the Soviet Union and Hungary.

The peak year of DDT production was 1963, the year after Carson's book was published. That year, Rotrosen said, about 183 million pounds of DDT was made in the United States. During his testimony he noted that in 1967, the last year for which statistics were available, approximately 103 million pounds were made in the United States, about 70 percent of which was exported. The major purchaser of exported DDT: the United Nations' World Health Organization, which used most of it to fight malaria.[53] The World Health Organization had consistently opposed DDT bans.

x   x   x

As the petitioners began their rebuttal the next week, one of the points stressed was that the chemical could easily and economically be replaced by other methods of control, ranging from other less persistent chemicals to an integrated pest management approach that relied more on information about the life cycles of pests and their interaction with the environment. The approach was intended to manage pest damage economically and with the least possible hazard to people, property, and the environment.

The environmentalists also sought to show that DDT's safety to humans hadn't been established, a contention that lingers unanswered decades later. Among their first witnesses was a neurophysiologist from the Albert Einstein College of Medicine in New York. Alan Steinbach testified on the compound's impact on the nervous system of animals. Gould's story began this way: "DDT has irreversible effects on the nervous systems of experimental animals, a neurophysiologist told the state Natural Resources Department today."[54]

Also called to the stand as the final phase of the hearing opened was George Wallace, the Michigan State University zoologist who had conducted early experiments on how DDT acted as a nerve poison to birds and encouraged Lorrie Otto and her "gals" to take action. Wallace had documented the decimation of robins on the East Lansing campus as a result of the compound's use to fight Dutch elm disease. "I watched hundreds of the birds die on my office floor," he testified.[55]

University of Wisconsin physician Dr. Theodore Goodfriend took the stand May 20 to testify there wasn't enough scientific evidence to suggest that DDT was "absolutely safe" for human use. The testimony of Goodfriend, assistant professor of internal medicine and pharmacology in the University of Wisconsin Medical School, noted Gould, "was almost directly against that of a witness for the chemical industry."[56]

The witness she referred to was Vanderbilt toxicologist Wayland Hayes, who had during the intervenor's portion of the hearing declared the chemical was "absolutely safe" for human use. Hayes returned to the stand and defended his comment. Richard Kienitz of the *Milwaukee Journal*'s Madison bureau quoted Hayes saying, "The point is, a latent effect is only latent until you can measure it in someone. We've already gone into it at (such) great length that we did try to find effects."[57]

Yannacone again honed in on Hayes's contentions based on research findings of concentrations in healthy adult males. Yannacone noted that research on DDT's effects on women and children was lacking. Hayes countered, saying there was no indication that infants were more susceptible to DDT than adults. Once again, though, by bringing children into the picture, Yannacone had used the hearing room to affect public opinion.

The hearing came to a close on May 21, with testimony from entomologists Paul DeBack of the University of California, Riverside, and Donald Chant of the University of Toronto, both of whom urged the use of integrated pest control methods.

It was left to Orie Loucks to summarize the case for the petitioners with a description of a systems analysis model of DDT's movement through an ecosystem.

"I was really nervous," Loucks recalled.[58] "For every part of that whole system, there was somebody who knew more about it than I did. I felt badly and wondered how some of the others felt." While Loucks may have worried about the feelings of his fellow scientists, most saw him as the best possible voice for the petitioners. He was highly respected among his colleagues and had street intelligence to go with it.

Yannacone had drilled Loucks about what to say and how. Experts from a variety of disciplines were called in to assist. In part, Yannacone was responding to prodding by Van Susteren. "By late March, Van Susteren was letting Yannacone know that this was an immense body of stuff, and he needed some way to bring it together," Loucks recalled.

"Yannacone asked me to do that. In the course of Yannacone probing, the whole body of work going into this systems model, he wanted someone to understand how biology was being captured by mathematics," Loucks recalled.[59]

The Loucks testimony was somewhat lost in newspaper coverage of that day, which focused on the fact that the historic hearing was coming to an end. But Yannacone wasn't playing to the press at this point. The target was Van Susteren.

Years later, Yannacone spoke about the hearing examiner. "Van Susteren was right down the middle. He was open-minded, but first and foremost a judge. He may not have had a black sheet on, but he was as good as any federal judge I've ever seen," Yannacone said.[60] "He was a walking encyclopedia of the law of evidence, and he wasn't intimidated by anyone—the media, Senator Nelson, NACA, our people. He wasn't affected by the nature of the witnesses, only what they delivered."

Gould was able to capture the essence of Loucks's remarks. The final paragraph of Gould's story on that last day of the hearing read: "Loucks noted that DDT levels tend to increase in living organisms as they move on up the food chain. DDT, he said, 'is capable of bringing about (an) upset in the Wisconsin regional ecosystem' by eliminating predators at the top of that food chain."[61] Humans, of course, are among the predators at the top.

Stafford and Yannacone went at it on that closing day, Loucks recalled. "This whole systems stuff, Stafford was just about hoarse objecting. Yannacone would then object. They were just about hoarse yelling at one another. Van Susteren would stand up and wave his arms and say, 'How is a stenographer going to make any sense of this?'"[62]

The same question might have been true for Van Susteren. His ruling would not come until June 10, 1970, more than a year after the hearing had concluded. "No concentrations, levels, tolerances, or amounts can be established as safe," he wrote.[63] That stood in sharp contrast to federal tolerance levels that had been set by the federal Food and Drug Administration. The ruling was billed as a spectacular victory for conservationists, noted a *Capital Times* editorial on June 16.

"So what?" was the response of some observers to Van Susteren's ruling, since DDT had been banned in Wisconsin six months earlier. There was much speculation about why it took Van Susteren more than a year to issue the ruling. Some charged the DNR with holding it up; others noted that Van Susteren's wife was gravely ill. Perhaps he was just being careful, understanding the importance of his ruling above and beyond the political fray that had been playing out in Wisconsin and several other states.

Lorrie Otto, who claimed to be the only private citizen present for all twenty-seven days of testimony,[64] took note of a comment made by Van Susteren after the reporters had left on the last day of the hearing. "The Wisconsin hearings were closed off when Maurice Van Susteren asked the lawyers to prepare their briefs," she wrote. "A few minutes later, he stood up, looked at the fabulous Victor Yannacone and his crew, and said, 'In all of my 20 years as a hearing examiner, I've never seen such legal talent nor have I ever been honored by such witnesses.'"[65]

She added this about the witnesses who testified for the petitioners: "Those witnesses, all 27 PHDs, came from two continents and three countries. All were experienced in the use of DDT. They were chosen from a group of 250 scientists. All stopped whatever they were doing and came to Madison on 24-hour notice. (One said, "I can't come but I'll come anyway!") These men[66] sat on the witness stand and were cross examined by five different attorneys including Wisconsin's public intervenor."

In the same correspondence, Otto continued to express frustrations about working through government bureaucracy. Patience is not a trait of citizens with grievances. She was aggravated about a variety of matters, including the fact that government officials had moved slowly or not at all on DDT, and, as a result, "that private citizens should have to do this, and do so much before getting it in front of the public and their officials."

CHAPTER SIXTEEN

ENVIRONMENT, FRONT AND CENTER

WHILE MAURICE VAN SUSTEREN'S RULING WOULD BE IM-portant, the hearing itself had in many ways been the story. It drew international attention to the still-young environmental movement. It proved that those concerned about what humans were doing to the environment weren't fringe voices; rather, they were engaged citizens and respected scientists.

Perhaps as a side benefit, the hearing also helped the news media better understand the importance of the environment as a beat to cover. Whitney Gould became the environmental reporter for her newspaper. Quincy Dadisman continued to cover the environment for the *Milwaukee Sentinel*. Young reporters fresh out of college aspired to work the environmental beat. News outlets large and small began devoting resources to covering the environment. And there was plenty to cover in the coming years.

Even as the Wisconsin DDT hearing wound down in spring 1969, attention had been shifting to other angles of the story. States were moving quickly to ban DDT and related compounds. Gaylord Nelson and others, including newly elected US representative David Obey of Wausau, who took office on April 1 that year after a special election, pushed for federal action.

The media was swarming over the story. Coverage, especially print, may have reached its peak in 1969. TV and radio news also covered the DDT story, but most of the in-depth treatment came in print. TV was rapidly becoming the major news source for many Americans, but newspapers were still reaching the vast majority of American households in the 1960s, and news magazines were flourishing.[1] In response to the threat from TV, some newspapers were aggressively adding staff. Gould was one of the reporters who got her job as news operations were expanded.[2]

The Wisconsin hearing had helped to galvanize public interest and open doors to new environmental story lines. The media had been introduced to the idea that human activities in one place could have dramatic impacts elsewhere. On June 22, 1969, an oil slick and debris in the Cuyahoga River caught fire in Cleveland, Ohio.[3] The Cuyahoga River fire lasted just thirty minutes and did little damage, but it became an oft-cited iconic emblem of the need for environmental regulation there and elsewhere in the United States.

On August 1, 1969, *Time* magazine reported on the fire and on the condition of the Cuyahoga: "Some River! Chocolate-brown, oily, bubbling with subsurface gases, it oozes rather than flows. 'Anyone who falls into the Cuyahoga does not drown,' Cleveland's citizens joke grimly. 'He decays.' . . . The Federal Water Pollution Control Administration dryly notes: 'The lower Cuyahoga has no visible signs of life, not even low forms such as leeches and sludge worms that usually thrive on wastes.' It is also—literally—a fire hazard."[4]

Public attention across the country was focusing on air and water pollution. In Wisconsin, paper mills, manufacturing facilities, municipal treatment plants, and other sources of pollution were undergoing scrutiny. Industry claims that environmental standards would devastate their operations sounded familiar to a public whose awareness was growing. The same case had been made about DDT.

The wonder chemical was still in the headlines. And it still generated controversy. In the wake of the federal seizure of Lake Mich-

igan coho salmon in March 1969, the *Milwaukee Journal* headlined
a story by reporter James Spaulding with "DDT Seems a Safe Pesticide for Man's Use." Spaulding wrote, "Despite the clamour of conservationists for a DDT ban, evidence of permanent harm to humans
from DDT accumulating in the environment has not been found."[5]
He noted that James Crow, professor and chairman of medical genetics at the University of Wisconsin in Madison, said there was no reason to believe that DDT was producing medical damage. Sometimes,
news accounts were contradictory. *Science News* reported in February 1969 that "Soviet workers occupationally exposed to DDT and
other organochlorine pesticides have shown disturbances of stomach
and liver functions after 10 years of contact with the pest destroyers."[6]

Trade publications like *Chemical & Engineering News* were mulling
the new world brought about by the emergence of ecological science.
A March 10, 1969, story headlined "PESTICIDES: Industry Losing
Battle" spoke of the need to integrate pesticide use with ecological
insights. *Motor News* took time in October 1969 to explore the issue,
despite the fact that it seemed unrelated to coverage of the American
automotive industry.

Time, Newsweek, Sports Illustrated, the *Christian Science Monitor*,
the *Los Angeles Times*, the *National Observer*, the *New York Times*, the
Philadelphia Inquirer, Outdoor Life, and *Science* magazine all weighed
in during the year with stories varying in focus.[7]

In the *Christian Science Monitor*, Harold Porter, president of the
National Plant Board, expressed concerns about a possible federal
ban on DDT. "We view with increasing alarm the growing reactions
against pesticides and the increasing restrictions on their use," the article quoted him as saying.[8] Meanwhile, the *Los Angeles Times* on March
6 speculated that DDT could bring about "lifeless oceans."[9]

Writing in the *Philadelphia Inquirer* on December 7, *London
Observer* columnist Gerald Leach speculated that bans on DDT and
the artificial sweetener cyclamate were overreactions and would harm
humans. Sugar, he wrote, "is a prime suspect in heart disease, or the

incontrovertible evidence from life insurance statistics that extra weight is the strongest factor predisposing to an early death."[10] As for DDT, he noted that while its use in developed countries had dropped sharply, having been replaced by safer pesticides, it remained the most widely distributed man-made chemical on Earth, even showing up in Antarctic penguins. "Most of it comes from the tropics, where for the past 20 years DDT and other persistent chemicals have saved literally millions of lives by decimating disease-carrying and crop-destroying insects. In India alone, it is estimated to have cut the incidence of malaria from 75 million to 5 million in a single decade."

Other stories noted that a federal DDT ban would heavily impact the South and cotton growers.

Leach's point on malaria would become the primary exhibit in an argument that stretched over decades and lingers to this day. The Wisconsin activists made it clear they weren't advocating a complete ban on DDT, but their actions helped lead to a federal ban that had international implications. As Robert Risebrough noted years later, that was an unintended consequence.

But despite ongoing controversy, another story line was emerging, too. *Time*, on July 11, pieced together an analysis of the pesticide controversy, explaining the pros and cons of a broadly effective but dangerously persistent chemical. The report included a graphic on biological magnification, showing how DDT content was multiplied about ten million times in living organisms. It showed that if zooplankton absorbed as little as 0.04 parts per million, as the chemical moved up the food chain, cormorants and other fish-eating birds showed concentrations at as high as 25 ppm. *Time*, in effect, was providing the nation with a primer on ecological science. "Long after exterminating the bugs at which it is aimed, DDT goes on performing its lethal work, washing from fields into rivers, lingering on the leaves of trees, floating about in the atmosphere for years—and contaminating everything it touches," the article claimed.[11]

New York Times reporter Gladwin Hill asked in a September 14 report, "Do people have a constitutional right to freedom from air pollution and other environmental hazards and annoyances?"[12]

The question arose from his coverage of a meeting in Warrenton, Virginia, of seventy-five of the nation's leading conservation lawyers. He wrote that the lawyers were focused on "the new field of 'environmental law.'" Among those on hand: Ralph Nader and Victor Yannacone.

Meanwhile, the Wisconsin environmental activists chided their foes, wondering aloud why scientists like Crow weren't testifying at the Madison hearings.

The Wisconsin press was still regularly turning to DDT for headlines. Legislative hearings and the ongoing Department of Natural Resources hearing generated their share of heat, but other stories focused on the debate among various forces about whether DDT was safe, or who was to blame for its misuse.

Wisconsin's newly installed Agriculture Secretary Donald Wilkinson spoke to Consolidated Badger Cooperative in April, advising caution in the use of pesticides while asking for a better public understanding of the facts about DDT use. "Agriculture is not the major contributor to pesticide pollution at this time, despite what some would like to have you believe," he said.[13] "The major contributors to DDT pollution now are communities which use it for fly, mosquito and Dutch elm disease control."

When University of Wisconsin faculty members and students halted scientific research on March 4, as part of a one-day national strike for peaceful uses of science, the DDT hearing was referenced. Scientists around the country observed this protest against the large amount of military research conducted on college campuses. Charles Kurland, a University of Wisconsin associate professor of zoology, said the protest was intended to make students aware of the misuse of science so they could work against it when they left the university.

"He [Kurland] said an example of the way scientists could influence politics was their testimony in Wisconsin recently about the harmful effects of DDT. The hearing stimulated the drafting of legislation seeking to ban DDT. The proposal has been introduced in the Assembly," read the *Milwaukee Journal*'s March 4, 1969, account of the protest.[14]

Similar views emerged at a University of Wisconsin faculty forum on participation by scientists in political decision making. "Science Must Quit Ivory Towers," read the March 19 headline in the *Capital Times*.

Wisconsin State Journal farm editor Robert Bjorklund took a different position on the issue: "The drawbacks of political action in scientific fields is that a scientist to be recognized must either be a member of scientists for something, or scientists against that something," he wrote in his "Weekly Focus on Farming" column.[15] "Apparently it is more difficult just to be a capable scientist seeking out such facts as people can use to make a wise decision." It is easy to imagine Bjorklund and Joseph Hickey or Hugh Iltis having a lively conversation on this topic.

Interest groups took sides in the ongoing debate. "Wisconsin agriculture needs to wage a tough battle to save one of its most basic tools for crop production—the use of pesticides—and possibly other chemicals," wrote Al Morrow in the January 11 *Wisconsin Agriculturalist*.[16] He noted that most or all Wisconsin vegetable growers and state farm organizations supported the chemical industry, including the Wisconsin Farm Bureau. (In February the Wisconsin Farmers Union overwhelmingly rejected a proposal that DDT be banned in Wisconsin. Citizens Natural Resources Association officer Carla Kruse, who was behind the effort to ban the pesticide, was also a Farmers Union member.[17])

Meanwhile the Wisconsin Bowhunters Association, representing about six thousand members, adopted a resolution endorsing a ban on "hard" pesticides—those that persist in the environment—such as DDT, when it met in January.[18]

Other groups also took a stand on DDT. The April meeting of the Wisconsin Conservation Congress, long a historically powerful group that advises the Department of Natural Resources, voted nearly unanimously at its 1969 statewide spring hearings to oppose use of hard pesticides such as DDT. Labor voiced an opinion in November, when the Wisconsin State AFL-CIO Conservation Committee went on record as opposing the use of DDT.

Newspaper opinion pieces and editorials, for the most part, leaned toward restricting DDT's use, especially as state legislative hearings began in 1969.

Conservative voices including the *Green Bay Press-Gazette* and *Appleton Post-Crescent* weighed in. The *Post-Crescent* called DDT "A Pesticide We Do Not Need" in a July 22 editorial. "Tough State Law for DDT Needed," read the headline on the Green Bay paper's July 27 editorial. *The Paper*, a short-lived newspaper in Oshkosh, proclaimed on July 24: "The Use of DDT Should Be Banned."

Daily newspapers weren't the only ones to weigh in. Taking note of the continued disagreements among scientists, politicians, and interest groups, the weekly *Rice Lake Chronotype* on May 7 said: "The public is confused, maybe not alarmed, but confused without question. What they need is straight answers, and facts, not political palaver or scientific semantics."[19]

Outdoors writers for several newspapers also had their say, most of them expressing concern about DDT's impacts on wildlife, especially fish. Farm writers held different views. In his weekly columns, the *Wisconsin State Journal*'s Bjorklund made it clear where he stood. He wrote on July 20: "It has become difficult even to question some proposals about DDT because anyone asking a question is immediately for the chemical industry and against the birds."[20] He added, "If someone wanted to beat America he could do it by crippling agriculture. And the way to control agriculture is to take its technologies away one by one."

On September 28, 1969, Bjorklund predicted that DDT wouldn't be banned, "but by public pressure and political reaction it will be eased out of the arsenal of weapons for beating the bugs."[21] Bjorklund covered portions of the DDT hearing and the legislature's efforts to ban DDT.

Don Johnson, the *Milwaukee Sentinel* outdoors reporter who was first to break the story of DDT in Wisconsin's fisheries, wrote in a column about the misuse of chemicals that nobody "really knows what the long-term, cumulative effects of many of these things will be."[22]

There was a bit of humor in some of the editorializing. The *Manitowoc Herald* headlined a May 24 editorial "Pass the Coho and DDT, Too." Noting that there was plenty of confusion over DDT concentrations in fish, the editorial said: "While the decision to eat fish containing DDT is a matter of choice, just like it being individual's decision to stop for an arterial when driving his car, there is sound reason for continued studies so that human and animal as well as environmental resources can be protected.

"The banning of DDT use in the state may be one way of forestalling any further harmful effects of the pesticide until there is more concensus [*sic*] on the chemical. Michigan already has chosen this course. Wisconsin should too."

Indeed, Michigan had chosen that course first, to the chagrin of the Wisconsin activists, who wanted to achieve that distinction. Lorrie Otto, in a July 10 letter to Charles Wurster, bemoaned this development, "Michigan is getting the headlines when Wisconsin could have so easily got them. We may come in as the caboose in the end!"[23]

"State to Ban Sale of DDT" shouted the *State Journal* of Lansing and East Lansing, Michigan, on April 17, 1969. An accompanying headline read "Michigan Action First in Country." Michigan agriculture director B. Dale Ball noted that other less persistent chemicals believed to have fewer harmful side effects remained available. "It is our desire to use materials that have the least harmful side effects," he said.[24] That the action came a week after the FDA expressed concerns about DDT levels in Lake Michigan coho salmon was a coincidence, he said. The Michigan ban, when finally approved in June, allowed some limited uses of the substance—by government officials and professional applicators—for control of bats, mice, and human body lice.

The Environmental Defense Fund had played a role in the Michigan ban, beginning efforts there shortly after its founding in 1967. At the time it sought court orders to stop cities from spraying DDT. Wurster, as early as 1967, had predicted troubles with the state's fishery due to the use of the pesticide.

Beyond the Midwest, Arizona had already declared a moratorium on the use of DDT in January 1969. In June, the administration of Governor Ronald Reagan in California announced it would ban DDT and DDD for household use and restrict their application on farms the following year.[25]

On the federal level, Senator Gaylord Nelson had been asking for a DDT ban since as early as 1966. He continued to push for federal action, and in 1969 the Nixon administration was moving in that direction. On May 19, 1969, Leslie Glasgow, an assistant secretary of the US Department of the Interior, said the use of hard pesticides like DDT should be prohibited within three to five years to protect fish, wildlife, and the human environment. "We've been talking for 10 years," he said. "It's time we make a move to do it."[26] Glasgow was speaking to news reporters before testifying before the Senate Commerce Subcommittee. His testimony that day was termed "one of the strongest warnings against agricultural pesticide dangers ever made by an official of a major government agency" in a *Milwaukee Journal* story compiled from press dispatches.

Nelson spoke that day, too, asserting, "I know of no other single environmental pollutant which is endangering the quality of life on earth more than DDT and other persistent pesticides. . . . In only one generation, it has contaminated the atmosphere, the seas, the lakes and the streams, and infiltrated the fatty tissue of most of the world's creatures."[27] Others would continue to take issue with Nelson's sweeping indictment, but Glasgow's comments proved prophetic.

A federal ban on DDT was still three years off, but by November 1969, federal agencies were taking action. On November 20, Agriculture Secretary Clifford Hardin ordered a ban on the use of DDT within thirty days in residential areas and a wider ban by 1971. The ban was endorsed by President Richard Nixon's newly created Council on Environmental Quality, an advisory group to the president. DDT spraying for Dutch elm disease, which had ignited the passions of citizen environmental activists, would come to an end.

Back in Wisconsin, the *Capital Times* weighed in the next day with an editorial headlined "Federal DDT Action Welcome; Wisconsin Dawdles on Problem." Hardin's action should "hearten conservationists everywhere," the newspaper said. It questioned waiting until 1971 for a broader ban, but fired its strongest volley at its home state and the delay in Van Susteren's decision. "Wisconsin could have played a proud role as a pioneer in enlarging the fight against DDT, but timidity and pressure by special interests have kept tied the hands of the state Department of Natural Resources. Nearly a year has gone by since the widely-publicized hearings on DDT conducted by the Department."[28]

History would prove the newspaper wrong about the state's role in the DDT story: the hearing played a crucial role in later actions. But the paper was correct in stating that the pesticide industry was clearly at work in the state during the lapse between the hearing and Van Susteren's ruling.

A newly created state Pesticide Review Board was in place by 1969, and the industry sought to transfer the DDT matter to that entity, which included a representative from the Department of Agriculture. Foes of DDT and other hard pesticides feared that the new board—which lacked a representative from the environmental science community—would be vulnerable to pressure from the agri-chemical industry.

Gould broke the story on September 23. All-capital letters proclaimed in a headline, "CHEMICAL FIRMS TRY TO BLOCK DDT RULING." She detailed efforts by the NACA attorney Willard Stafford, who had filed a brief with the DNR asking that the petitioners' complaint be dismissed and the matter shifted to the Pesticide Review Board.

Yannacone heaped scorn on the move in a telephone interview with Gould: "It is an affront to the state of Wisconsin and the people of Wisconsin and to the people of the United States for the NACA to make a move at this late stage to prevent the full impact of the first direct confrontation involving DDT with any degree of scientific sophistication and legal due process from being presented and a finding of fact and legal determination from being made under Wisconsin law."[29]

The same article documented the CNRA's impatience with the DNR. CNRA president Frederick Baumgartner, Gould reported, had telegrammed DNR secretary Lester Voigt, asking that the department finish its work without delay. Voigt and Van Susteren cited the length of testimony, a shortage of court reporters, and a pileup of other business for delays.

The DNR did release the complete transcript of the hearing in October. Testimony, exhibits, and the index ran to approximately 4,500 pages. It weighed forty pounds. The DNR made it available at a cost of $675. Van Susteren's decision was still seven months away.

Despite activists' concerns about the pace of efforts to ban DDT in Wisconsin, legislative action marked much of 1969. And the environmentalists had their say as action proceeded.

Efforts to legislatively address the pesticide problem had actually begun in 1967, with a bill to create the Pesticide Review Board. Canning and farm industry spokesmen opposed the bill, with Wisconsin Farm Bureau lobbyist William KasaKaitas leading the way. KasaKaitas argued that laws already in place were sufficient. Conservation groups pushed back, as did citizens including Mrs. Virginia M. Kline, who

Walter Scott, a state conservation official, weighs testimony from the Wisconsin DDT hearing. It amounted to forty pounds and approximately 4,500 pages. While working for the Wisconsin Conservation Department, which later became the Wisconsin Department of Natural Resources, Scott helped organize the Citizens Natural Resources Association. *WHi Image ID 102667, Madison Newspapers Inc.*

was described by reporter John Patrick Hunter of the *Capital Times* as "a Madison housewife."[30]

Creation of the board was still being argued in 1969. Supporters of two bills to create the board who showed up at a legislative hearing in March included representatives of the Wisconsin Resource Conservation Council, the Wisconsin Federation of Women's Clubs, and the Racine Garden Club. The Federation of Women's Clubs had become a strong voice for conservation in Wisconsin and the nation in the 1950s and '60s. The Conservation Council's leadership included Martin Hanson, who would prepare the fliers warning of DDT in fish later that year. The EDF also had a hand in the legislation. University of Wisconsin law professor James MacDonald took a leave of absence to work for the EDF on the creation of a model pesticide control act that included the establishment of a board to regulate use of pesticides, require their registration, and call for detailed scientific data about their effects on the environment before they could be used.[31]

Lacking the drama of the DDT hearing and efforts to ban the compound, creation of the Pesticide Review Board was nonetheless an important effort to update pesticide control measures in an age when the use of these substances had become essential to mainstream agriculture. The board—which would be comprised of representatives of the heads of the DNR, the Wisconsin Department of Agriculture, and the Wisconsin Department of Health and Social Services—was eventually created by the legislature and signed into law by Governor Warren Knowles on June 29, 1969.

But efforts for an outright ban of DDT continued. The bill sponsored by State Senators Martin Schreiber and Fred Risser in January 1969 moved forward. Representatives Lewis Mittness of Janesville and Norman Anderson of Madison introduced a companion bill in the assembly. Even as the DDT hearing proceeded in fits and spurts at the Hill Farms State Office Building, more public attention was focused on the chemical's fate in the state capitol.

Schreiber, who would later serve as governor from 1977 to 1979, tied his bill to the DDT hearing. "There is unqualified evidence of the uncontrollable and destructive nature of DDT," he told the *Milwaukee Sentinel* in 1969. "Experts have clearly stated the potential for environmental disaster if we permit its continued use."[32]

State politicians were clearly listening to their constituents, regardless of political affiliation. The assembly bill to ban DDT included sixteen Democratic and eleven Republican cosponsors. The environment, it seems, had risen above partisan politics. But that doesn't mean the bills didn't set off fireworks as they were argued.

Some familiar faces showed up when the Assembly Agriculture Committee took up the matter in April. Gould was on hand for the April 9 hearing, at which sponsor Mittness claimed that humankind was on the verge of "slowly committing suicide by using persistent pesticides in the U.S. We're worried about the war in Vietnam, the fiscal crisis, student unrest. . . . But 24 hours a day we're spewing into our environment pollutants that could determine the course of mankind."[33]

Botany professor Grant Cottam from the University of Wisconsin in Madison argued for the bill, as did Dr. N. T. Shaidi, a University of Wisconsin pediatrician and hematologist who sought to link DDT to aggravation of a blood disease. "He related that a girl being treated at U.W. Hospitals for the disease, a form of anemia, died after exposure to the pesticide," wrote Gould.

Others argued against the bill. University of Wisconsin entomologist Ellsworth Fisher, who had testified at the DNR hearing, was back, saying that most alternative pesticides were more toxic than DDT. Charles Creuzinger, a vegetable grower from Sturtevant, said DDT was "a must" in the production of carrots, and a ban would impose hardships on growers of lettuce, celery, and some fruits.[34]

The opposing witnesses were joined by Laurence Motl of the DNR, who said he feared the legislative action merely against DDT "will cause the public and some legislators, too, to relax with the feeling that the danger has been dealt with, the problem has been solved and that further action is not necessary."[35] A state Pesticide Review Board would provide more comprehensive oversight of all pesticides, he said. Motl's opposition put the DNR in accord with the Department of Agriculture, which opposed a ban and also favored the Pesticide Review Board.

Otto, who had long expressed impatience with and distrust of the natural resources agency, sent Walter Scott a blistering letter over the DNR's position.

"We are in real trouble now! And all because of the DNR!" she wrote.[36] "For three years the DNR banned DDT on all land under it's [sic] control. Yet, in front of the Legislature, Laurence Motl would never support a statewide ban."

The DNR's support for a Pesticide Review Board was tied to the hold-up of the release of Van Susteren's ruling, she charged. "Well now finally your big baby has been born but you tell me that it really isn't much better than your old permit system except that you can get press and public support. What the lawyers are telling me about it is that this new law makes our hearings mute. . . . While Mr. Stafford raised the flag of victory in a battle he did not win, the Department has lost the entire show and gained the disrespect and bad faith of the public. And this you fellows are never going to recover from. We all gave too much of ourselves, so that we are left soiled and hurt and disillusioned."

But legislative action proceeded. Final approval of the Pesticide Review Board had come on July 22, when the state assembly passed the bill on a ninety-six to one vote. The state senate had earlier unanimously approved a similar measure. The only assembly opponent was Mittness, who argued the legislation would serve as an excuse to avoid a state ban.[37]

He was wrong. A few days before approving the Pesticide Review Board bill, the assembly passed the bill to ban DDT on a ninety-nine to zero vote. Later in 1969, the state senate took up the matter. *Wisconsin State Journal* farm editor Bjorklund noted in a September 25 story that "the great DDT fight in Wisconsin changed markedly Wednesday.

"It is no longer a fight or even a debate, since only opponents of DDT appeared to support an Assembly-passed bill that would outlaw sale of DDT except in emergencies."[38]

It was an anticlimactic if satisfying moment for the citizens who had worked for nearly a decade to see DDT banned. The state senate got around to voting on the DDT ban on January 8, 1970. Governor Knowles signed the law a few days later on Friday, January 13. Knowles, who would later be inducted into the Wisconsin Conservation Hall of Fame, said the ban "clearly shows Wisconsin's determination to confront directly the most apparent threats to a healthy environment."[39]

The first Earth Day would be celebrated later that year, and its founder, Gaylord Nelson, would continue to push for a federal ban on DDT.

President Richard Nixon's administration took steps in that direction later the same year. Nixon created the Environmental Protection Agency in 1970. The act reorganized how the federal government handled environmental regulation, as the various functions previously had been housed in several other units of government. That set the stage for EPA's first administrator, William Ruckelshaus, to make a sweeping decision two years later.

On June 14, 1972, Ruckelshaus announced a ban on virtually all interstate sales and shipments of DDT. Ruckelshaus initiated the action despite the fact that the National Academy of Sciences, the American Medical Association, the US Surgeon General, the World Health Organization, and other high-level groups had spoken out in favor of continued use of DDT to fight disease and protect crops. A lengthy EPA scientific hearing had resulted in a recommendation

for continued use of the pesticide. Hearing Examiner Edmund Sweeney wrote in his "recommended findings, conclusions and orders"
that "DDT is not a carcinogenic hazard to man. The uses of DDT
under the regulations involved here do not have a deleterious effect
on freshwater fish, estuarine organisms, wild birds or other wildlife.
The evidence of this proceeding supports the conclusion that there is
a present need for the essential uses of DDT."[40]

Ruckelshaus took his action under the Federal Insecticide, Fungi-
cide and Rodenticide Act, the general law that provided for regulation of pesticides. The law, passed in 1947, was an updated version of
the Federal Insecticide Act of 1910, the first federal law in the United
States regulating pesticides.

The DDT story, and the controversy that surrounds it, has continued for decades. The pesticide was banned for agricultural uses
worldwide by the 2001 Stockholm Convention on Persistent Organic
Pollutants, an international treaty signed by 128 parties and 151 sig-
natories. Under the same agreement, the use of DDT is still permitted in countries that need it, such as tropical countries that continue
to employ DDT to control malaria.

EPILOGUE

THE DDT STORY IN WISCONSIN IS A FASCINATING CHAPTER in state and national history, one of citizen engagement and activism that in many ways hasn't been replicated in the nearly half-century since the story played itself out.

"The little army of private citizens behind the scenes was really the key," said the former *Capital Times* reporter Whitney Gould, who recalled the events of decades earlier from her home in Milwaukee.[1] There were other keys, too.

Scientists entered the public arena and made a difference. Some suffered bruises for their efforts. But they became engaged nonetheless.

Proximity didn't hurt the cause: DDT spraying for Dutch elm disease hit people close to home. When enough people began to question its impact, the story took on a life of its own.

The media played a big role. Newspapers were still flourishing, with large news holes and enough reporters to chase down stories. TV and radio reporters dutifully followed, and national coverage was widespread.

When Wisconsin citizens marched into municipal buildings with dead robins, or came to meetings waving copies of *Silent Spring*, reporters knew they had the definition of news: man bites dog. Or, in this case, man bites robin.

Wisconsin's rich conservation tradition was a factor. The list of the original members of the Citizens Natural Resources Association reads like a who's who of conservation activists in the state at that time. They came from many walks of life, and many of them were business leaders who took on the mantle of citizen conservationist.

The administrative laws that enabled citizens in Wisconsin to make their case were not common in other states. "Wisconsin was the source of many concepts of law and government," noted attorney Victor Yannacone from his law office in Patchogue, New York, one spring day as this book was coming together.[2]

"Wisconsin saw that it could deliver services to people with administrative services. . . . Wisconsin had a judicial component that allowed for review of administrative actions and actually applied principles of old English law, where you go to a judge and ask for declaratory judgment. That was a direct result of the Progressive tradition to challenge the actions of administrative government."

Aldo Leopold's influence was a factor. *A Sand County Almanac* didn't enjoy widespread popularity until the late 1960s and '70s, as the new environmental movement took shape. But Leopold's ideas and influence permeated the educational culture at the University of Wisconsin in Madison and elsewhere in the academic community. One of his legacies was working in cooperation with other academics in an interdisciplinary manner. This interdisciplinary approach was used effectively in the Department of Natural Resources hearing, during which the expertise of mathematicians, lawyers, physicians, scientists from a variety of specialties, and everyday citizens like Lorrie Otto were employed.

"You cannot think of the land ethic as being something created in a book," noted Orie Loucks as he reflected on that period.[3] "Leopold was talking to a lot of people in Madison and Wisconsin at that time. You had a living statement of Wisconsin's vision of conservation from the 1940s. And within a few years you have Rachel Carson working on persistent pesticides as used by agriculture. A lot of what Leopold was talking about was the abuses of agriculture. Would Rachel Carson have been sharing her manuscript with Leopold? You bet."

The fact that the Wisconsin activists' foes initially underestimated them and the Environmental Defense Fund played a big role in the final outcome.

As Charles Wurster and others noted years later, the chemical industry learned its lesson in Madison. "If this whole DDT show we put on 40 years ago was done today, we wouldn't win. There's too much of a corporate propaganda machine going on out there. We'd get shot down."[4]

But DDT wasn't the last agricultural chemical to make headlines in Wisconsin. In the 1980s, the pesticide aldicarb, used primarily to kill the Colorado potato beetle, was found to be leaching into groundwater in central Wisconsin. A lengthy controversy unfolded, and the compound's manufacturer eventually pulled it from the market in the state rather than risk a ban. As a direct result of that controversy, Wisconsin passed what was considered a model groundwater quality law in 1984.

There are parallels to the DDT and aldicarb stories and a direct connection between Long Island, New York, and Wisconsin in both cases. Aldicarb contamination of drinking water in Long Island led its manufacturer to remove it from the market in Suffolk County, New York, in 1979. That set the stage for the later action in Wisconsin.

Similarly, the first local action taken against DDT came on Long Island. There, environmentalists filed a lawsuit against the Long Island Mosquito Commission in 1966. A temporary injunction halted the use of the substance, and the case went to trial that December. DDT was never used again on Long Island. One of the scientists who assisted the Long Island environmentalists: Charles Wurster. The plaintiff in the case: Carol Yannacone. Her attorney: husband Victor Yannacone. "It marked the beginning of what we now call environmental law," recalled Wurster years later in *Return of the Peregrine: A North American Saga of Tenacity and Teamwork*.[5]

Following that action, Wurster, Yannacone, and a small group of others, mostly scientists, who believed that the environment could be

best served in a legal setting, incorporated the EDF in 1967. Soon
they were at work on DDT in Michigan. Then came Wisconsin.

But those were the early days of the environmental movement. Tar-
gets were easy to find. They were everywhere. The CNRA, still in existence today but not a major environmental force in the state, turned its
attention to other water quality concerns soon after the DDT battles,
focusing on paper wastes and other pollutants contaminating major
rivers in Wisconsin. The federal Clean Water Act, passed in 1972, one
of a series of environmental laws put in place by Congress, proved a
powerful weapon in those fights.

The EDF continues to be a force for environmental action, but it
has long since dropped its unofficial "sue the bastards" motto. Today,
it explains its mission on its website: "We are passionate, pragmatic
environmental advocates who believe in prosperity *and* stewardship.
Grounded in science, we forge partnerships and harness the power of
market incentives."[6]

Environmental advocacy groups mushroomed in the years following the DDT battles. Some became as entrenched and intransigent
as the groups they opposed. When asked whether a citizens' effort
such as the one that successfully fought the indiscriminate use of DDT
would succeed today, Yannacone, always a bit of a cynic, responded,
"No. The pampered princes and princesses of privilege who have taken
over the [environmental] movement do not have the fire in their belly
that people of generations before did."[7]

Over time, the forces that came together to fight DDT in Wisconsin and elsewhere went their separate ways. Hunting and fishing organizations and environmental groups have since often seemed to find
as many differences as areas of agreement.

The major environmental issues of today are also more complex
and difficult to understand. The misuse of DDT was an issue of global
importance, but the fact that it had a local component, thanks to
Dutch elm disease spraying, helped people understand the pesticide's
impact on the environment.

Complex issues of today, such as global climate change, are harder for people to grasp. For his part, Wurster isn't confident that much progress can be made on that front.

"We have a much bigger problem with climate change, but we can't do anything about it. We can't get anything done in Congress. The big difference is the magnitude of the enemy. [In 1968–1969] we caught them with their pants down. They thought it was just a public relations problem. They didn't grasp that we had all this scientific knowledge, and by time they realized it was happening, it was too late," he recalled in a 2012 interview.[8]

"With climate change, who's the foe? Oil companies, the largest corporations in the world. They have a multi-million-dollar propaganda machine. Now these huge industries have their pants very much up. There are all sorts of think tanks and propaganda organizations saying it isn't so. I'm not so optimistic."

Gould made some of the same points as she looked back on the DDT battles and compared them to twenty-first-century environmental challenges.

"One big lesson . . . and it's a somewhat ambiguous lesson, has to do with both the promise and limitations of citizen activism. By promise, I mean it has to do with the way in which citizens, when they band together and focus on common goals, can get something wonderful accomplished. These people did that. They really did. Against huge odds. The money—the power—was all against them, but they won in the end, and the environment won.

"But the limitations of citizen involvement are also underscored here. When you're dealing with global environmental crises such as climate change and even the broader spread of chemicals in the environment and the use of fossil fuels, it's really difficult for a band of citizens to make a dent, because the levers of power are more diverse. They are global in scope. There are so many forces arrayed against reform. . . . There are some days when I'm really optimistic. When I see some little victory here or there it gives me hope. And then there are other days, when I look at continued spilling of oil in the Gulf of Mexico, when I'm just in despair. I think, my God, have we not learned a thing."[9]

Yes, it was a long time ago. Yes, the environmental movement was young and naive. But Wisconsin citizens made a difference. Their deeds might have been described in the words of anthropologist Margaret Mead, who is credited with saying, "Never doubt that a small group of thoughtful, committed citizens can change the world. Indeed, it is the only thing that ever has." Another Mead quote is equally relevant: "No society has ever yet been able to handle the temptations of technology to mastery, to waste, to exuberance, to exploration and exploitation. We have to learn to cherish this earth and cherish it as something that's fragile, that's only one, it's all we have. We have to use our scientific knowledge to correct the dangers that have come from science and technology."[10]

⊠   ⊠   ⊠

As for the characters who acted out the DDT battle in Wisconsin, most continued to work on causes in which they believed.

Lorrie Otto emerged as a national figure in the native landscaping movement. Frequently featured in the media in flowing gowns and looking like nature's fairy godmother, she earned honorifics like "Nature Lady," "Queen of the Prairie," and the "heart and soul of natural landscaping." In many ways, she was the heart and soul of the DDT battles in Wisconsin. She stirred the pot time and again, giving countless hours to the effort.

Orie Loucks was soon engaged in efforts to block the US Navy's Project Sanguine, an underground communications system for the navy proposed for the Clam Lake area of northern Wisconsin in the 1970s. William Reeder was also active in opposition to the project. Opponents of the project expressed concerns about the effects of high ground currents and electromagnetic fields on the environment. Faced with opposition, the navy built a scaled-down version in the 1980s under the name Project ELF.

After leaving Wisconsin in 1978, Loucks focused his efforts on understanding and analyzing global carbon sequestration and the regional effects of air pollutants while serving as director of the Holcomb Research Institute at Butler University. He ended his professional career in 2004 after spending fourteen years as the Ohio Eminent Scholar in Applied Ecosystem Studies at Miami University.

Reeder left Wisconsin in 1978 to take a position at the University of Texas, where he stayed until 1992. He returned to Madison upon retiring and remains a fixture at the Zoological Museum he directed while on the University of Wisconsin zoology faculty.

Joseph Hickey, Hugh Iltis, and Gene Roark, who all cofounded the Wisconsin chapter of the Nature Conservancy in 1960, continued to work for land preservation in the state. At this writing, Roark was president of the Wisconsin Conservation Hall of Fame Foundation's Executive Board and remained active in a number of conservation organizations. Iltis, whose home overlooks the UW–Madison Arboretum, was busy converting his slides of plants from many parts of the world to digital format. Hickey, a beloved teacher at the university, left his mark on hundreds of students who, as noted by Roger Tory Peterson, "moved into and built up the structures of modern conservation and environmental study."[11]

Robert Risebrough was completing a manuscript about eggshell thinning in California condors as this book was being written. The cause of the thinning: DDT wastes dumped into waterways decades ago by Montrose Chemical Corporation, the last major US manufacturer of the compound. Charles Wurster, living in Seattle, Washington, was in the process of wrapping up a manuscript for a book of his own about DDT and other pesticides. Dan Anderson's ongoing research includes a project at Clear Lake, California, the site of early DDT findings.

As for Victor Yannacone, he is no longer associated with the EDF, having left the organization in an acrimonious split shortly after the Wisconsin hearing. He continues to practice law in Patchogue, New York, on Long Island, with a portion of his work devoted to environmental law, a branch that he helped create.

People associated with the DDT story who were inducted into the Wisconsin Conservation Hall of Fame include Hickey and Otto. Gaylord Nelson was an early inductee, as was Governor Warren Knowles. Their names also are attached to the state's premier land preservation fund, the Knowles-Nelson Stewardship Fund. A. D. Sutherland and Virgil Muench of the Izaak Walton League, co-petitioners in the DNR hearing, are also inductees, as is Martin Hanson, the Mellen conservationist who circulated the fliers about DDT in fish, and Emily Earley, the Madison woman who was one of the leaders of "the little army of private citizens" cited by Gould. Hanson died shortly before being inducted. Earley died shortly after, having been feted at a well-attended ceremony in Madison that was organized by Roark. Walter Scott, the guy behind the scenes at the Wisconsin Conservation Department and the DNR, was inducted in 1995. In addition to his daily duties at the state agency, he founded the *Passenger Pigeon*, the journal of the Wisconsin Society for Ornithology, and, for decades, worked on developing a list of Wisconsin's largest trees.

At this writing, Whitney Gould was retired and living in Milwaukee, where she frequently makes presentations on architecture and, occasionally, the DDT battles.

x   x   x

The DDT story, with its deep roots in Wisconsin, remains a pivotal and controversial topic in the history of the modern environmental movement. The Wisconsin activists made it clear throughout that they recognized the pesticide's value, especially in areas of human health.

Their point was that its misuse was having a major and unnecessarily negative impact on the state and region's ecosystem.

In the wake of its banning in the United States, DDT's devastation of wildlife was halted and, in many cases, reversed. The peregrine falcon, bald eagle, and brown pelican—all driven to near extinction—have recovered sufficiently to be removed from the federal endangered species list.

DDT proponents point to a dramatic spike in the number of people worldwide infected with malaria after the substance was banned in the United States. In India alone, rates went from sixty thousand in 1962 to six million by 1976. In the 2011 book *DDT and the American Century*, author David Kinkela cites those numbers, but adds, "The rising rates of malaria had less to do with the discontinued use of DDT than with the fallacious logic of [insect] eradication, the administrative burdens of eradication, and pesticide resistance. Indeed, the shift [from chlorinated hydrocarbons such as DDT] to organophosphates [such as parathion, malathion, methyl parathion, chlorpyrifos, diazinon, dichlorvos, phosmet, fenitrothion, tetrachlorvinphos, and azinphos-methyl], which endangered many farmworkers, was partly a response to the impact of insect resistance. Over time, the use of DDT to benefit public health and agricultural production increased the rate and rise of insect resistance. Not only did this impact crop yields, but it significantly reduced the effectiveness of DDT for malaria control programs. In Central America alone, the rate of DDT resistance was reported to be nearly 80 percent for malaria-bearing insects."[12]

The causes of the rise in malaria and other diseases following DDT's banning in the United States will continue to be argued. It is a highly charged topic that is driven at least in part by ideology. As this book and many others have demonstrated, it is also a debate that highlights differences of opinion among scientists.

Risebrough, for one, has struggled with the question of unintended consequences from the banning of DDT. When interviewed for this book, he was pondering addressing the topic in an essay for a general audience.

"I think a small amount of DDT could be used and wouldn't harm wildlife. I've been trying to locate any evidence to support that," he said. The American ban didn't preclude use of the compound in other parts of the world, but he noted it had a chilling effect. "Funding was deliberately withheld from malaria programs because of good intentions. Some people said, 'We in America don't want DDT, so we shouldn't thrust it on the rest of the world. If DDT is bad here, then. . . .' It was a dogma that emerged from all of that. But it's also all tied up with people who don't particularly like regulation and is part of a diatribe against environmentalists. I think there's an obligation to respond, given the political climate [that has emerged in twenty-first-century America]."[13]

Yannacone agreed that DDT might have uses in today's world to fight diseases such as malaria. "DDT, by itself, if it didn't metabolize, was not terribly harmful. In the environment, and biomagnifying in the food chain, it is very dangerous," he said. "I have a long-running discussion with a scientist who works in Africa and with malaria, and he would really like to use DDT in the huts where people live. In the old days, if they had used DDT to paint the inside of the walls of the huts, the danger would have been minimal. But it was sprayed all over and got into webs and systems where you didn't want it to go. It's the classic problem with the chemical industry: a little is good, so let's use a lot.

"In areas where mosquitoes are not resistant, you could go in and paint the walls," Yannacone said. "The problem is: Why do mosquitoes become resistant to DDT as fast as they do? They can build resistance and can have a resistant population in less than two seasons. I often wonder why insect physiologists aren't out there studying pesticide resistance. Nobody seems interested, and there's no money for the research."[14]

Here in the United States, Dutch elm disease continues its slow death march across the landscape, and the elm is no longer the dominant tree species in Wisconsin and other states where it once graced city streets. Cities and their residents still deal with dead elms, but the remaining number of trees is so low that municipal budgets are no longer burdened with huge costs for treatment of the disease and tree removal.

Today people eat fish from many Wisconsin streams and lakes without much worry of pesticide contamination, although many compounds continue to enter our waterways. But Lake Michigan, which played a pivotal role in the DDT story, is beset by a host of other environmental problems, most prominently invasive species such as the zebra and quagga mussels.

Pesticides remain essential to conventional, large-scale agriculture, which is asked to play an ever larger role in feeding a world whose population has doubled since 1968, when the DDT hearing began. DDT's impact on human health has never fully been resolved. And many questions remain about the impacts of other pesticides on humans and other life-forms.

The story lines are many. In March 2013, media across the globe reported that the US government was being sued by a coalition of beekeepers, conservationists, and food security advocates over pesticides linked to serious harm in bees.

The lawsuit accused the Environmental Protection Agency of failing to protect the insects—which pollinate three-quarters of all food crops—from nerve agents that it says should be suspended from use. The nerve agents in questions—neonicotinoids—are now the world's most widely used insecticides. In April 2013, the European Union partially suspended use of three neonicotinoids for a two-year period. Several EU members, including the United Kingdom, opposed the move.

Elsewhere, researchers are focusing on the impact of toxic pesticides on a widespread decline in grassland bird numbers in the United

States. Researchers are looking into the extent to which lethal pesticides, such as organophosphate and carbamate insecticides, are responsible for the decline in grassland bird populations.

On Long Island, which gets all of its water supply from one aquifer, environmentalists and agricultural interests continue to clash over how to balance the use of pesticides for farm production with the need to protect water quality.

These are but a few examples of ongoing concerns about pesticides. Stories on conflicts like these are common. The battle lines remain to a large degree unchanged, with agricultural interests and the chemical industry resisting regulation and environmental groups seeking more government intervention.

The DDT battles were in many ways the start of this ongoing debate, which has stretched across parts of two centuries. There is little reason to believe the debate will be resolved anytime soon.

x   x   x

"It was a long time ago" was a common refrain when people associated with the Wisconsin DDT battles reflected on a story that had garnered international attention. Memories fade. Stories change. Details slip into the fog of history. It would be easy to conclude we are left only with papers stored on shelves in boxes of archived collections. But that would not do justice to the Wisconsin DDT story and the people who made it happen. Their efforts raised awareness about a whole range of ecological issues and provided a real-life test of the concepts that are wrapped into Aldo Leopold's land ethic.

And the Wisconsin battles left us with citizens who set an example by becoming involved.

Roger Tory Peterson was eighty-four years old when he came to Wisconsin for Joseph Hickey's memorial service on September 4, 1993. He came alone and left alone, but not before giving a eulogy for his old friend from the Bronx County Bird Club. "He knew the meaning of conservation; the value of birds, animals, forests, waters, and soil; the joy and well-being to be had from their study and contemplation," Peterson noted. "He felt that it was a sacred responsibility to pass these things on to the future. A person like Joe does not really die. He has left too much of an imprint on other people. His spirit lives on."[15]

Peterson might well have been speaking about many of the activists who took part in Wisconsin's DDT battles. Certainly, it was true of Lorrie Otto, Fred Ott, and other members of the Citizens Natural Resources Association. It was no less true of the other scientists who stepped out of the laboratory and into the public fray, and brave souls like Walter Scott, who juggled bureaucratic duties with what he knew needed to be done.

One thing is clear: virtually every reference to the history of DDT mentions the impact of Wisconsin's battles.

Reflecting on the story she covered from start to finish, Whitney Gould put it this way, "The DDT chapter was one chapter in a long book that is still being written on whether we can learn to live peacefully on this Earth."[16]

ACKNOWLEDGMENTS

THE LIST OF PEOPLE WHO DESERVE ACKNOWLEDGMENT FOR helping make this book a reality could go on for pages. But my editors wouldn't like that, so I'll keep it to a few paragraphs.

My wife, Nick Schultz, offered constant support and asked important questions as the project proceeded. This book would not have been possible without her help.

Several people gave freely of their time to help me understand the story and place it in the context of the era. They include Roy Gromme, Whitney Gould, and Susan Nehls, daughter of Joseph Hickey. Without their insights, it would have been difficult to fit together the pieces of this sometimes complicated story.

I am forever grateful for the support and encouragement I received from Wisconsin Historical Society Press senior editor Kathryn Thompson. Wisconsin Historical Society Press developmental editor Laura Kearney's sharp eye, patience, and wise counsel made this book so much better than the draft that landed on her desk. To would-be writers, I offer this advice: everyone needs an editor.

The staff at the Nelis R. Kampenga University Archives & Area Research Center at the University of Wisconsin–Stevens Point provided invaluable assistance. Wisconsin's network of area research centers is a treasure to be used and enjoyed by people all across the state.

My friend and mentor George Rogers of Stevens Point was kind

enough to review some early chapters and offer support and guidance. I can't think of a man with more knowledge on more topics
than George, which is why I sought his help.

Others who went out of their way to help were my friend Dave
Zweifel, editor emeritus of the *Capital Times* of Madison, and Amy
Kimmes, assistant managing editor at the *Wausau Daily Herald*.

I am of the belief there is no such thing as a self-made man or
woman. Anyone who achieves a measure of success in life received
a helping hand somewhere along the way. To whatever extent I have
found success in my own endeavors, this has certainly been the case.
To all those who reached out to help me, I offer my humble thanks.
You know who you are.

NOTES

PREFACE

1. After a peregrine meeting at Cornell University in 1969, the governments of the United States, Canada, and Mexico were asked to do whatever was in their powers to protect the remaining populations of peregrine falcons. In 1970, the US Department of the Interior listed the peregrine as endangered. The use of DDT was banned in 1972. Congress approved the Endangered Species Act in 1973.

The first peregrine breeding season in a new breeding barn at Cornell University occurred in the spring of 1971. Eventually more than four thousand captive-produced peregrine falcons were released into the wild. Once extinct east of the Mississippi River, they now breed naturally in at least forty states across the country. They were removed from the Endangered Species List in 1999.

PROLOGUE

1. Edward O. Wilson, afterword to *Silent Spring*, by Rachel Carson, 40th anniversary edition (New York: Mariner Books, 2002).

2. Otto frequently cited that comment from a local official in Bayside, Wisconsin, in public remarks, including her 1999 induction into the Wisconsin Conservation Hall of Fame. She wore a brightly colored pair of tennis shoes to the formal induction ceremony in Stevens Point.

3. Thomas Dunlap, *DDT, Scientists, Citizens and Public Policy* (Princeton, NJ: Princeton University Press, 1981), 152.

4. Ibid., 153.

CHAPTER 1

1. The full speech is at nobelprize.org, the official website of the Nobel Prize.

2. "Chlorinated Hydrocarbons (Organochlorines)—DDT," US Fish and Wildlife Service, www.fws.gov/contaminants/Info/DDT.html.

3. Dunlap, *DDT, Scientists, Citizens and Public Policy*, 35.

4. Ibid., 37.

5. Aldo Leopold, *A Sand County Almanac with Other Essays on Conservation from Round River* (New York: Oxford University Press, 1966), 190.

CHAPTER 2

1. "Wisconsin State Symbols," Wisconsin.gov, www.wisconsin.gov/state/core/wiscon sin_state_symbols.html.

2. "Fostering Clean Air through Environmental Law," *New York Times*, May 14, 1995. "I saw the dead birds on campus, and then we began to see some that were alive, with tremors," Wurster recalls. He quickly dedicated himself to finding out the cause.

3. Charles Wurster, interview with the author, March 3, 2012.

4. "The Green Lake Convention," meeting notes by Helen Northrup and Clara Hus-song in *Passenger Pigeon* (Wisconsin Society for Ornithology) 19, no. 2 (Summer 1957): 76, University of Wisconsin Digital Collections.

5. Wisconsin Historical Society image collection, WHi Image ID 73094.

6. Lorrie Otto recalled the encounter with the Bayside village manager in an essay titled "CNRA, DDT and Me," in *CNRA—The First 50 Years* (Citizens Natural Resource Association, 2001).

7. Clarence Cottam and Elmer Higgins, *DDT: Its Effect on Fish and Wildlife*, US Department of the Interior Fish and Wildlife Service Circular 11 (Washington, DC: GPO, 1946).

8. "In Memoriam: Clarence Cottam," *Auk* 92 (January 1975): 122–123. On these pages and elsewhere in the tribute, Cottam's willingness to speak forcefully about issues that concerned him is documented.

9. Bill Christofferson, *The Man from Clear Lake: Earth Day Founder Senator Gaylord Nelson* (Madison: University of Wisconsin Press, 2004). Christofferson summarizes Nelson's role in the DDT battles in Chapter 24.

10. Jerry Apps, interview with the author, September 29, 2010.

11. George Wallace to "Mrs. Owen Otto," March 4, 1966, box 3, file 1, Lorrie Otto Papers, 1930–2008, Wisconsin Historical Society Archives, Madison.

12. Joseph Hickey, interview with Thomas Dunlap, 1973, Wisconsin Historical Soci-ety Archives, Madison.

13. Dunlap is a professor of history at Texas A&M University and the author of several books, including *DDT: Scientists, Citizens and Public Policy* (Princeton, NJ: Princeton University Press, 1981), which grew out of his doctoral dissertation at UW–Madison.

14. Wurster to Otto (under the State University of New York at Stony Brook letter-head), November 3, 1965, box 3, file 1, Lorrie Otto Papers.

CHAPTER 3

1. Roark was a cofounder of the Wisconsin chapter of the Nature Conservancy. Hickey was another cofounder.

2. Gene Roark, interview with the author, June 23, 2010.

3. Joseph Hickey, oral history transcript, recorded in Madison on July 18, 1978, by Frederick Greeley (associate professor of wildlife biology at the University of Massachusetts). A cover letter from Greeley to Hickey, along with the transcript, is dated November 16, 1978. The transcript is in the Hickey family collection, made available courtesy of Joseph's daughter, Susan Nehls.

4. E. H. Fisher and C. L. Fluke, *DDT: Its Present Uses and Limitations* (Madison: University of Wisconsin Extension Service of the College of Agriculture, October 1945).

5. William G. Moore, "The Wisconsin Ban on DDT: Old Law, New Content," *Gargoyle* (University of Wisconsin Law School) 16, no. 2 (Fall 1985).

6. Howard Mead, interview with the author, April 3, 2012. Mead and his wife, Nancy, were longtime publishers of *Wisconsin Trails* magazine. His family and Schmidt's were neighbors and among those who took their concerns to the Madison City Council.

7. Cottam's uncle, Clarence Cottam, hired and worked with Rachel Carson at the US Fish and Wildlife Service, Department of the Interior. He wrote about the dangers of pesticides as early as 1946. Carson cited Cottam's work in Chapter 10 of *Silent Spring*.

8. Potter would advance the concept of "bioethics" to describe his view that all human choices not only have short-term consequences on the ecosystem and all life systems and societies but also have long-term consequences for the future—some of which are predictable, others not.

9. A more complete treatment of Baldwin's position can be found in an oral history interview, "My Half Century at the University of Wisconsin," privately published by Baldwin in 1995, University of Wisconsin Archives, Oral History Project.

10. "Critique of 'Insecticides and People,'" prepared by the University of Wisconsin Department of Entomology, February 21, 1963, Hugh Iltis private collection.

11. Iltis's letter to Dr. H. B. McCarty, director, Division of Radio-Television Education, is dated March 19, 1963. A copy was made available to the author by Iltis.

12. The letters exchanged by Voigt and Pound are in box 3, file 5, Lorrie Otto Papers.

13. The Lorrie Otto Papers, box 3, file 5, includes a quote from this speech in her handwriting, citing the *Journal of Environmental Quality*.

14. Dan Anderson, interview with the author, April 3, 2012.

15. Wurster, interview with the author, March 2, 2012.

16. The text of Foster's comments is in the Hickey family collection, made available courtesy of Susan Nehls.

17. Orie Loucks, interview with author, March 27, 2012.

18. Victor Yannacone, interview with the author, June 6, 2012.

CHAPTER 4

1. As stated in an invitation sent to citizens in counties around the state, printed on paper featuring the letterhead of the Wisconsin Conservation Commission, box 1, call no. M72–421, file 4, Citizens Natural Resources Association of Wisconsin Records, 1950–1974, Wisconsin Historical Society Archives, Madison.

2. As fate would have it, the hackberry tree is similar in form to the American elm, and it was sometimes recommended as a replacement tree when Dutch elm disease struck the elms.

3. *CNRA—The First 50 Years*, 3.

4. As stated in the preamble and pledge adopted at the CNRA's organizational meeting December 16, 1950, from Roy Gromme's personal collection, Oconomowoc. Gromme's father, Owen, was a founding member of the CNRA. Roy would later serve as president.

5. "Submitted by Walter Scott," read the list, in box 1, call no. M72–421, file 4, Citizens Natural Resources Association of Wisconsin Records.

6. The invitation to the first meeting of the group is in box 1, file 1, Citizens Natural Resources Association of Wisconsin Records.

7. Alvin Throne letter to IWLA members, December 17, 1950, in box 1, call no. M72–421, file 4, Citizens Natural Resources Association of Wisconsin Records. Throne's letter is also the source for the reference to the decline in IWLA membership in Milwaukee.

8. Sutherland letter, dated December 20, 1950, is in box 1, call no. M72–421, file 5, Citizens Natural Resources Association of Wisconsin Records.

9. Arthur Molstad of Milwaukee was the Wisconsin Conservation Commission chairman.

10. A copy of the December 27, 1950, letter is in the personal collection of Roy Gromme. Walter Scott's letter was on plain stationery, not on paper with the Wisconsin Conservation Department letterhead.

11. William Knoll's comments were transcribed in a note from Scott to CNRA founding members, box 1, call no. M72–421, file 5, Citizens Natural Resources Association of Wisconsin Records.

12. Scott's comments were in a note he sent to other founders of CNRA. The note is in the personal collection of Roy Gromme.

13. *CNRA—The First 50 Years*, 1.

14. Scott to Wallace Grange, February 20, 1951, box 1, call no. M72–321, file 5, Citizens Natural Resources Association of Wisconsin Records.

15. The resolution, undated but likely passed in 1959 and signed by CNRA president Aroline Schmitt—who used *Mrs. Max J. Schmitt* as her signature—is in the personal collection of Roy Gromme.

16. Ibid.

17. Maxine Roberts, interview with author, June 6, 2001.

18. Roy Gromme, interview with author, August 16, 2010.

19. *CNRA—The First 50 Years*, 17.

20. Ibid.

CHAPTER 5

1. Gary Werner, interview with the author, May 29, 2013. Werner is executive director of the Partnership for the National Trails System, based in Madison, Wisconsin.

2. From a July 10, 1975, University of Wisconsin–Stevens Point news release. Files on the Baumgartners are located in the UWSP University Relations and Communications office.

3. Ted Baumgartner, e-mail correspondence with the author, March 21, 2012.

4. Dr. Byron Shaw, a colleague of Frederick Baumgartner, interview with the author, June 30, 2011.

5. Directly below the CNRA letterhead, Baumgartner typed "Office of the President—CNRA, c/o Department of Natural Resources, Wisconsin State University, Stevens Point." Most of Baumgartner's other correspondence was on plain stationery and addressed from his Stevens Point residence. Letter, October 8, 1968, box 1, call no. M75–368, file 5, Citizens Natural Resources Association of Wisconsin Records.

6. Russell Lynch earned his conservation stripes as what is believed to be the first full-time natural resources reporter for a major daily newspaper, the *Milwaukee Journal*. He won numerous awards and was inducted posthumously into the Wisconsin Conservation Hall of Fame.

7. With the transition of the Conservation Department to the Department of Natural Resources under government reorganization, the citizens' board that oversaw it also had a name change.

8. Warren Knowles to Baumgartner, December 11, 1968, box 1, call no. M75–368, file 4, Citizens Natural Resources Association of Wisconsin Records.

9. Baumgartner to Knowles, January 14, 1969, box 1, call no. M75–368, file 4, Citizens Natural Resources Association of Wisconsin Records.

10. Thomas Dunlap, "DDT on Trial: The Wisconsin Hearing, 1968–1969," *Wisconsin Magazine of History* 62, no. 1 (Autumn 1978): 11.

11. Ellsworth Fisher to Baumgartner, March 28, 1969, box 1, call no. M75–368, file 4, Citizens Natural Resources Association of Wisconsin Records.

12. Baumgartner to Walter Scott, February 3, 1969, box 1, call no. M75–368, file 4, Citizens Natural Resources Association of Wisconsin Records.

13. Baumgartner to Elvis Stahr, February 13, 1969, box 1, call no. M75–368, file 4, Citizens Natural Resources Association of Wisconsin Records.

14. Roland Clement to Baumgartner, July 7, 1969, box 1, call no. M75–368, file 4, Citizens Natural Resources Association of Wisconsin Records.

15. Roy Gromme, interview with the author, March 27, 2012.

16. Baumgartner to Charles Wurster, undated, box 1, call no. M75–368, file 5, Citizens Natural Resources Association of Wisconsin Records.

17. UW–Stevens Point news release, July 10, 1975. The news release was made available through the office of University Relations and Communications at UW–Stevens Point.

18. Linda D. F. Shalaway, "The Birds and Baumgartners of Little Lewis Hollow," *Oklahoma Today* 32, no. 3 (Summer 1982): 27.

19. Biographical material on Bertha Pearson comes from a biographical sketch in the collection of the Marathon County Historical Society. It can be accessed online at www.marathoncountyhistory.org/PeopleDetails.php?PeopleId=386&View=P&ItemName.

20. *Final Report of the Illinois State Council of Defense of Illinois 1917–1918–1919* (State of Illinois, July 1, 1919), 25.

21. "Miss Bertha Pearson Wins Conservation Award," *Wausau Record-Herald*, May 18, 1966. Pearson was awarded the Wildlife Conservation Award by the Wisconsin Federation of Women's Clubs. The organization had a long track record of interest in conservation.

22. Copies of Pearson's remarks to the commission in July 1964 and her report to the CNRA board are in the private collection of Roy Gromme.

23. Ibid.

24. The presenter was Al Berkman of Wausau, a fellow CNRA officer. His summary of the award and comments about Pearson are in the private collection of Roy Gromme.

25. Harvey Hazeltine Scholfield's September 2004 comments are from an oral history of the Scholfield family compiled by Lynne Scholfield and made available to the author.

26. The Marathon County Historical Society biographical sketch of Berkman notes that the North Central Watershed Association, the Kiwanis Club of Greater Wausau, and the Wausau Chamber of Commerce honored Berkman with a "1969 Al Berkman Night—Mr. Conservation." Subsequent articles in the *Wausau Daily Herald* note that people affectionately referred to him by that moniker.

27. From the Marathon County Historical Society biographical sketch of Berkman.

28. "Marathon Sets Proud Record," *Milwaukee Sentinel*, January 2, 1961.

29. Carla Kruse to Fred Harrington and Glenn Pound, November 21, 1968, box 1, call no. M75–368, file 4, Citizens Natural Resources Association of Wisconsin Records.

30. Carla Kruse's obituary, *Baraboo News Republic*, September 29, 2009.

31. Wisconsin Historical Society, *Dictionary of Wisconsin History*, "Freethinkers in Wisconsin," www.wisconsinhistory.org/dictionary/index.asp?action=view&term_id=11488&term_type_id=1&term_type_text=people&letter=f.

32. Harold Kruse, interview with the author, January 5, 2010.

33. Loucks, interview with the author, April 3, 2012.

34. *CNRA—The First 50 Years*, 84.

35. *Passenger Pigeon* (Wisconsin Society for Ornithology) 26, no. 3 (Autumn 1964): 113, University of Wisconsin Digital Collections.

36. Gretchen Kruse, e-mail to the author, May 8, 2012.

37. Harold Kruse, interview with the author, January 5, 2010.

CHAPTER 6

1. "Doing What Comes Naturally, How Lorrie Otto, the 'Prairie Lady,' Evolved into an Environmental Activist," *Milwaukee Journal*, June 28, 1992.

2. "Queen of the Prairie," *Milwaukee Journal Sentinel*, August 26, 1999.

3. Ibid.

4. The Lorrie Otto Papers, 1930–2008, at the Wisconsin Historical Society Archives in Madison provide a wealth of examples of each of these traits. Examples are cited throughout this book.

5. Charles Wurster, November 3, 1965, letter to "Mrs. Owen Otto," box 3, file 1, Lorrie Otto Papers.

6. "Bird Mortality after Spraying for Dutch Elm Disease with DDT," *Science* 146, no. 3666 (April 2, 1965): 90.

7. *CNRA—The First 50 Years*, 20.

8. Otto to Joan Wolfe, a Michigan conservationist and frequent correspondent with Otto, August 26, 1968, box 7, file 7, Lorrie Otto Papers.

9. Lorrie Otto, interview with Robert Steele (graduate student at the University of Wisconsin–Stevens Point), August 28, 1996, transcript, p. 10, Wisconsin Conservation Hall of Fame archives at Schmeeckle Reserve, University of Wisconsin–Stevens Point.

10. Ibid.

11. Frederick Baumgartner letter, October 8, 1968, box 1, call no. M75–368, file 5, Citizens Natural Resources Association Records.

12. Otto, interview with Steele, 10.

13. *CNRA—The First 50 Years*, 25.

14. Gromme's message, which appeared in a 1967 CNRA newsletter, was reprinted in *CNRA—The First 50 Years*, 23.

15. *CNRA—The First 50 Years*, 23.

16. Ibid., 24.

17. Don Johnson to Otto, 1969, box 7, file 3, Lorrie Otto Papers.

18. From the author's notes on the induction ceremony.

CHAPTER 7

1. Roy Gromme, interview with the author, March 27, 2011.

2. William George Bruce, *History of Milwaukee, City and County* (Chicago, IL: S. J. Clarke Publishing Co., 1922), 320.

3. "Historic Designation Study Report, Old World Third Street Historic District," City of Milwaukee, 2001, www.city.milwaukee.gov/ImageLibrary/Groups/cityHPC/DesignatedReports/vticnf/HDOldWorldThird.pdf.

4. "Ott Proved a Saving Angel to Museum, Zoo, Wildlife," *Milwaukee Journal Sentinel*, April 13, 2008.

5. Ibid.

6. Roy Gromme, interview with the author, March 27, 2011.

7. Frederick Baumgartner to Elvis Stahr, February 13, 1969, box 1, call no. M75–368, file 4, Citizens Natural Resources Association of Wisconsin Records.

8. Roland C. Clement to Baumgartner, July 7, 1969, box 1, call no. M75–368, file 4, Citizens Natural Resources Association of Wisconsin Records.

9. *CNRA—The First 50 Years*, 27.

10. Rachel Carson Trust tally sheet, June 30, 1969, box 1, call no. M75–368, file 5, Citizens Natural Resources Association of Wisconsin Records.

11. Arthur Godfrey's address was footnoted and referenced by David Archibald, managing director of the Arboretum and Wildlife Refuge at UW–Madison, in Archibald's keynote address to the Symposium on Prairie and Prairie Restorations, according to the *Proceedings of a Symposium on Prairie and Prairie Restoration: first held on September 14 and 15, 1968 at Knox College, Galesburg, Illinois*. The proceedings were published in 1970. Archibald's address is available online at http://digicoll.library.wisc.edu/cgi-bin/EcoNatRes/EcoNatRes-idx?type=article&did=EcoNatRes.NAPC01.DArchibald&id=EcoNatRes.NAPC01&isize=M.

12. Godfrey to Lorrie Otto, February 6, 1969, box 7, file 3, Lorrie Otto Papers.

13. *CNRA—The First 50 Years*, 27.

CHAPTER 8

1. "Joe Hickey, Birder," *Defenders Magazine*, February 1982, 15. The magazine is published by Defenders of Wildlife, a national conservation organization focused on wildlife and habitat conservation and the safeguarding of biodiversity.

2. "The Bronx Age, Nine New York Teen-Agers and Their Birding Revolution," *Birder's World*, October 1989, 24.

3. Ibid., 28.

4. Aldo Leopold to Hickey, January 8, 1947. The letter is among records in the Hickey family collection, made available courtesy of Susan Nehls.

5. Hickey, oral history by Greeley.

6. Ibid., 5–6.

7. Ibid., 6.

8. "Joe Hickey, Birder," 12.

9. Ibid.

10. Ibid., 7.

11. Ibid.

12. Thomas Dunlap, *DDT, Scientists, Citizens and Public Policy*, 130.

13. Hickey, oral history by Greeley, 7.

14. Ibid., 7.

15. Ibid.

16. From Hickey's remarks to the National Audubon Society upon receiving the Audubon Medal in 1984. A copy of his remarks is in the Hickey family collection, made available courtesy of Susan Nehls.

17. Hickey, oral history by Greeley, 8–9.

18. Joseph J. Hickey, ed., *Peregrine Falcon Populations: Their Biology and Decline [Proceedings of an International Conference Sponsored by the University of Wisconsin, 1965]*, (Madison: University of Wisconsin Press, 1969), 383.

19. Ibid., 447.

20. Hickey, oral history by Greeley, 9.

21. *Peregrine Falcon Populations*, 565–566.

22. Dunlap, *DDT: Scientists, Citizens and Public Policy*, 100.

23. Hickey, oral history by Greeley, 9.

24. Ibid., 10.

CHAPTER 9

1. Rita Gray Beatty, *The DDT Myth: Triumph of the Amateurs* (New York: John Day Co., 1973), 78.

2. From Ott's obituary, *Milwaukee Journal Sentinel*, April 13, 2008.

3. A copy of Hickey's remarks is in the Hickey family collection, made available courtesy of Susan Nehls.

4. David R. Zimmerman, "Death Comes to the Peregrine Falcon," *New York Times Magazine*, August 9, 1970, provides a fascinating account of the peregrine's perils. The narrative on Hagar is taken from this piece.

5. Ibid., 43.

6. *Peregrine Falcon Populations*, 256.

7. "Death Comes to the Peregrine Falcon," 44.

CHAPTER 10

1. Dan Anderson, "Joe Hickey the Scientist: A Story of Discovery" (unpublished essay), 1. Anderson shared the essay with the author.

2. Hickey, oral history by Greeley, 10.

3. "Joe Hickey the Scientist," 3.

4. Hickey, oral history by Greeley, 11.

5. Anderson, interview with the author, April 3, 2012.

6. Ibid.

7. Ibid.

8. "Joe Hickey the Scientist," 3.

CHAPTER 11

1. Ernstine Brehmer, Letter to the Editor, *Sheboygan Press*, April 25, 1960.

2. Kathy Brady, "Pesticides and Politics: A Wisconsin Town Battles Bugs and Bureaucracy," *Wisconsin Magazine of History* 93, no. 4 (Summer 2010): 3. While it focuses on Whitewater, Kathy Brady's account of the push and pull between citizens concerned about birds and city officials worried about trees is one that repeated itself across a wide swath of the country as Dutch elm disease marched on.

3. Ibid., 8.

4. Editorial, *La Crosse Tribune*, April 15, 1969. The editorial also noted that the 100,000 pounds of DDT shipped into the state in 1968 had a cash value of only $17,500. The bulk of the chemical—58,000 pounds—was used to fight Dutch elm disease in Wisconsin. Another 44,500 pounds was used to combat the leafhopper, a threat to carrot crops. Another 14,000 pounds went to spray apple trees in commercial orchards, with the remainder used for cherry trees, potatoes, and snap beans. Most of the DDT produced in the United States was going to other countries, the newspaper noted.

5. Robert Stack, Dean K. McBride, and H. Arthur Lamey, "Dutch Elm Disease," North Dakota State University Extension Bulletin 324, revised 1994.

6. Tim Lang, interview with the author, October 26, 2010. Information about the arrival of the disease is according to plant pathologist George E. Hafstad, "Dutch Elm

Disease Report," Wisconsin Department of Agriculture 1965. The report is among materials in the Lorrie Otto Papers.

7. "Dutch Elm Disease Report," 1.

8. Mead, interview with the author, April 12, 2012.

9. "Birds, Bees, Butterflies Case Rests on a Robin," *Milwaukee Sentinel*, October 8, 1965.

10. "State Ignores Report on Elm Tree Injection," *Milwaukee Journal*, November 11, 1965.

11. "Village Accused of 'Spraying Poison,'" *Milwaukee Sentinel*, February 8, 1966.

12. "Hold Up DDT Spraying of Elms for Further Study of Hazards," *Whitefish Bay Herald*, February 10, 1966.

13. "Village Accused of 'Spraying Poison.'"

14. "DDT Program Gets Full OK," *Milwaukee Sentinel*, February 15, 1966.

15. Ibid.

16. Ibid.

17. "Bayside Halts Spraying, Bids Wildlife Back," *Milwaukee Sentinel*, February 3, 1966.

18. Otto frequently wrote personal comments on materials she collected. This article is in box 3, file 4 of the Lorrie Otto Papers.

19. "The Worry about DDT," *Milwaukee Journal*, February 22, 1966.

20. "Elm War Decision: Strong DDT Again," *Milwaukee Journal*, November 7, 1966.

21. "DDT and DED," *Twin City News-Record* (Neenah-Menasha, Wisconsin), November 13, 1969.

22. "Public Concern Cited as Reason for DDT Reversal," *Janesville Gazette*, December 17, 1969.

23. "Cigarettes, DDT," *Milwaukee Sentinel*, February 21, 1969.

24. A copy of Norman Borlaug's letter to Betty Chapman, dated October 4, 1971, is in the personal files of Hugh Iltis and was made available to the author.

25. Mead, interview with the author, April 4, 2012.

26. James Zimmerman to Otto Festge, March 9, 1967, box 3, file 6, Lorrie Otto Papers.

27. "DDT Abandoned by City Forester," *Capital Times*, March 22, 1967.

28. Mead, interview with the author, April 4, 2012.

29. "DDT Abandoned by City Forester."

30. Ibid.

31. The Conservation Department would soon be reorganized and renamed the Department of Natural Resources.

32. Written copy of Scott's remarks at the DNR hearing on DDT, box 3, file 6, Lorrie Otto Papers.

33. "City Must Spray Elms," *Wisconsin State Journal*, August 10, 1967.

34. "Urge Halt to Use of DDT on Trees," *Capital Times*, October 26, 1967.

35. "Council Votes Ban on DDT for Elms," *Wisconsin State Journal*, October 27, 1967.

CHAPTER 12

1. "State Fish Swimming in DDT Waters," *Milwaukee Sentinel*, January 7, 1966.

2. *CNRA—The First 50 Years*, 21.

3. Don L. Johnson, "Finally, the DDT Story," *Dunn County News*, September 17, 2000.

4. Otto, interview with Steele.

5. *CNRA—The First 50 Years*, 21.

6. "State Fish Swimming in DDT Waters."

7. Johnson, "Finally, the DDT Story."

8. "Fishermen Upset by Lake Pesticides," *Milwaukee Sentinel*, January 29, 1966.

9. "Finally, the DDT Story."

10. "Lake Michigan Fish Contain Most Pesticides," *Grand Rapids Press*, November 23, 1963.

11. Letter, October 8, 1968, box 1, call no. M75–368, file 5, Citizens Natural Resources Association of Wisconsin Records.

12. "DDT Found in Fish from 31 Counties," *Milwaukee Journal*, April 30, 1967.

13. Ibid.

14. "Lake Pesticides Reported Nearing 'Lethal Level,'" *Milwaukee Sentinel*, February 2, 1968.

15. "A Plea to Save Lake Michigan from Pesticides," *Milwaukee Journal*, August 3, 1968.

16. Walter Scott, "Problems and Problem Areas," box 4, file 6, Lorrie Otto Papers.

17. Lorrie Otto to Victor Yannacone, September 17, 1968, box 4, file 6, Lorrie Otto Papers.

18. "Officials to Meet on Controversy Over Coho, DDT," *Milwaukee Sentinel*, April 9, 1969.

19. United Press International, "Michigan Fears Loss of Fishery," *Milwaukee Journal*, April 24, 1969.

20. Ibid.

21. "State Fish Called Safe Despite DDT," *Milwaukee Sentinel*, April 30, 1969. Dadisman covered the hearing for the paper.

22. "Governors Ask Higher Limit on DDT Content of Fish," *Milwaukee Journal*, September 3, 1969.

CHAPTER 13

1. The author visited the Hanson retreat in April 2005 to gather information for a biography commissioned by the Wisconsin Conservation Hall of Fame. Martin Hanson was inducted into the Hall of Fame in April 2009, a few months after his death.

2. Paul G. Hayes, "The Last Lord of Camelot North," *Milwaukee Journal Magazine*, February 20, 1994.

3. Ibid.

4. Christofferson, *The Man from Clear Lake*, 242.

5. Ibid.

6. Ibid., 245.

7. Thomas Huffman, "Protectors of the Land & Water: The Political Culture of Conservation and the Rise of Environmentalism in Wisconsin, 1958–70" (doctoral thesis, University of Wisconsin–Madison, 1989).

8. "Drive against DDT Taken to Resorts," *Appleton Post-Crescent*, April 9, 1969.

9. "Threat to State Tourism Raised Unless the Legislature Bans DDT," *Wisconsin State Journal*, April 10, 1969.

10. "Alfonsi Asks, Keep DDT Threat Quiet," *Waukesha Daily Freeman*, April 11, 1969.

11. Martin Hanson to Paul Alfonsi, April 12, 1969, box 5, file 3, Lorrie Otto Papers.

12. "'Asinine' Publicity Cited," *Rhinelander Daily News*, April 16, 1969.

13. "Bradley Claims Handbill Harms Tourism," *Oshkosh Northwestern*, April 11, 1969.

14. "Fishing Season and DDT," *Wausau Record-Herald*, April 17, 1969.

15. "Startling Message on DDT," *Janesville Gazette*, April 10, 1969.

16. "Alfonsi Asks, Keep DDT Threat Quiet."

17. "Dispute DDT Risk to Fish Eaters Despite Warning," *Vilas County News-Review*, April 10, 1969.

18. "Hansen's [*sic*] DDT Warning Troubles Resort Owners," *Capital Times*, April 14, 1969.

19. The Associated Press reported on Knowles's statement, and the story ran in newspapers across the state, including the *Green Bay Press-Gazette*, on April 20, 1969.

CHAPTER 14

1. Harmon Henkin, "DDT on Trial," *Environment* 11, no. 2, January–February 1969–December 1969: 14.

2. "Legal Action Started over Spray Plan," *Milwaukee Sentinel*, September 26, 1968.

3. William G. Moore, "The Wisconsin Ban on DDT: Old Law, New Content," *Gargoyle* (University of Wisconsin Law School) 16, no. 2 (Fall 1985): 2.

4. Dunlap, "DDT on Trial: The Wisconsin Hearing, 1968–1969," 6.

5. Moore, "The Wisconsin Ban on DDT," 4.

6. Dunlap, "DDT on Trial: The Wisconsin Hearing, 1968–1969," 6.

7. Moore, "The Wisconsin Ban on DDT," 5.

8. Roy Gromme, interview with the author, March 27, 2012.

9. CNRA news release, May 5, 1969, box 5, file 7, Lorrie Otto Papers. The news release also announced that the EDF had reorganized to escalate its efforts to ban DDT. It named Dr. Joseph Hassett of the University of New Mexico executive director of the organization and put Victor Yannacone on a monthly retainer to be paid from the Rachel Carson Trust.

10. Volunteer list, box 7, file 5, Lorrie Otto Papers.

11. William Reeder, interview with the author, February 25, 2013.

12. Loucks, interview with the author, March 27, 2012.

13. Otto letter to the *New Yorker*, February 8, 1969, box 7, file 3, Lorrie Otto Papers. Robert Rudd was one of two summation witnesses for the environmentalists. The other was Orie Loucks.

14. Reeder, interview with the author, February 25, 2013.

15. Whitney Gould, interview with the author, July 9, 2010.

16. Loucks, interview with the author, April 3, 2012.

17. Lynne Eich, interview with the author, March 2012.

18. Moore, "The Wisconsin Ban on DDT," 6.

19. Wurster, interview with the author, March 3, 2012.

20. Peg Watrous to Lorrie Otto, February 19, 1969, box 7, file 7, Lorrie Otto Papers.

21. Anderson, interview with the author, April 3, 2012.

22. "DDT Bugs Students, Too, They Tell Officials," *Wisconsin State Journal*, December 13, 1968.

23. "'DDT Commandos' Invade State Hearing," *Milwaukee Journal*, December 13, 1968.

24. Yannacone, interview with the author, June 12, 2012.

25. Wurster, interview with the author, September 7, 2012.

CHAPTER 15

1. Gould, interview with the author, July 9, 2010. Gould was with the *Capital Times* from 1967 to 1984, when she was lured to the *Milwaukee Journal*. She stayed with that paper when it merged with the *Milwaukee Sentinel* and retired in 1997 after serving as its architecture critic, focusing on the importance of inviting, livable cities and their relationship to the natural world.

2. Dunlap, "DDT on Trial: The Wisconsin Hearing, 1968–1969," 10.

3. Ibid.

4. Ibid.

5. "Wisconsin Ponders Ban of Controversial DDT," *Sunday Oregonian* (Portland, Oregon), December 22, 1968, box 5, file 7, Lorrie Otto Papers.

6. Gould, interview with the author, July 9, 2010.

7. Dunlap, "DDT on Trial: The Wisconsin Hearing, 1968–1969," 15.

8. "Scientist Warns of DDT Peril to Sex Life," *Capital Times*, January 14, 1969.

9. Lorrie Otto scribbled this note on a copy of the news article, "Scientist Warns of DDT Peril to Sex Life," box 5, file 7, Lorrie Otto Papers. She frequently wrote comments on photocopies of news articles and other materials.

10. "DDT Found in Mother's Milk," *Milwaukee Journal*, May 6, 1969.

11. "Claim Babies Get Too Much of DDT," *Capital Times*, May 6, 1969.

12. Wurster, interview with the author, March 2, 2012.

13. Dunlap, "DDT on Trial: The Wisconsin Hearing, 1968–1969," 9.

14. Ibid., 11.

15. "DDT Quiz Lapses into Legal Squabble," *Capital Times*, December 3, 1969.

16. Dan Anderson, e-mail to the author, March 27, 2012.

17. Hugh Iltis, interview with the author, June 5, 2012. As World War II continued, Hugo Iltis's sister-in-law Lizzy needed to prove her lineage to the Nazis. In doing so, she learned that Gregor Mendel showed up in her family tree.

18. Gould, interview with the author, June 1, 2012.

19. "Biologist Blasts DDT, Pesticides," *Capital Times*, December 4, 1968.

20. "U.W. Ecologist Blames DDT for Polluting Lakes, Large and Small," *Capital Times*, December 10, 1969.

21. Dunlap, "DDT on Trial: The Wisconsin Hearing, 1968–1969," 9.

22. Yannacone, interview with the author, June 9, 2012.

23. Otto to Carol Yannacone, 1968, box 7, file 2, Lorrie Otto Papers.

24. Gould, interview with the author, July 9, 2010.

25. Loucks, interview with the author, March 27, 2012.

26. "Test for DDT," *New York Times*, December 1, 1968. The editorial appeared just a day before the hearing began.

27. "The DDT Fight: David vs. Goliath," *Capital Times,* December 16, 1968.

28. "Cite Dangers to Fish at Hearings on DDT," *Capital Times*, January 13, 1969.

29. "Scientist Testifies of DDT Harm to Mallard Ducks' Reproduction," *Capital Times*, January 16, 1969.

30. Otto note on "Scientist Testifies of DDT Harm to Mallard Ducks' Reproduction," box 5, file 7, Lorrie Otto Papers.

31. "DDT Foes Close Case with 'Ecological Hazard' Plea," *Capital Times*, January 17, 1969. A copy of the story with Otto's note is in box 4, file 7, of the Lorrie Otto Papers.

32. "Madison DDT Hearings Bolster Nation-Wide Concern," *Capital Times*, March 25, 1969.

33. "Chemical Unit Defends DDT Use," *Capital Times*, March 20, 1969.

34. Dunlap, "DDT on Trial: The Wisconsin Hearing, 1968–1969," 20.

35. Ibid., 17.

36. "DDT Poses No Threats to Health, Professor Tells Resumed Hearing," *Wisconsin State Journal*, April 30, 1969.

37. Dunlap, "DDT on Trial: The Wisconsin Hearing, 1968–1969," 20.

38. "U.W. Entomologist Backs DDT Use for Vegetable Crops," *Wisconsin State Journal*, May 3, 1969.

39. "DDT Wiping Out Bird Species, Hearing Is Told," *Milwaukee Sentinel*, May 13, 1969.

40. Robert Risebrough, interview with the author, June 6, 2012.

41. Ibid.

42. Ibid.

43. Hickey, oral history by Greeley, 10.

44. "DDT Defendant Delights Pesticide's Foes with Testimony on Residues," *Capital Times*, May 8, 1969.

45. Ibid.

46. Ibid.

47. Otto note on the *Capital Times*, May 8, 1969, report, box 4, file 7, Lorrie Otto Papers.

48. "Stress of Modern Life Rather Than DDT Harms State Birds, UW Expert Testifies," *Green Bay Press-Gazette*, May 8, 1969.

49. Ibid.

50. "DDT Proponents Keep Up Steady Barrage of Arguments," *Capital Times*, May 5, 1969.

51. "Shell Co. Game Manager Denies DDT Is Harmful to Wildlife," *Capital Times*, May 13, 1969.

52. The *Capital Times* relied on a report from the *London Observer* for its April 17 coverage of the Sweden ban.

53. "Book Hurt DDT Sales, Hearing Told," *Milwaukee Sentinel*, May 15, 1969.

54. "DDT Permanently Injures Animals," *Capital Times*, May 20, 1969.

55. Ibid.

56. "U. Pharmacologist Won't Term DDT 'Safe' for Humans," *Capital Times*, May 21, 1969.

57. Richard Kienitz, "Meaning of Safety Argued at DDT Hearing," *Milwaukee Journal*, May 21, 1969. Kienitz, of the paper's Madison bureau, had long since become a regular at the hearing as the newspaper grasped its importance.

58. Loucks, interview with the author, April 3, 2012.

59. Ibid.

60. Yannacone, interview with the author, June 12, 2012.

61. "Massive DDT Trial Testimony Closes," *Capital Times*, May 22, 1969.

62. Loucks, interview with the author, April 3, 2012.

63. "Examiner's Summary of Evidence and Proposed Ruling," Petition of Citizens Natural Resources Association Inc., and Wisconsin Division, Izaak Walton League of America Inc., for a Declaratory Ruling on Use of Dichloro-Diphenyl-Trichloro-Ethane, Commonly Known as DDT, in the State of Wisconsin, 3-DR-1, Wisconsin Department of Natural Resources, May 21, 1970. Van Susteren's ruling was an exhaustive summary of approximately 4,500 pages of testimony, exhibits, and related information.

64. It's a matter of definition: Hugh Iltis, the University of Wisconsin in Madison botanist who testified at the hearing, said in a June 4, 2012, interview with the author that he was on hand throughout. Was he a private citizen or a scientist? Several others interviewed by the author claimed that they, too, were at the hearing each day. But it remains a fact that Otto played the most active role among citizen activists who were not scientists.

65. The undated letter, addressed "Dear Sirs," was likely sent to EDF officials, although that is not clear. The letter is in box 7, file 14, of the Lorrie Otto Papers.

66. And one woman: Lucille Stickel.

CHAPTER 16

1. "Sixty Years of Daily Newspaper Circulation Trends," Communic@tions Management Inc., May 6, 2011. The firm is a Canadian company that provides consulting advice in media economics, media trends, and the impact of new technologies on the media.

2. Dave Zweifel, editor emeritus of the *Capital Times*, interview with the author, June 5, 2012.

3. Ohio History Central, www.ohiohistorycentral.org/entry.php?rec=1642.

4. "America's Sewage System and the Price of Optimism," *Time*, August 1, 1969.

5. "DDT Seems a Safe Pesticide for Man's Use," *Milwaukee Journal*, box 4, file 9, Lorrie Otto Papers.

6. "DDT Workers Affected in U.S.S.R.," *Science News*, February 15, 1969, 166.

7. Lorrie Otto's archival materials contain copies of articles from publications listed. Many were found in box 4.

8. "Second Thoughts Emerge on U.S. Decision to Ban DDT," *Christian Science Monitor*, December 30, 1969.

9. "Lifeless Oceans? DDT Could Bring About Such a Result," *Los Angeles Times*, March 6, 1969.

10. "Cyclamate, DDT Bans May Be Overreactions," *Philadelphia Inquirer*, December 7, 1969.

11. "Pesticide into Pest," *Time*, July 11, 1969, 56.

12. "Conservation Lawyers Move to Defend the 'Quality of Living,'" *New York Times*, September 14, 1969.

13. "Cities, Not Farms, Key Cause of Pesticide Woes—Wilkinson," *Green Bay Press-Gazette*, April 20, 1969.

14. "UW Researchers Join Protest of Military Use of Science," *Milwaukee Journal*, March 4, 1969. The protest against the military use of science took an ugly turn in Madison the following year. A bomb caused massive damage to the university's Sterling Hall, which housed the Army Mathematics Research Center. Researcher Robert Fassnacht was killed, three others were injured, and the blast caused significant damage to the physics department. Neither Fassnacht nor the physics department were involved with or employed by the Army Mathematics Research Center.

15. "Science, DDT, and All Things for All Men," *Wisconsin State Journal*, August 31, 1969.

16. "Fight to Save Farm Chemicals," *Wisconsin Agriculturist*, January 11, 1969.

17. "Living with DDT and Liking It," *Stevens Point Journal*, March 13, 1969.

18. "WBA Hits Opponents of Bow Deer Hunting," *Capital Times*, January 20, 1969.

19. "Let's Have Straight Answers," *Rice Lake Chronotype*, May 7, 1969.

20. "Too Many Controls Threaten Farms," *Wisconsin State Journal*, July 20, 1969.

21. "Environmentalists Take Aim at Fertilizers," *Wisconsin State Journal*, September 28, 1969.

22. "Toxic Menace Also Threat in Waters around World," *Milwaukee Sentinel*, August 15, 1969.

23. Lorrie Otto to Charles Wurster, July 10, 1969, box 7, file 5, Lorrie Otto Papers.

24. "State to Ban Sale of DDT," *State Journal* (Lansing–East Lansing, MI), April 17, 1969.

25. "California to Ban Home Use of DDT," *Chicago Sun-Times*, June 13, 1969.

26. "US Official Urges National DDT Ban," *Milwaukee Journal*, May 20, 1969.

27. Ibid.

28. "Federal DDT Action Welcome; Wisconsin Dawdles on Problem," *Capital Times*, November 21, 1969.

29. "Chemical Firms Try to Block DDT Ruling," *Capital Times*, September 23, 1969.

30. "Won't Back Pesticide Council," *Capital Times*, May 17, 1967.

31. "UW Law Prof Writes Model Pesticide Bill," *Milwaukee Sentinel*, April 26, 1969.

32. "Bill Urges Complete Ban on DDT," *Milwaukee Sentinel*, February 1, 1969.

33. "State DDT Ban Can Alert World to Pollution Dangers," *Capital Times*, April 10, 1969.

34. Ibid.

35. Ibid.

36. Otto to Walter Scott, September 22, 1969, box 7, file 14, Lorrie Otto Papers.

37. "State Board on Pesticide Curbs OK'd," *Milwaukee Journal*, July 23, 1969.

38. "No DDT Supporters at Hearing to Ban It," *Wisconsin State Journal*, September 25, 1969.

39. "Knowles Approves Ban on DDT Sales," *Milwaukee Journal*, February 13, 1970.

40. "Consolidated DDT Hearing: Hearing Examiner Edmund M. Sweeney's Findings, Conclusions and Orders, issued April 25, 1972, Environmental Protection Agency." The document can be viewed and downloaded from the EPA's website at www.epa.gov/history/topics/ddt/1972_EPA_DDT_hearing.PDF.

EPILOGUE

1. Gould, interview with the author, June 1, 2012.

2. Yannacone, interview with the author, June 12, 2012.

3. Loucks, interview with the author, March 27, 2012.

4. Wurster, interview with the author, June 14, 2011.

5. Tom J. Cade and William Burnham, eds., *Return of the Peregrine: A North American Saga of Tenacity and Teamwork* (Boise, ID: Peregrine Fund, 2003), 19.

6. Environmental Defense Fund website, www.edf.org.

7. Yannacone, interview with the author, June 12, 2012.

8. Wurster, interview with the author, September 7, 2012.

9. Gould, interview with the author, August 9, 2010.

10. Mead made the comment at the first Earth Day demonstration, April 22, 1970, in New York City. A radio excerpt reproduced by Voice of America, January 17, 2010, can be heard at http://learningenglish.voanews.com/content/margaret-mead-1901-1978-one-of-the-most-famous-anthropologists-in-the-world-124869344/112571.html.

11. Roger Tory Peterson remarks, Joseph Hickey's memorial service, September 4, 1993, Hickey family collection, made available courtesy of Susan Nehls.

12. David Kinkela, *DDT and the American Century: Global Health, Environmental Politics and the Pesticide that Changed the World* (Chapel Hill: University of North Carolina Press, 2011), 173.

13. Risebrough, interview with the author, June 6, 2012.

14. Yannacone, interview with the author, June 12, 2012.

15. Peterson remarks, Joseph Hickey's memorial service.

16. Gould, interview with the author, August 9, 2010.

INDEX

ABOUT THE AUTHOR

Bill Berry grew up in Green Bay and earned undergraduate degrees from the University of Wisconsin–River Falls. After more than twenty years as a reporter, columnist, and editor for several daily newspapers, he redirected his energy to communicate about conservation and agriculture. This work has taken him across the United States to learn and write about private lands conservation. A columnist for the *Capital Times* of Madison, he lives in Stevens Point with his wife and is the father of two daughters.

Photo by Tom Charlesworth